NORM AND ACTION

International Library of Philosophy
and Scientific Method

Editor: Ted Honderich

A catalogue of books already published in the
International Library of Philosophy and Scientific Method
will be found at the end of this volume

NORM AND ACTION

A LOGICAL ENQUIRY

by

Georg Henrik von Wright

ROUTLEDGE & KEGAN PAUL
LONDON AND HENLEY

THE HUMANITIES PRESS
ATLANTIC HIGHLANDS, NEW JERSEY

First published 1963
by Routledge & Kegan Paul Ltd
39 Store Street
London WC1E 7DD and
Broadway House, Newtown Road,
Henley-on-Thames
Oxon. RG9 1EN

Reprinted 1965, 1971 and 1977

Reproduced and printed in Great Britain by
Redwood Burn Limited
Trowbridge & Esher

ISBN 0 7100 3616 7

PREFACE

THE present work is a thoroughly revised version of the first of the two series of Gifford Lectures on 'Norms and Values', which I gave at the University of St. Andrews in 1959 and 1960. The content of the second series was published in 1963 in the International Library of Philosophy and Scientific Method under the title *The Varieties of Goodness*. The latter work and the present are substantially independent of one another. There is, however, a minor amount of overlap between the discussion of the ontological status of prescriptions in Chapter VII of this book and the discussion in the last three chapters of *The Varieties of Goodness*.

In 1951 I published in *Mind* a paper with the title 'Deontic Logic'. In it I made a first attempt to apply certain techniques of modern logic to the analysis of normative concepts and discourse. Since then there has been a growing interest in the logic of norms among logicians and, so far as I can see, among legal and moral philosophers also. Moreover, the name *deontic logic*, originally suggested to me by Professor C. D. Broad, seems to have gained general acceptance.

The thoughts which are contained in the present work are the fruits, partly of criticism of ideas in my early paper, and partly of efforts to develop these ideas further. I should like to say a few words here about the growth of my thoughts and the plan of this book. Readers who have no previous familiarity with deontic logic may skip this part of the Preface.

In my original paper the two 'deontic operators', O for obligation and P for permission, were regarded as interdefinable. O was treated as an abbreviation for $\sim P \sim$. The operators were prefixed to what I regarded as names of acts, $A, B, \ldots$ and to molecular compounds of such names. The acts were conceived of as act-categories, such as, *e.g.*, murder or theft, and not as act-individuals, such as, *e.g.*, the murder of Caesar. Act-categories were treated as 'proposition-like entities', *i.e.*, entities on which the truth-functional operations of negation, conjunction, disjunction, etc., can be performed. The meanings of expressions such as OA or $P(A \ \& \ \sim B)$ I regarded as propositions to the effect that certain categories of acts are obligatory or permitted. Thus the possibility of combining the expressions by means of truth-connectives was taken for granted. I also, however, implicitly regarded these meanings as norms enjoining or permitting acts. It did not then occur to me that this made the applicability of truth-connectives to the expressions problematic. Since the expressions OA, etc., obviously could not themselves be regarded as names of acts, iterated use of the operators O and P was not allowed by the rules of the calculus. Expressions such as OOA were accordingly dismissed as meaningless.

I have since come to entertain doubts on practically all issues of importance in my first publication on deontic logic. These doubts have been of two kinds. Some concern the *validity* of certain logical principles of obligation-concepts, which I had originally accepted. Others concern the *interpretation* of the symbols and expressions of the calculus.

One of my doubts of the first kind relates to the nature of permissive norms. Is permission an independent normative concept, or can it be defined in terms of obligation (and negation)? If it can be so defined, what is the correct way of defining it? These questions are discussed in the last four sections (13–16) of Chapter V and briefly touched upon in various places elsewhere in the book.

Other doubts of the first kind have to do with the principles of distributivity of the deontic operators and the various principles of 'commitment'. When these principles are formulated in a more refined logical symbolism it turns out that they do not possess the unrestricted validity which I originally claimed for them. These various laws of the 'old system' are discussed and corrected in the last four sections (15–18) of Chapter IX.

My dissatisfaction and doubts relating to questions of interpreting the calculus were even more serious, and became in the end destructive of the entire original system.

If A denotes an act, what does $\sim A$ mean? Does it signify the *not-doing* of the thing, the doing of which is symbolized by A? Or does it signify the *undoing* of that thing, *i.e.*, the doing of something which results in an opposite state of affairs? If the first answer is the right one the question will arise what we are to understand by 'not-doing': the mere fact that a certain thing is not done, or the forbearance of some agent from doing this thing, when there is an opportunity to do it? If the second answer is correct, how shall we then distinguish between leaving something undone and undoing it?

These and similar considerations made it plain that the symbolism for acts which I had been using was inadequate for expressing logical features of action, which are of obvious relevance to a logic of obligation-concepts. The same inadequacy would have been there had I regarded *A*, *B*, etc., not as names of categories of acts, such as manslaughter or window-opening, but as sentences describing states of affairs, such as that a man is dead or a window open. In short, the symbolism of so-called propositional logic was inadequate for symbolizing the various modes of action. New logical tools had to be invented. A Logic of Action turned out to be a necessary requirement of a Logic of Norms or Deontic Logic.

We could say that formal logic, as we know it to-day, is essentially the logic of a *static* world. Its basic objects are possible states of affairs and their analysis by means of such categories as thing, property, and relation. There is no room for *change* in this world. Propositions are treated as definitely true *or* false— not as now true, now false. Things are viewed as having or lacking given properties and not as changing from, say, red to not-red.

Acts, however, are essentially connected with changes. A state which is not there may come into being as a result of human interference with the world; or a state which is there may be made to vanish. Action can also continue states of affairs which would otherwise disappear, or suppress states which would otherwise come into being. A necessary requirement of a Logic of Action is therefore a Logic of Change.

Our first step towards building a Deontic Logic will be to survey the traditional logical apparatus with a view to constructing out of its ingredients a new apparatus which is adequate for dealing, at least in gross outline, with the logical peculiarities of a world in change. This is done in Chapter II, which contains the fundamentals of a Logic of Change. After a general discussion of the concept of action in Chapter III the fundamentals of a Logic of Action are presented in Chapter IV. The elements of Deontic Logic are not treated until Chapters VIII and IX.

In my 1951 paper I took it for granted that the expressions which are formed of the deontic operators and symbols for acts can be combined by means of truth-connectives. This assumption would be warranted if the expressions in question could be safely regarded as the 'formalized counterparts' of sentences which express propositions. If, however, the expressions are also intended to be formalizations of norms, then it is not certain that the assumption is warranted. Propositions, by definition, are true or false. Norms, it is often maintained, have no truth-value.

The question whether norms are true or false challenges the question, what norms *are*. It is readily seen that the word 'norm' covers a very heterogeneous field of meaning, that there are many different things which are or can be called by that name. These things must first be classified, at least in some crude manner, before a discussion of the relation of norms to truth can be profitably conducted. This I have tried to do in Chapter I. *One* of the many types of norm which there are, I call *prescriptions*. After a more detailed analysis of the structure of norms, with the main emphasis on prescriptions, in Chapter V, the discussion of norms and truth is resumed in Chapter VI. No attempt is made to settle the problem for all norms. The view that prescriptions have no truth-value, however, is accepted.

The deontic sentences of ordinary language, of which the expressions of deontic logic may be regarded as 'formalizations', exhibit a characteristic ambiguity. Tokens of the same sentence are used, sometimes to enunciate a prescription (*i.e.*, to enjoin, permit, or prohibit a certain action), sometimes again to express a proposition to the effect that *there is* a prescription enjoining or permitting or prohibiting a certain action. Such propositions are called norm-propositions. When expressions of deontic logic are combined by means of truth-connectives we interpret them as sentences which express norm-propositions.

The conception of deontic logic as a logic of norm-propositions challenges the question, what it means to say of prescriptions, or of norms generally, that they *exist*. Wherein does the 'reality' of a norm lie? This is the ontological problem of norms. Some aspects of it, relating chiefly to the existence of prescriptions, are discussed in Chapter VII. I find the problem extremely difficult, and do not feel at all satisfied with the details of my proposed solution to it. But I feel convinced that, if deontic logic is going to be anything more than an empty play with symbols, its principles will have to be justified on the basis of considerations pertaining to the ontological status of norms.

I still adhere to the opinion of my original paper that iteration of deontic operators to form complex symbols, such as OO or PO or $O \sim P$, etc., does not yield meaningful results. Some kind of 'iteration', however, is certainly possible. For there can be prescriptions (and maybe norms of other types too) concerning the obligatory, permitted, or forbidden character of acts of giving (other) prescriptions. In a symbolic language, which contained expressions for such norms of higher order, deontic operators would occur inside the scope of other deontic operators. No attempt is here made to develop the adequate symbolism. But some problems concerning higher order norms (prescriptions) are discussed informally in the last chapter (X) of this book.

The building of a Deontic Logic has thus turned out to be a much more radical departure from existing logical theory than I at first realized. The more I have become aware of the complications connected with the subject, the more have I been compelled to narrow my claims to be able to treat it in a systematic and thorough way. What is here accomplished, if anything, covers only a small part of the ground which has to be cleared before Deontic Logic stands on a firm footing.

The main object of study in this book is *prescriptions*. Originally, I had planned to include in it also a fuller treatment of that which I call *technical norms* about means to ends, and the closely related topic of *practical inference* (necessity). But I have come to realize that this is an even more extensive and bewildering conceptual jungle than the topic of prescriptions. I therefore eventually decided not to attempt to penetrate it here. But I think that a theory which combines a logic of prescriptions with a logic of practical necessities is an urgent desideratum for the philosophy of norms and values.

I have lectured on norms and deontic logic both before and after my Gifford Lectures in 1959. I wish to thank my classes collectively for the stimulating opportunities which lecturing has given me to present ideas—often in an experimental and tentative form. In particular, I wish to thank two of my colleagues individually. These are Professor Jaakko Hintikka, whose criticism has effected profound revisions of some of my earlier views in the Logic of Action, and Mr. Tauno Nyberg, by whose advice and assistance I have greatly profited in preparing these lectures for publication.

GEORG HENRIK VON WRIGHT

CONTENTS

CONTENTS

xvi

I

ON NORMS IN GENERAL

1. THE word 'norm' in English, and the corresponding word in other languages, is used in many senses and often with an unclear meaning. It can hardly be said to be a well-established term in the English philosophic vocabulary. This can be said, however, of the adjective 'normative'.

'Norm' has several partial synonyms which are good English. 'Pattern', 'standard', 'type' are such words. So are 'regulation', 'rule', and 'law'. Directions of use and prescriptions are perhaps not often called 'norms', but we should not hesitate to call them 'normative'.

Since the field of meaning of 'norm' is not only heterogeneous but also has vague boundaries, it would probably be futile to try to create a General Theory of Norms covering the whole field. The theory of norms must be somehow restricted in its scope.

When constructing a restricted theory of norms, however, it is as well to remember that the various meanings of 'norm' are not logically unrelated. The word is not 'ambiguous' in the ordinary sense. A restricted theory of norms runs the risk of being defective if it does not pay due attention to conceptual affinities and logical relationships between the various parts of the whole field of meaning.

In this chapter I shall try to single out and briefly characterize some of the chief meanings of the word 'norm' or, as we could also say, species or types of norms.

2. We have said that *one* of the meanings of 'norm' is *law*. The word 'law', however, is used in at least three typically different

1

senses. First, we speak of the *laws of the state*. Secondly, we speak of the *laws of nature*. Thirdly, we speak of *laws of logic* (and mathematics).

Obviously, the laws of nature and the laws of the state are very different. Yet the identity of name is no pure coincidence.

Thus, with the Greeks the conception of the world as a *kosmos* or harmonious order seems to have been connected historically with their conception of the city-state as a just and lawful order for a human community. The natural philosophy of the pre-Socratics has been called a projection of ideals of a social order on to the entire universe. In the philosophy of Plato we could say, this idea of the world as a *kosmos* is projected back on to human conditions and made a pattern or standard of the good life.

With the Greek conception of law as the conditions of equilibrium and harmony may be contrasted the Hebrew (Old Testament) conception of it as the expression of a commanding sovereign will. The idea of God as lawgiver may be regarded as an analogy or a projection on to a supernatural plane of the idea of a sovereign chief or king in a human community. As the king gives laws to those over whom he is set to rule, so in a similar manner God rules the whole universe by His law or 'word'. The Christian idea of a king 'by the grace of God' is a projection back on to human affairs of this idea of a supreme lord of the universe. The idea of the worldly kingdom is given a foundation in the same supernatural idea, for which it originally set the pattern.

As *we* tend to see it, the laws of nature and the laws of the state are *toto coelo* logically different in spite of affinities in the origins of the ideas of the two 'laws'. The difference can be briefly characterized as follows:

The laws of nature are *descriptive*. They describe the regularities which man thinks he has discovered in the course of nature. They are true or false. Nature does not, except metaphorically, 'obey' its laws. If a discrepancy is found to exist between the description and the actual course of nature it is the description, and not the course of nature, that must be corrected.—This is a superficial characterization of what the laws of nature are. But I think it is *basically* correct.

The laws of the state are *prescriptive*. They lay down regulations for the conduct and intercourse of men. They have no truth-value. Their aim is to influence behaviour. When men disobey the laws

2

the authority behind the laws tries, in the first place, to correct the behaviour of men. Sometimes, however, the authority alters the laws—perhaps in order to make them conform more to the capacities and demands of 'human nature'.

The contrast 'prescriptive/descriptive' can be used for distinguishing norms from things which are not norms. The laws nature are descriptive, not prescriptive—and *therefore* they are not norms. That is: we thus delineate the use of the word 'norm'; we draw the boundaries of the concept. Under another use of the term the laws of nature can perfectly well be called 'norms'.

Someone may think that the attribute 'prescriptive' gives the clue to a general characterization of norms. Normative discourse is prescriptive discourse, it is often said. With prescriptive discourse is then contrasted descriptive, and sometimes also evaluative, discourse.

To identify the meaning of 'normative' with that of 'prescriptive' and 'norm' with 'prescription' would, however, be too narrowing. Besides, 'prescriptive' and 'prescription' are words with a vague meaning and must be made more precise in order to be useful. As we shall soon see, there are things which we may without hesitation wish to call norms, but to which the attributes 'prescriptive' and 'descriptive' both appear equally inappropriate.

3. Let us briefly consider the meaning of 'law' in the phrase 'laws of logic (mathematics)'. The laws of logic were often in the past also called the Laws of Thought.

On closer inspection we find that there are, in logic and mathematics, several *types* of proposition which are or may be called 'laws'. We need not here inquire into these distinctions. As examples of laws of logic, we shall instance the Law of Excluded Middle in the formulation 'Every proposition is either true or false' and the Law of Contradiction in the formulation 'No proposition is both true and false'.

Are such laws 'descriptive' or 'prescriptive'? If the first, *what* do they describe? The way people think? This suggestion is not very satisfactory. For, first of all, it is not clear in itself what it *means* to think according to the law, for example, that no proposition is both true and false. Secondly, the idea that the laws of logic describe how people think seems difficult to reconcile with the notion that these laws are *a priori* and thus true independently of experience—including experience of how people think.

The *a priori* nature of the laws of logic seems easier to reconcile with a view of them as prescriptive laws. Shall we then say that the laws of logic prescribe how we *ought to* think and how we *may* and *must not* think? Perhaps we can say this, but it is also obvious on reflection that the *sense* in which the laws of logic 'prescribe' (order, permit, prohibit) is a different sense from that in which the laws of the state prescribe.

Here the idea suggests itself that the laws of logic and mathematics prescribe how one ought to think and calculate in order to think and calculate correctly. The laws of logic do not aim at making people think correctly, as the laws of the state can be said to aim at making people behave in a certain way. The laws of logic provide a standard whereby to judge *whether* people think correctly or not. This seems to be a good way of characterizing the difference between the two types of law and the different senses in which they 'prescribe'.

Yet to say that the laws of logic prescribe how people have to think in order to think correctly is a challenging and dangerous way of talking. It suggests that the 'prescriptive' function of the laws of logic is secondary to a 'descriptive' function of them as stating principles of correct thinking. Primarily, the laws of logic and mathematics state *truths* about the logical and mathematical entities—propositions, relations, inferences, numbers, etc. This they also do overtly when formulated in the usual way, as, *e.g.*, when we say, 'Every proposition *is* either true or false.'

Thus the view of the laws of logic as prescriptive of the way people ought to think leads to a view of these laws as being, primarily, descriptive. What, on this new view, the laws of logic describe is not, however, how people think, but how the logical entities are constituted.

This view of logic (and mathematics) is connected with great difficulties. It seems to presuppose a peculiar 'ontology' of the logical (mathematical) entities. This ontology is sometimes called *Platonism* or *Realism* in the philosophy of logic (mathematics). On this view, the laws of logic (mathematics) are at the same time very much like and yet significantly different from the laws of nature. Both types of law have a truth-value. But laws of the first type are necessarily true; laws of the second type contingently so.

Both types of law describe the properties and relations of some entities. But the entities with which laws of the first type deal are eternal and imperishable, whereas the entities with which the laws of the second type deal are mutable and contingently existing. This is a superficial characterization. But I think it catches hold of something typical.

The main alternative to a realistic (Platonistic) position in the philosophy of logic (mathematics) is sometimes called a *nominalist* or *conventionalist* position. It has many variants. Some of them seem just as implausible and difficult to defend as some radically Platonistic view. I shall here refrain from giving even a superficial characterization of the conventionalist position as such. I shall only hint at the status which the *laws* of logic (mathematics) will acquire if we reject a Platonistic philosophy.

We could then compare these laws to the *rules of a game*. Playing a game is an activity, and so is thinking and calculating. The rules of, say, chess determine which moves are permitted and which not, and sometimes require a certain move to be made. *In a similar sense* it may be suggested, the rules of logic determine which inferences and affirmations are 'possible' (correct, legitimate, permitted) in thinking. Of a person who does not play in accordance with the rules of chess, we would say either that he plays *incorrectly* or that he does not play *chess*. We would say the first, *e.g.*, if he wanted to follow the rules but did not know or understand what they demanded of him. Or we would say it if he is trying to cheat his opponent. We would say the second, *e.g.*, if he did not care about following the rules, or consciously and consistently played according to different rules. *In a similar sense*, the suggestion runs, we say of a person who does not infer according to the rules of logic either that he infers incorrectly or that he does not 'infer' at all. And we say the one or the other on roughly the same grounds as those which determine our reactions to the player.

The 'Platonist' would argue that the above analogy breaks down at this point: Whereas the man who plays against the rules of a game sins only against the *rules*, the man who thinks against the rules of logic is in conflict with *truth*. The rules of a game are man-made and can be altered by convention or at will. The standards of truth are not conventional. That there is some truth in this argument is obvious. What this truth is and what

5

implications it has for the analogy between the laws of logic and the rules of a game is, however, *not* obvious.

We raised the question whether the laws of logic and mathematics are descriptive or prescriptive. We have found that neither characterization appears quite to the point. These laws may be called descriptive, but not in the same clear sense in which the laws of nature are descriptive. They may also be called prescriptive, but in a rather different sense from that in which the laws of the state are prescriptive. The comparison of the laws of logic (mathematics) to the rules of a game suggested a new characterization of these laws. According to this new characterization, the laws of logic (mathematics) neither describe nor prescribe, but *determine* something. Irrespective of what we think of the comparison in other respects, we can agree to the usefulness of this characterization. It suits the laws of logic (mathematics) *better* than either the attribute 'descriptive' or the attribute 'prescriptive'.

4. The rules of a game are the prototype and standard example of a main type of norm. We shall here reserve the name *rule* as a technical term for this type.

Playing a game is a human activity. It is performed according to standardized patterns, which can be called *moves* in the game. The rules of the game *determine*, as I shall say, these moves or patterns—and thereby also the game 'itself' and the activity of playing it. We could say that, when viewed from the point of view of the game itself, the rules determine which are the *correct* moves, and when viewed from the point of view of the activity of playing, the rules determine which are the *permitted* moves. It is understood that moves which are not correct are *prohibited* to players of the game, and that a move which is the only correct move in a certain situation in the game is *obligatory* when one is playing the game.

The *rules of grammar* (morphology and syntax) of a natural language are another example of the same main type of norm as the rules of a game. To the moves of a game as patterns correspond the set forms of correct speech. To play or the activity of playing a game corresponds speech or the activity of speaking (and writing) a language. Of a person who does not speak according to the rules of grammar, we say either that he speaks incorrectly or that he does not speak *that language*. The grounds for saying the one or the other are very much the same as the grounds for saying of a person either that he plays a game incorrectly or does not play *it* at all. But the rules of grammar have a much greater flexibility and mutability than the rules of a game. They are in a constant process of growth. What the rules *are* at any given moment in the history of a language may not be possible to tell with absolute completeness and precision.

The rules of a logical and mathematical *calculus* are in some respects even more like the rules of a game (such as, *e.g.*, chess) than are the rules of grammar of a natural language. (Games and calculi have a much poorer 'history' than natural languages.) In at least one important respect, however, the rules of a calculus are more like rules of grammar than like rules of a game. Calculating, like speaking a language, is a play with *symbols*. Calculi and languages have a *semantic* dimension, which games, on the whole, lack.

5. A second main type of norms, beside rules, I shall call *prescriptions* or *regulations*. We have already met with one sub-type of such norms, *viz.* the laws of the state.

I shall regard the following features as characteristic of norms which are prescriptions:

Prescriptions are *given* or *issued* by someone. They 'flow' from or have their 'source' in the will of a norm-giver or, as we shall also say, a norm-*authority*. They are, moreover, addressed or directed to some agent or agents, whom we shall call norm-*subject(s)*. The authority of a norm can normally be said to want the subject(s) to adopt a certain conduct. The giving of the norm can then be said to manifest the authority's will to make the subject(s) behave in a certain way. In order to make its will *known* to the subject(s), the authority *promulgates* the norm. In order to make its will *effective*, the authority attaches a *sanction* or threat of punishment to the norm. In all these respects the norms which we call prescriptions differ characteristically from the norms which we call rules.

Generally speaking, prescriptions are commands or permissions, given by someone in a position of authority to someone in a position of subject. Military commands are an example of prescriptions. So are the orders and permissions given by parents to children. Traffic-rules and other regulations issued by a magistrate

7

largely have this character too. The decisions of a law-court may be said to have a prescriptive aspect or component.

6. A group of norms which are in some respects like rules and in other respects like prescriptions are *customs*.

Customs may be regarded as a species of habits. A habit is primarily a regularity in an individual's behaviour, a disposition or tendency to do similar things on similar occasions or in recurrent circumstances. Habits are acquired and not innate. Customs may be regarded as *social* habits. They are patterns of behaviour for the members of a community. They are acquired by the community in the course of its history, and imposed on its members rather than acquired by them individually.

Customs have to do with the way people greet each other, eat, dress, get married, bury their dead, etc. Ceremony, fashion, and manner are sister-categories of custom. It is a custom of my country, but not of the Anglo-Saxon countries, to thank the hosts or the heads of a family when the meal is finished. This is regularly done. A member of the community who—either exceptionally or habitually—does not do this is regarded with disapproval. A 'foreigner' to the community may be excused for not knowing or not adopting the custom.

Habits and customs, *qua* regularities of behaviour, show a certain resemblance to the regularities of nature, which natural scientists study. Social anthropology is largely a *science des mœurs*. It is 'descriptive' in much the same sense in which natural science is descriptive.

Yet there is a difference 'in principle' between regularities of behaviour, such as customs, and laws of nature. This difference is *not* that the former regularities are 'statistical' and admit of exceptions, the latter regularities 'nomic' and exceptionless. There seems to be no objection to calling *some* statistical regularities 'laws of nature'. It is not the bare existence of exceptions to a rule that constitutes the difference 'in principle' between customs and regularities in nature. The difference lies in the *way* in which exceptions may occur. There is a sense in which the human individual can 'break' the rule of custom and in which the course of nature cannot 'break' its (causal or statistical) laws.

We can characterize this difference between customs and laws of nature by saying that the former present a genuinely normative

8

or prescriptive aspect which the latter lack. Customs are 'norm-like' in the sense that they *influence* conduct; they exert a 'normative pressure' on the individual members of the community whose customs they are. The existence of this pressure is reflected in the various punitive measures whereby the community reacts to those of its members who do not conform to its customs. In this respect customs are entirely unlike laws of nature, and resemble, not so much norms which are rules, as norms which are prescriptions.

Yet there are important differences too between customs and prescriptions. Customs, first of all, are not *given* by any authority to subjects. If we can speak of an authority behind the customs at all this authority would be the community itself, including both its past and present members. Customs could aptly be characterized as *anonymous* norms or prescriptions. But this characterization must not encourage any mysticism about the nature of the community as norm-giver.

Another difference between customs and prescriptions is that the former do not require promulgation by means of symbolic marks. They need not be 'written down' anywhere in so many words. On this ground they could also be called *implicit* prescriptions. It is an interesting problem whether, within an animal or other community without a language, customs which exert a normative pressure on the members are (logically) possible.

There are some respects in which customs are more like rules than like prescriptions. Customs determine, or as it were 'define', ways of living which are characteristic of a certain community. A member who does not live in accordance with custom is seldom sought out for punishment in the same way as he who breaks the laws. The awkwardness of his position is more like that of a child who stands aside and does not want to join in the games of his playmates. He becomes a 'stranger' to his community rather than an 'outlaw'.

7. A third main type of norms, beside rules and prescriptions, are those which I shall call *directives* or *technical norms*. They are, approximately speaking, concerned with the *means* to be used for the sake of attaining a certain *end*.

'Directions for use' are examples of technical norms. In them is presupposed that the person who follows the directions, aims at the thing (end, result), with a view to the attainment of which those directions are laid down.

I shall regard as the standard formulation of technical norms, conditional sentences, in whose antecedent there is mention of some wanted thing, and in whose consequent there is mention of something that must (has to, ought to) or must not be done. An example would be 'If you want to make the hut habitable, you ought to heat it'.

Shall we say that the sentence quoted is 'descriptive' or 'prescriptive'? The proper answer, it seems to me, is that it is neither.

Compare the sentence under discussion with the sentence 'If the house is to be made habitable, it ought to be heated'. This last sentence I would not hesitate to call (purely) descriptive. It says that heating the house is a *necessary condition* of making the house habitable. This is (or is not) true, independently of whether any-one wants to make the house habitable and aims at this as an end. An equivalent formulation of the sentence would be 'Unless the house is heated, it will not be habitable'. We could say that the normal use of either is to make a statement about men's living conditions. The truth which the statement affirms is a kind of primitive 'law of nature'.

A statement to the effect that something is (or is not) a necessary condition of something else I shall call an *anankastic statement*. A (type of) sentence the normal use of which is for making an anankastic statement, I shall call an *anankastic sentence*. A sentence which is used for making an anankastic statement can also be said to express an *anankastic proposition*.

It would be a mistake, I think, to identify technical norms with anankastic propositions. There is, however, an essential (logical) connexion between the two. In giving the directive 'If you want to make the hut habitable, you ought to heat it', it is (logically) *presupposed* that if the hut is not being heated it will not become habitable.

Another confusion to be avoided is that between technical norms and what I propose to call *hypothetical norms*. By the latter I understand, approximately speaking, norms concerning that which ought to or may or must not be done should a certain contingency arise. Hypothetical norms, too, are usually formu-lated by means of conditional sentences. For example: 'If the dog barks, don't run.' This sentence would normally be used for prescribing a certain mode of conduct, in case a certain thing should happen. The norm which the sentence enunciates is a prescription.

In the 'background' of a hypothetical norm (prescription) too there is often an anankastic proposition. Why must I not run, if the dog starts to bark? If I run, the dog may attack me. Therefore, if I want to escape being attacked by the barking dog I must not run. Here the technical norm—or the underlying anankastic proposition—explains why the hypothetical prescription was given to me. But this connexion is accidental, not essential. Neither the technical norm nor the anankastic relationship is (logically) presupposed in the giving of the hypothetical norm (prescription). Even if there existed no technical norm or anankastic relationship in the background, the hypothetical order not to run, if— could be given to a person. (Cf. Ch. IX, Sect. 3.)

A man argues with himself: 'I want to make the hut habitable. Unless it is heated, it will not become habitable. Therefore I ought to heat it.' I shall call this type of argument a *practical inference*. In it the person who conducts the argument extracts, as it were, a prescription for his own conduct from a technical norm. Such 'autonomous' prescriptions given by a man to himself are, however, very unlike the 'heteronomous' prescriptions, categorical or hypothetical, given by a norm-authority to some norm-subject(s). It is doubtful whether one should call the former 'prescriptions' at all. (Cf. Ch. V, Sect. 8.)

8. What is the position of so-called moral norms (principles, rules) in the division of norms into main groups?

An answer to the question might be easier if we could give obvious examples of moral norms. This, however, is not altogether easy. One example which appears relatively uncontroversial (as an example) is the principle that promises ought to be kept. It is, however, an example of a moral norm of a rather special character. Other examples would be that children ought to honour their parents, that one must not punish the innocent, or that one should love one's neighbour as oneself.

Are moral norms to be classified along with rules of a game, *i.e.*, do they determine (define) a practice? It seems to me that, *on the whole*, moral norms are *not* like rules (in the sense which we

11

here give to the term). But some moral norms present this aspect too. It is an aspect of the obligation to keep promises that this obligation is inherent in or is a logical feature of the institution of giving and taking promises. 'By definition', one could say, promises ought to be kept. But this is only one aspect, beside others, of the obligation in question.

Are moral norms to be classified with the *customs* of a society (community)? It is noteworthy that the word 'moral' derives from the Latin *mos*, which means custom. Some moral philosophers have sought to reduce ethics to a branch of a general *science des mœurs*. It seems to me that *some* moral ideas can be profitably viewed by the philosopher too against a background of the customs (traditions) of a community. This might be true, for example, of moral ideas in matters relating to sexual life. Other moral norms, however, seem to have no significant place in this perspective. To try to explain the obligation to keep promises, for example, in terms of the 'normative pressure' of customs seems utterly out of place.

Are moral norms prescriptions? If we think they are, we must also be able to tell *whose* prescriptions *to whom* they are. Who *gave* the moral law?

A contract is a kind of promise. The legal obligations which people have under contract are therefore obligations to keep a kind of promise. The legal norms which institute these obligations are prescriptions. They can truly be called somebody's prescriptions to somebody—in spite of the fact that their authority is not a human individual or 'physical' person. But the *moral* norm to the effect that promises ought to be kept cannot become identified with the sum total of such legal prescriptions 'supporting' it. The laws of the state frequently have a 'moral content' or are concerned with 'moral matters'. The same is true of the prescriptions which parents issue for the conduct of children. In the moral life of man prescriptions thus play a prominent role. This is no mere accident; it is a logical feature of morality. But this logical tie between moral norms and prescriptions does not, so far as I can see, reduce the former to a species of the latter.

Some think that moral norms are the commands of God to men. The moral law is the law of God. To take this view of morality is to regard moral norms as prescriptions. These prescriptions, however, are not only of a very special *kind*. They must, perhaps, be thought of as prescriptions in a special *sense* of the term. This is so because of the peculiar nature of the (supernatural) authority who is their source.

The chief alternative in the history of ethics to the view of morality as the laws of God is a teleological view of it. On the first view, moral norms are a kind of prescription—or prescriptions in some special sense of the term. On the second view, moral norms are a kind of technical norm or directives for the attainment of certain ends. But what end or ends? The happiness of the individual or the welfare of a community? Eudaimonism and utilitarianism are variants of a teleological ethics. It would seem that the ends, relative to which certain modes of conduct are morally obligatory or permissible, cannot be specified independently of considerations of good and evil. This holds true also of happiness and welfare as proposed ultimate ends of moral action.

In view of the difficulties encountered by both a law-conception of moral norms and a teleological conception of them, it might be suggested that moral norms are *sui generis*. They are 'conceptually autonomous', a group of norms standing by themselves, and not prescriptions for conduct in conformity with the will of a moral authority or directives for the attainment of moral ends. The view of moral norms as *sui generis* is sometimes called the *deontologist* position in ethics.

This is not the place for detailed criticism of deontologism in ethics. As a proposed way out of difficulties, this position seems to me to be definitely unsatisfactory. The peculiarity of moral norms, as I see them, is not that they form an autonomous group of their own; it is rather that they have complicated logical affinities to the other main types of norm and to the value-notions of good and evil. To understand the nature of moral norms is therefore not to discover some unique feature in them; it is to survey their complex relationships to a number of *other* things.

9. The norms of various categories, of which we have so far been talking, are mainly norms concerned with that which ought to or may or must not be *done*. Laws of nature and other anankastic propositions are, on the whole, not concerned with action; but these we have decided not to call 'norms'.

There is, however, a group of norms which are immediately

concerned, not with action, but with things that ought to or may or must not *be*. German writers sometimes make a distinction between *Tunsollen* and *Seinsollen*.[1] In Anglo-Saxon writings the distinction is not very often referred to.[2]

Following G. E. Moore,[3] I shall call norms which are concerned with being rather than with doing, *ideal rules*. Ideal rules are referred to, for example, when we say that a man ought to be generous, truthful, just, temperate, etc., and also when we say that a soldier in the army should be brave, hardy, and disciplined; a schoolmaster patient with children, firm, and understanding; a watchman alert, observant, and resolute; and so forth.

We also say of cars, watches, hammers, and other implements, which are used to serve various purposes, that they ought to have certain properties and should not have others. The question may be raised whether such statements should be counted as stating ideal rules or as anankastic propositions about the relations of means to ends. That question will not be discussed here.

Ideal rules are closely connected with the concept of *goodness*. The properties which we say a craftsman, administrator, or judge ought to possess are characteristic, not of *every* craftsman, administrator, or judge, but of a *good* craftsman, administrator, or judge. The person who has the properties of a good so-and-so in a supreme degree, we often call an *ideal* so-and-so. The same holds true of watches, cars, and other things which serve various human purposes.

The features which ideal rules require to be present in good members of a class or kind of human beings can be termed the *virtues* characteristic of men of that class or kind. In an extended sense of 'virtue', roughly corresponding to the Greek *arete*, the characteristic properties of good instruments are often called virtues also.

It is natural to call ideal rules concerning men in general, as distinct from men of a particular class or profession, *moral* rules or ideals. It is useful to distinguish between moral *principles*, which

[1] See, for example, Nicolai Hartmann, *Ethik* (1925), Teil I, Abschnitt VI, Kap. 18–19. Max Scheler, in *Der Formalismus in der Ethik und die materiale Wertethik* (1916), uses the terms 'ideales Sollen' and 'normatives Sollen'.

[2] An exception is G. E. Moore, who draws the distinction very neatly in his paper 'The Nature of Moral Philosophy' (in *Philosophical Studies*, 1922).

[3] *Op. cit.*, pp. 320 f.

are norms of moral action, and moral *ideals*, which set the pattern of a good man.

It may be thought that ideal rules are reducible to norms of action. The concepts of a brave, generous, just, etc., *act*, it may be argued, are primary to the concepts of a brave, generous, just, etc., *man*. The man who does brave acts is 'by definition' a brave man, and so forth. This, however, would be to take a much too simple-minded view of the relationship in question. Yet it is also clear that 'education' (in the broadest sense) towards ideals will have to make use of prescriptions and other norms of conduct.

There is a certain similarity between ideal rules and technical norms. Striving for the ideal resembles the pursuit of an end. It would, however, be a mistake to think of the ideal rules as norms concerning means to ends. In order to be a good teacher, a man ought to have such and such qualities. In order to fetch a book from the top shelf of his bookcase, he ought to use a ladder. But those qualities of a man which determine his goodness as a teacher are not *causally* related to the ideal—as the use of a ladder may be a causal prerequisite of fetching a book from a shelf. The former relation is conceptual (logical). The ideal rules determine a concept, *e.g.* the concept of a (good) teacher or soldier. In this they are similar to rules of a game. It is because of this similarity that we have given them here the name 'rules'.

10. Our discussion, in the preceding sections, of the field of meaning of the word 'norm' has led us to distinguish between three major groups or types of norms. We have called them *rules*, *prescriptions*, and *directives*.

As a prototype of rules we instance the rules of a game. Rules of grammar also belong to this type of norm. Perhaps the so-called laws or rules of logic and mathematics should also be counted as belonging to it.

As prescriptions we count commands, permissions, and prohibitions, which are given or issued to agents concerning their conduct. The laws of the state are prescriptions.

Directives we also call technical norms. They presuppose ends of human action and necessary relationships of acts to these ends.

In addition to these three main groups of norms we mentioned three minor groups of particular importance. They are *customs*, *moral principles*, and *ideal rules*. It is characteristic of the minor groups that they show affinities to more than one of the major groups—they fall, so to speak, 'between' the major groups.

Thus, customs resemble rules in that they determine, *quasi* define, certain patterns of conduct—and prescriptions in that they exert a 'normative pressure' on the members of a community to conform to those patterns.

On the nature of moral principles there has been much controversy and disagreement. Some philosophers regard them as a kind of prescription—say, as the commands or laws of God to men. Others regard them as some sort of technical norm or directive of how to secure ends of a peculiar nature. Irrespective of which view one accepts as basically true, one cannot deny that moral principles have important relationships both to prescriptions *and* to technical norms. The prescriptive aspect of morality, moreover, is related to custom. The 'technical' aspect of morality is related to ideals of the good life and man.

Ideal rules, finally, can be said to hold a position between technical norms about means to an end and rules which determine a pattern or standard.

II

PRELIMINARIES ON LOGIC.
THE LOGIC OF CHANGE

---

1. THE author became interested in the logic of norms and normative concepts (also called 'deontic logic') through the observation that the notions of 'ought to', 'may', and 'must not' exhibit a striking analogy to the modal notions of necessity, possibility, and impossibility. His interest in modal logic again had been awakened by the observation that its basic concepts show an analogy to the basic concepts of so-called quantification-theory, the notions of 'all', 'some', and 'none'.

Familiarity on the part of the reader with the techniques of modal logic and quantification-theory is, however, neither presupposed nor needed for understanding the arguments in this book.

Modal logic and quantification-theory may be said to rest on a more elementary branch of logical theory, so-called propositional logic. The orthodox logical techniques used in this work nearly all belong to this elementary theory. We shall in the next two sections briefly recapitulate its fundamentals. This recapitulation, however, is too summary to give anyone who is not already familiar with the subject a working knowledge of its techniques.

By the 'techniques' of propositional logic I mean, principally, the construction of so-called *truth-tables* and the transformation of expressions into so-called *normal forms*. These techniques are described in any up-to-date text-book on (mathematical or symbolic) logic.

17

2. The objects which propositional logic studies are usually called by logicians and philosophers *propositions*.

Propositions may be said to have two 'counterparts' in language. One of these is (indicative) *sentences*. An example would be the sentence 'London is the capital of England'. Sentences *express* propositions. Propositions can be called the *meaning* or *sense* of sentences.

The second linguistic counterpart of propositions is *that*-clauses. A that-clause, in English, consists of the word 'that' followed by a sentence. For example, 'that London is the capital of England' is a that-clause. That-clauses have the character of *names* of propositions. Propositions can be called the *reference* of that-clauses.

Names of propositions must not be confused with names of sentences. A conventional way of naming a sentence is to enclose (a token of) this sentence within quotes. This method we used above when we gave an example of a sentence.

When we speak *about* sentences and propositions we have to refer to them by means of their names. Thus, for example, when we say that the German sentence 'London ist die Hauptstadt Englands' expresses the proposition that London is the capital of England. Instead of the phrase 'expresses the proposition' we could also have used the word 'means'.

By *expressions* or *formulae* of propositional logic we understand certain (linguistic) structures which are built up of two kinds of signs, called *variables* and *constants*. As variables we shall use lower-case letters p, q, r, etc. The constants which we use are the signs $\sim$, &, v, $\rightarrow$, and $\leftrightarrow$. The formulae we also call *p-expressions*. They are defined recursively as follows:

(i) Any variable is a formula.
(ii) Any formula preceded by $\sim$ is a formula; any two formulae joined by &, v, $\rightarrow$, or $\leftrightarrow$ is a formula.

The variables themselves we also call *atomic* formulae. A formula which is not atomic is called *molecular*, or is said to be a molecular complex or compound of atomic formulae.

For the building up of molecular formulae, as we do it here, *brackets* are needed. For our use of brackets we adopt the convention that the sign & has a stronger binding force than v, $\rightarrow$, and $\leftrightarrow$; the sign v than $\rightarrow$ and $\leftrightarrow$; and the sign $\rightarrow$ than $\leftrightarrow$. Thus, for example, we can instead of: $(((p \ \& \ q) \vee r) \to s) \leftrightarrow t$, write simply: $p \ \& \ q \vee r \to s \leftrightarrow t$.

(Brackets are a third kind of signs of propositional logic and should be mentioned in a full recursive definition of formulae. They are, however, signs of a 'subsidiary' nature. Under a different way from ours of defining the formulae, one can dispense with the use of brackets altogether.)

We shall have to think of the letters p, q, r, etc., in expressions of propositional logic as standing for or representing (arbitrary) sentences which express propositions. The p-expressions could be called sentence-*schemas*. What the techniques of propositional logic literally 'handle' are thus schemas for arbitrary sentences and their compounds. This is, perhaps, a reason why some logicians prefer to call propositional logic by the name 'sentential logic' or 'sentential calculus'. We shall sometimes call it by the name *p-calculus*.

3. An important point of view, from which so-called 'classical' propositional logic studies its objects, propositions, is the truth-functional point of view.

In classical propositional logic truth and falsehood are the two *truth-values*. It is assumed that every proposition has one, and one only, truth-value. If there are n logically independent propositions there are evidently 2^n possible ways in which they can be true and/or false together. Any such distribution of truth-values over the n propositions will be called a *truth-combination*.

If the truth-value of one proposition is uniquely determined for every possible truth-combination in some n propositions, then the first proposition is called a *truth-function* of the n propositions. It is not difficult to calculate that there exist in all $2^{(2^n)}$ different truth functions of n logically independent propositions.

The following truth-functions are of special interest to us:

The *negation* of a given proposition (is the truth-function of it which) is true, if and only if, the given proposition is false. If p expresses a proposition, then $\sim p$ will, by convention, express the negation of this proposition. $\sim$ is called the negation-sign.

The *conjunction* of two propositions (is the truth-function of them which) is true, if and only if, both propositions are true. If p and q express propositions, $p \ \& \ q$ expresses their conjunction. $\&$ is called the conjunction-sign.

The *disjunction* of two propositions is true, if and only if, at least one of the propositions is true. If p and q express propositions, $p \lor q$ expresses their disjunction. $\lor$ is called the disjunction-sign.

The (material) *implication* of a first proposition, called the *antecedent*, and a second proposition, called the *consequent*, is true if, and only if, it is not the case that the first is true and the second false. If p and q express propositions, $p \rightarrow q$ expresses their implication.

The (material) *equivalence* of two propositions is true if, and only if, both propositions are true or both false. If p and q express propositions, $p \leftrightarrow q$ expresses their equivalence.

The *tautology* of n propositions is the truth-function of them which is true for all possible truth-combinations in those n propositions. The tautology has no special symbol.

The *contradiction* of n propositions is the truth-function of them which is false for all possible truth-combinations in those n propositions. Like the tautology, the contradiction has no special symbol.

Truth-functionship is transitive. If a proposition is a truth-function of a set of propositions, and if every member of the set is a truth-function of a second set of propositions, then the first proposition, too, is a truth-function of the second set of propositions.

Thanks to the transitivity of truth-functionship, every formula of propositional logic or p-expression expresses a truth-function of the propositions expressed by its atomic constituents. Which truth-function of its atomic constituents a given p-expression expresses can be calculated (decided) in a so-called *truth-table*. The technique of constructing truth-tables is assumed to be familiar to the reader.

Two formulae, f_1 and f_2, are called *tautologously equivalent*, if the formula $f_1 \leftrightarrow f_2$ expresses the tautology of its atomic constituents.[1]

The formulae f and $\sim\sim f$ are tautologously equivalent. That this is the case is called the Law of Double Negation. 'Double negation cancels itself.'

---

[1] f, g, and f_1, f_2, etc., are here used as so-called meta-variables. They represent arbitrary formulae or p-expressions. The constant-signs of propositional logic are used 'autonymously' for the purpose of building up molecular compounds of meta-variables. Such compounds represent arbitrary p-expressions of the corresponding molecular structure.

The formulae $\sim(f_1 \& f_2)$ and $\sim f_1 \vee \sim f_2$ are tautologously equivalent, and so are the formulae $\sim(f_1 \vee f_2)$ and $\sim f_1 \& \sim f_2$. These are the Laws of de Morgan. The first says that the negation of a conjunction of propositions is tautologously equivalent to the disjunction of the negations of the propositions. The second says that the negation of a disjunction of propositions is tautologously equivalent to the conjunction of the negations of the propositions.

Conjunction and disjunction are associative and commutative. Thanks to their associative character, the truth-functions can be generalized so that one can speak of the conjunction and disjunction of any arbitrary number n of propositions.

The formulae $f_1 \& (f_2 \vee f_3)$ and $f_1 \& f_2 \vee f_1 \& f_3$ are tautologously equivalent, and so also the formulae $f_1 \vee f_2 \& f_3$ and $(f_1 \vee f_2) \& (f_1 \vee f_3)$. These are called Laws of Distribution.

The formula $f_1 \rightarrow f_2$ is tautologously equivalent to $\sim f_1 \vee f_2$ and also to $\sim(f_1 \& \sim f_2)$. The formula $f_1 \leftrightarrow f_2$ again is tautologously equivalent to $f_1 \& f_2 \vee \sim f_1 \& \sim f_2$. These equivalences may be said to show that implication and equivalence is definable in terms of negation, conjunction, and disjunction.

Formulae may become 'expanded' or 'contracted' in accordance with the laws that a formula f is tautologously equivalent to the formulae $f \& f$ and $f \vee f$ and $f \& (g \vee \sim g)$ and $f \vee g \& \sim g$.

Thanks to these equivalences and the transitivity of truth-functionship, every formula of propositional logic may be shown to possess certain so-called *normal forms*. A normal form of a given formula is another formula which is tautologously equivalent to the first and which satisfies certain 'structural' conditions. Of particular importance are the (perfect) *disjunctive* and the (perfect) *conjunctive* normal forms of formulae. The techniques of finding the normal forms of given formulae are assumed to be familiar to the reader.

Given n atomic formulae, one can form 2^n different conjunction-formulae such that every one of the atomic formulae or its negation-formula is a constituent in the conjunction. (Conjunction-formulae which differ only in the order of their constituents, *e.g.* $p \& \sim q$ and $\sim q \& p$, are here regarded as the same formula.)

It is easily understood in which sense these 2^n different conjunction-formulae may be said to 'correspond' to the 2^n different truth-combinations in the propositions expressed by the atomic formulae. The conjunction-formulae are sometimes called *state-descriptions*. The conjunctions themselves can be called *possible worlds* (in the 'field' or 'space' of the propositions expressed by the atomic formulae).

The (perfect) disjunctive normal form of a formula is a disjunction of (none or) some or all of the state-descriptions formed of its atomic constituents. If it is the disjunction of them all the formula expresses the tautology of the propositions expressed by its atomic constituents. This illustrates a sense in which a tautology can be said to be *true in all possible worlds*. If again the disjunctive normal form is 0-termed the formula expresses the contradiction of the propositions expressed by its atomic constituents. A contradiction is *true in no possible world*. Propositions which are true in some possible world(s) but not in all are called *contingent*.

Sentences which express contingent propositions we shall call *descriptive* or *declarative* sentences.[1]

4. What is a proposition?—An attempt to answer this question in a satisfactory way would take us out on deep waters in philosophy. Therefore we shall confine ourselves to a few scattered observations only. In the first place I should like to show that the term 'proposition', as commonly used by logicians and philosophers, covers a number of different entities which, for the specific purposes of the present study, we have reason to distinguish.

Someone may wish to instance that it is raining as an example of a proposition. Or that Chicago has more inhabitants than Los Angeles. Or that Brutus killed Caesar.

Is it not the case that the proposition that it is raining has one and one only truth-value? Surely, someone may say, it must be either raining or not raining and cannot be both. But, of course, it can be raining in London to-day but not to-morrow; and it can be raining to-day in London but not in Madrid; and it can to-day be raining and not raining in London, *viz.* raining in the morning but not in the afternoon. So, in a sense, it is quite untrue to say

---

[1] We shall, for the sake of typographical convenience, throughout avoid the use of quotes round symbolic expressions such as p, $\sim p$, $p \& q$, etc. When mentioning the expressions, we use the expressions themselves 'autonymously'. When speaking of the meanings of the expressions, we shall use locutions of the type 'the proposition expressed by p', 'the state of affairs described by $p \& q$', etc.

that the proposition that it is raining has one and one only truth-value, or to say that it cannot be both raining and not raining.

When we insist that it cannot be both raining and not raining we mean: raining and not raining at the same place and time. Or, as I shall prefer to express myself: on one and the same *occasion*. But a proposition may be true on one occasion and false on another.

These observations give us a reason for making a distinction between *generic* and *individual* propositions. The individual proposition has a uniquely determined truth-value; it is either true or false, but not both. The generic proposition has, by itself, no truth-value. It has a truth-value only when coupled with an *occasion* for its truth or falsehood; that is, when it becomes 'instantiated' in an individual proposition.

We cannot here discuss in detail the important notion of an occasion. It is related to the notions of space and time. It would not be right, however, to identify occasions with 'instants' or 'points' in space and time. They should rather be called spatio-temporal *locations*. Two occasions will be said to be *successive* (in time), if, and only if, the first occasion comes to an end (in time) at the very point (in time) where the second begins.

Occasions are the 'individualizers' of generic propositions. Their logical role in this regard is related to old philosophic ideas of space and time as the *principia individuationis*.

Occasions must not be confused with (logical) *individuals*. Individuals could be called 'thing-like' logical entities. Not all logical individuals, however, are called 'things' in ordinary parlance. 'London' and 'the author of Waverley' refer to individuals; but neither a city nor a person is it natural to call a thing. The counterparts of individuals in language are proper names and so-called definite descriptions (uniquely descriptive phrases).

When a sentence which expresses a proposition contains proper names and/or definite descriptions the corresponding logical individuals, we shall say, are *constituents* of the expressed proposition. But the occasion for a proposition's truth or falsehood we shall not call a constituent of the proposition.

It should be observed that it is not the occurrence of individuals among its constituents which decides whether a proposition is generic or individual. That Brutus killed Caesar is an individual proposition. But this is not so because of the fact that the

23

proposition is about the individuals Brutus and Caesar; it is due to the logical nature of the concept (universal) of being killed. A person *can* be killed only once, on one occasion. That Brutus kissed Caesar is not an individual proposition. This is so because a person can be kissed by another on more than one occasion.

It may be suggested that only generic propositions among the constituents of which there are no logical individuals are eminently or fully generic. Generic propositions among the constituents of which there are individuals might then be called semi-generic or semi-individual. A further suggestion might be that semi-generic propositions 'originate' from fully generic propositions by a process of substituting for some universal in the generic proposition some individual which falls under that universal. But we need not discuss these questions here.

The relation of universal to logical individual must be distinguished from the relation of generic proposition to individual proposition. But the two relations, though distinct, are also related.

Sometimes there are intrinsic connexions between a logical individual and the spatio-temporal features which constitute an occasion for a proposition's truth or falsehood. The individuals to which geographical names refer have a fixed location on the surface of the earth. The proposition that Paris is bigger than New York is false now, but was true two hundred years ago. The occasion on which the proposition is true or false has only the *temporal* dimension. This is so because the individuals which are constituents of the proposition have intrinsically a fixed spatial location. If individually the same town could move from one country to another it might be true to say that Paris was bigger than New York at the time when the former was situated in China. As things are, logically, to say this does not even *make sense*.

The distinction which we are here making between *individual* and *generic* propositions must not be confused with the well-known distinction between singular or *particular* propositions, on the one hand, and universal or *general* propositions, on the other hand. As far as I can see, the division of propositions into individual and generic applies only to particular propositions. General propositions such as, *e.g.*, that all ravens are black, or that water has its maximum density at 4° C, have a determined truth-value but are *not* instantiations, in the sense here considered, of some generic propositions. There are no 'occasions' for the truth or falsehood of general propositions. Such propositions are therefore also, as has often been noted, in a characteristic way independent of time and space.

To propositional logic in the traditional sense it is not an urgent problem whether we should conceive of its objects of study, propositions, as generic or individual. It is perhaps true to say that *primarily* propositional logic is a formal study of individual (particular) propositions. If we conceive of its objects as generic propositions we must supplement such statements as that no proposition is both true and false by a (explicit or tacit) reference to one and the same occasion. And we must bear in mind that it is only *via* the notion of an occasion that the notion of truth and of truth-function reaches generic propositions.

For the formal investigations which we are going to conduct in the present work the distinction between individual and generic propositions is of relevance. We shall here have to understand the variables p, q, etc., of propositional logic as schematic representations of sentences which express *generic* propositions. Thus, for example, we could think of p as the sentence 'The window is open', but not as the sentence 'Brutus killed Caesar'. A further restriction on the interpretation of the variables will be introduced in the next section.

5. When a (contingent) proposition is true there corresponds to it a *fact* in the world. It is a well-known view that truth 'consists' in a correspondence between proposition and fact.

There are several types of fact. Here we shall distinguish three types:

Consider the propositions (true at the time when this was written) that the population of England is bigger than that of France and that my typewriter is standing on my writing-desk. The facts which answer to these propositions and make them true we commonly also call *states of affairs*.

Consider the proposition that it is raining at a certain place and time. Is the fact which would make this proposition true, rainfall or the falling of rain, also a state of affairs? We sometimes call it by that name. But the falling of rain is a rather different sort of state of affairs from my typewriter's standing on my writing-desk.

One could hint at the difference with the words 'dynamic' and 'static'. Rainfall is something which 'goes on', 'happens' over a certain period of time. Rainfall is a *process*; but my typewriter's being or standing on my writing-desk we would not, in ordinary speech, call a process.

Consider the proposition that Brutus killed Caesar. The corresponding fact nobody—with the possible exception of some philosophers—would call by the name 'state of affairs'. Nor would we call it 'process', although processes certainly were involved in the fact, *e.g.*, Brutus's movements when he stabbed Caesar and Caesar's falling to the ground and his uttering of the famous words. The type of fact which Caesar's death exemplifies is ordinarily called an *event*. Like processes, events are facts which *happen*. But unlike the happening of processes, the happening of events is a *taking place* and not a *going on*.

The three types of fact which we have distinguished are thus: states of affairs, processes, and events. It is not maintained that the three types which we have distinguished are exhaustive of the category of facts. The truth of *general* propositions raises special problems which we shall not discuss here at all.

Just as we can distinguish between generic and individual propositions, so we can distinguish between generic and individual states of affairs, processes, and events. Whether we should also distinguish between generic and individual facts is a question which I shall not discuss. Someone may wish to defend the view that facts are necessarily *individual* states of affairs, processes, and events.

Rainfall is a generic process, of which the falling of rain at a certain place and time is an instantiation. Dying is a generic event, of which, *e.g.*, Caesar's death is an instantiation. The superiority with regard to population of one country over another is a generic state of affairs, of which the present superiority with regard to population of England over France is an instantiation. But in the past the relative size of the populations of the two countries was the reverse. Thus, there is also a generic or semigeneric state of affairs, *viz.* the superiority with regard to population of England over France, which is instantiated in the present situation.

A sentence which expresses a contingently true proposition will be said to *describe* the fact which makes this proposition true.

(Cf. above, p. 22, on the term 'descriptive sentence'.) Thus, *e.g.*, the sentence 'Caesar was murdered by Brutus' describes a fact.

Facts can also be *named*. The name of a fact is a substantive-clause such as, *e.g.*, 'Caesar's death' or 'the present superiority with regard to population of England over France'. One also speaks of *the fact that*, *e.g.*, Caesar was murdered by Brutus. This may be regarded as an abbreviated way of saying that the proposition that Caesar was murdered by Brutus is true ('true to fact'). The phrase 'that Caesar was murdered by Brutus' names a proposition. Cf. above, p. 18.)

Even if we do not want to distinguish between individual and generic facts, it seems appropriate and natural to say that sentences which express contingent generic propositions describe generic states of affairs or processes or events. Thus, *e.g.*, the sentence 'It is raining' can be said to *describe* a generic process, the *name* of which is 'rainfall'.

To propositional logic, as such, it makes no difference whether we think of the true-making facts of propositions as states of affairs or processes or events. But to the study of deontic logic these distinctions are relevant. This is so because of the paramount position which the concept of an *act* holds in this logic.

We have already stipulated that the variables p, q, etc., should be understood as schematic representations of sentences which express generic propositions. We now add to this the stipulation that the sentences thus represented should describe *generic states of affairs*.

6. The three types of fact (and, correspondingly, of proposition), which we have distinguished, are not logically independent of one another.

We shall not here discuss the question how processes are related to events and to states of affairs. Be it only observed that the beginning and the end (stopping) of a process may be regarded as events.

There is a main type of event which can be regarded as an *ordered pair* of two states of affairs. The ordering relation is a relation between two occasions which are successive in time. We shall not here discuss the nature of this relation in further detail. Simplifying, we shall speak of the two occasions as the earlier and the later occasion. The event 'itself' is the *change* or transition from the state of affairs which obtains on the earlier occasion, to the state which obtains on the later occasion. We shall call the first the *initial* state, and the second the *end*-state.

The event, for example, which we call the opening of a window, consists in a change or transition from a state of affairs when this window is closed, to a state when it is open. We can also speak of the event as a *transformation* of the first state to the second. Alternatively, we can speak of it as a transformation of a world in which the initial state obtains, or which contains the initial state, into a world in which the end-state obtains, or which contains the end-state. Such transformations will also be called *state-transformations*.

Sometimes an event is a transition, not from one state to another state, but from a state to a process (which begins) or from a process (which ceases) to a state. Sometimes an event is a transition from one process to another process. Sometimes, finally, it is a transition from one 'state' of a process to another 'state' of the same process—*e.g.*, from quicker to slower or from louder to weaker.

Events of these more complicated types we shall, in general, not be considering in this inquiry. 'Event' will, unless otherwise expressly stated, always mean the transition from a state of affairs on a certain occasion to a state of affairs (not necessarily a different one) on the next occasion. If the occasion is specified the event is an individual event; if the occasion is unspecified the event is generic.

7. We introduce a symbol of the general form T, where the blanks to the left and to the right of the letter T are filled by p-expressions. The symbol is a schematic representation of sentences which describe (generic) events. The event described by pTq is a transformation of or transition from a certain initial state to an end-state, *viz.* from the (generic) state of affairs described by p to the (generic) state of affairs described by q. Or, as we could also put it: pTq describes the transformation of or transition from a p-world to a q-world. The states of affairs will also be called 'features' of the worlds.

We shall call expressions of the type T *atomic* T-expressions. We can form molecular compounds of them. By a T-*expression* we shall understand an atomic T-expression or a molecular compound of atomic T-expressions.

T-expressions may be handled in accordance with the rules of the p-calculus (propositional logic). As will be seen, there also exist special rules for the handling of T-expressions. The rules for handling T-expressions, we shall say, define the *T-calculus*.

Let p mean that a certain window is open. $\sim p$ then means that this same window is closed ($=$not open). $\sim pTp$ again means that the window is being opened, strictly speaking: that a world in which this window is closed changes or is transformed into a world in which this window is open. Similarly, $pT \sim p$ means that the window is being closed (is closing). We could also say that $\sim pTp$ describes the event called 'the opening of the window' and that $pT \sim p$ describes the event named 'the closing of the window'.

Consider the meaning of pTp. The letter to the left and that to the right of T describe the same generic state of affairs. The occasions on which this generic state is thought to obtain are successive in time. Hence pTp expresses that the state of affairs described by p obtains on both occasions, irrespective of how the world may have otherwise changed from the one occasion to the other. In other words: pTp means that the world remains *unchanged* in the feature described by p on both occasions. It is a useful generalization to call this too an 'event' or a 'transformation', although it strictly speaking is a 'not-event' or a 'not-transformation'.

In a similar manner, $\sim pT \sim p$ means that the world remains unchanged in the generic feature described by $\sim p$ on two successive occasions.

Again let p mean that a certain window is open. pTp then means that this window remains open and $\sim pT \sim p$ that it remains closed on two successive occasions.

We shall call the events or state-transformations, described by pTp, $pT \sim p$, $\sim pTp$, and $\sim pT \sim p$, the four *elementary (state-) transformations* which are possible with regard to a given (generic) state of affairs or feature of the world. The four transformations, be it observed, are *mutually exclusive*; no two of them can happen on the same pair of successive occasions. The four transformations, moreover, are *jointly exhaustive*. On a given occasion the world either has the feature described by p or it lacks it; if it has this feature it will on the next occasion either have retained or lost it;

if again it lacks this feature it will on the next occasion either have acquired it or still lack it.

By an *elementary* T-expression we understand an atomic T-expression in which the letter to the left of T is either an atomic p-expression or an atomic p-expression preceded by the negation-sign, and the letter to the right of T is this same atomic p-expression either with or without the negation-sign before itself.

8. We shall in this section briefly describe how every state-transformation—strictly speaking: proposition to the effect that a certain change or event takes place—may be regarded as a truth-function of elementary state-transformations.

Consider the meaning of pTq. A p-world changes to a q-world. p and q, let us imagine, describe logically independent features of the two worlds. The p-world either has or lacks the feature described by q. It is, in other words, either a p & q-world or a p & $\sim q$-world. Similarly, the q-world is either a p & q-world or a $\sim p$ & q-world. The event or transformation described by pTq is thus obviously the same as the one described by $(p$ & q v p & $\sim q) T(p$ & q v $\sim p$ & $q)$.

Assume that the p-world is a p & q-world and that the q-world is a p & q-world too. Then the transition from the initial state to the end-state involves no change at all of the world in the two features described by p and q respectively. The schematic description of this transformation is $(p$ & $q) T(p$ & $q)$, and the transformation thus described is obviously the same as the *conjunction* of the two elementary transformations described by pTp and qTq.

Assume that the p-world is a p & q-world and that the q-world is a $\sim p$ & q-world. Then the transition from the initial state to the end-state involves a change from 'positive' to 'privative' in the feature described by p. The transformation described by $(p$ & $q) T(\sim p$ & $q)$ is obviously the same as the conjunction of the elementary transformations described by $pT \sim p$ and qTq.

Assume that the p-world is a p & $\sim q$-world and the q-world a p & q-world. The world now changes from being a $\sim q$-world to being a q-world, but remains unchanged as p-world. The transformation described by $(p$ & $\sim q)T(p$ & $q)$ is the conjunction of the elementary transformations described by pTp and $\sim qTq$.

Assume, finally, that the p-world is a p & $\sim q$-world and the

30

q-world a $\sim p$ & q-world. The world now changes from p-world to $\sim p$-world and from $\sim q$-world to q-world. The transformation described by $(p$ & $\sim q)T(\sim p$ & $q)$ is the conjunction of the elementary transformations described by $pT \sim p$ and $\sim qTq$.

Thus the atomic T-expression pTq is identical in meaning with the following disjunction-sentence of conjunction-sentences of elementary T- expressions:

(pTp) & (qTq) v $(pT \sim p)$ & (qTq) v (pTp) & $(\sim qTq)$ v $(pT \sim p)$ & $(\sim qTq)$.

From the example which we have been discussing it should be plain that every atomic T-expression can become transformed into a molecular complex (disjunction-sentence of conjunction-sentences) of elementary T-expressions. Thus every atomic T-expression expresses a truth-function of elementary state-transformations. Since truth-functionship is transitive, it follows that every molecular complex too of atomic T-expressions expresses a truth-function of elementary state-transformations.

Consider an arbitrary T-expression. We replace its (not-elementary) atomic constituents by disjunction-sentences of conjunction-sentences of elementary T-expressions. The original T-expression has thus become transformed into a molecular complex of elementary T-expressions. These last will be called the T-*constituents* of the original T-expression.

It follows from what has been said that every T-expression expresses a truth-function of (the propositions expressed by) its T-constituents. Which truth-function it expresses can be investigated and decided in a truth-table. This truth-table differs from an 'ordinary' truth-table of propositional logic only in the feature that certain combinations of truth-values are excluded from it. The excluded combinations are those, and only those, which would conflict with the principle that, of the four elementary T-expressions which answer to a given atomic p-expression, *no two* must be assigned the value 'true', and *not all* may be assigned the value 'false'.

If a T-expression expresses the tautology of its T-constituents we shall call (the proposition expressed by) it a T-*tautology*. An example of a T-tautology is (pTp) v $(pT \sim p)$ v $(\sim pTp)$ v $(\sim pT \sim p)$.

The negation of a T-tautology is a T-*contradiction*. An example of a T-contradiction is (pTp) & $(pT \sim p)$. It follows that $\sim(pTp)$ v $\sim (pT \sim p)$ is a T-tautology.

31

We consider, finally, some special formulae.

The first is $(p \vee \sim p)Tp$. Its normal form is $(pTp) \vee (\sim pTp)$. The formula, in other words, expresses a true proposition if, and only if, on the later of two successive occasions the world has the feature described by p, independently of whether it had this feature or lacked it on the earlier of the two occasions.

The second is $(p \vee \sim p)T(p \vee \sim p)$. It is a T-tautology. Its normal form is $(pTp) \vee (pT \sim p) \vee (\sim pTp) \vee (\sim pT \sim p)$.

A special rule must be given for dealing with T-expressions in which contradictory p-expressions occur. This is necessary because of the fact that a contradictory formula has no perfect disjunctive normal form. Or, as one could also put it: its normal form 'vanishes', is a 0-termed disjunction. The rule which we need is simply this: An atomic T-expression, in which the p-expression to the left or right of T expresses the contradiction of the propositions expressed by its atomic p-constituents, expresses a T-contradiction. The intuitive meaning of this is obvious: since a contradictory state of affairs cannot obtain, it cannot change or remain unchanged either. Nor can it come into existence as a result of change.

9. Consider an arbitrary T-expression. We replace the (not-elementary) atomic T-expressions of which it is a molecular complex by disjunction-sentences of conjunction-sentences of elementary T-expressions. Thereupon we transform the molecular complex thus obtained into its (perfect) disjunctive normal form. (See above Section 3.) This is a disjunction-sentence of conjunction-sentences of elementary T-expressions and/or their negation-sentences.

It may happen that some (or all) of the conjunction-sentences contain two (or more) elementary T-expressions of different type but of the same variable (atomic p-expression). For example: $(pTp) \& (\sim pT \sim p)$. Since the four elementary types of state-transformations are mutually exclusive, such conjunction-sentences are contradictory. We omit them from the normal form.

Consider next the negation-sentence of some elementary T-expression, e.g., the formula $\sim(pTp)$. Since the four elementary types of state-transformations are jointly exhaustive, the negation of the formula for one of the types will be tautologously equivalent to the disjunction of the unnegated formulae for the three other types. Thus, *e.g.*, the formula $\sim(pTp)$ is tautologously equivalent to the disjunction-formula $pT\sim p$ v $\sim pTp$ v $\sim pT\sim p$.

Because of the joint exhaustiveness of the four elementary types of state-transformations, we can replace each negated elementary T-expression by a three-termed disjunction-sentence of (unnegated) elementary T-expressions. We make these replacements throughout in the above perfect disjunctive normal form of the molecular complex—having omitted from the normal form the contradictory conjunctions, if any, which occur in it. Thereupon we distribute the conjunction-sentences which contain disjunction-sentences as their members into disjunction-sentences of conjunction-sentences of elementary T-expressions. The formula thus obtained we call the *positive normal form* of the original arbitrary T-expression. It is a disjunction-sentence of conjunction-sentences of elementary T-expressions. No negated T-expressions occur in it.

10. p-expressions, we have said (Section 5), may be regarded as (schematic) descriptions of (generic) states of affairs. T-expressions again are schematic descriptions of generic changes. Thus, in a general sense, p-expressions could be called 'state-descriptions' and T-expressions 'change-descriptions'. Following an established terminology, however, we here make a restricted use of the term *state-description* to mean a conjunction-sentence of n atomic p-expressions and/or their negation-sentences (cf. Section 3). By analogy, we shall make a restricted use of the term *change-description* to mean a conjunction-sentence of some n elementary T-expressions of n different atomic variables (p-expressions). Thus, for example, (pTp) & $(qT\sim q)$ is a change-description.

n atomic p-expressions (variables p, q, etc.) determine 2^n different possible state-descriptions. To each state-description of n atomic p-expressions there correspond 2^n possible change-descriptions. n atomic p-expressions therefore determine in all $2^n \times 2^n$ or 2^{2n} different possible change-descriptions. Thus, for example, to the state-description p & $\sim q$ there correspond the four change-descriptions (pTp) & $(\sim qT\sim q)$ and (pTp) & $(\sim qTq)$ and $(pT\sim p)$ & $(\sim qT\sim q)$ and $(pT\sim p)$ & $(\sim qTq)$.

Given n atomic p-expressions, we can list in a table the 2^n state-descriptions and the 2^{2n} change-descriptions which answer to the atomic variables. This is a list for the case of two atomic variables, p and q:

State-descriptions	Change-descriptions
$p \mathbin{\&} q$	$(pTp) \mathbin{\&} (qTq)$ $(pTp) \mathbin{\&} (qT\sim q)$ $(pT\sim p) \mathbin{\&} (qTq)$ $(pT\sim p) \mathbin{\&} (qT\sim q)$
$p \mathbin{\&} \sim q$	$(pTp) \mathbin{\&} (\sim qT\sim q)$ $(pTp) \mathbin{\&} (\sim qTq)$ $(pT\sim p) \mathbin{\&} (\sim qT\sim q)$ $(pT\sim p) \mathbin{\&} (\sim qTq)$
$\sim p \mathbin{\&} q$	$(\sim pT\sim p) \mathbin{\&} (qTq)$ $(\sim pT\sim p) \mathbin{\&} (qT\sim q)$ $(\sim pTp) \mathbin{\&} (qTq)$ $(\sim pTp) \mathbin{\&} (qT\sim q)$
$\sim p \mathbin{\&} \sim q$	$(\sim pT\sim p) \mathbin{\&} (\sim qT\sim q)$ $(\sim pT\sim p) \mathbin{\&} (\sim qTq)$ $(\sim pTp) \mathbin{\&} (\sim qT\sim q)$ $(\sim pTp) \mathbin{\&} (\sim qTq)$

The positive normal-form of a T-expression which contains n variables for states of affairs is a disjunction-sentence of (none or) one or two . . . or 2^{2n} conjunction-sentences of n elementary T-expressions. If the disjunction has no terms the T-expression expresses a T-contradiction. If it has 2^{2n} terms the T-expression expresses a T-tautology.

III

ACT AND ABILITY

1. THE concept of a human act is of basic importance to the questions which are discussed in this book. It is not one of the aims of deontic logic to clarify this concept. The notion of an act is more like a tool, which this logic has to use for other purposes of clarification. Considering, however, the complex and obscure nature of this notion, we must try to throw light on some of its aspects before we can be reasonably sure that our use of it as a tool in deontic logic stands on a firm basis.

I find it surprising that the concept of a human act has, *as such*, been relatively little discussed in philosophic literature. The same is true of the related notions of activity and behaviour. Traditional philosophic discussion, bearing on these concepts, has concentrated on the problem of the so-called freedom of the will. In this discussion it is all too often taken for granted that it is clear what action *is*. In fact, much of what has been said about the problem of freedom can be shown to be void of interest, because based on some logically defective notion of acting.

In our discussion of acts we renounce every pretension of being systematic, and shall try to confine ourselves to a necessary minimum of conceptual distinctions and observations. The freedom of the will we shall not discuss at all. But of the related topic of the *ability to act* (do), we shall have to say something.

2. The notion of a human act is related to the notion of an event, *i.e.* a change in the world. What is the nature of this relationship? It would not be right, I think, to call acts a kind or species of

35

events. An act *is* not a change in the world. But many acts may quite appropriately be described as the bringing about or *effecting* ('at will') of a change. To act is, in a sense, to *interfere* with 'the course of nature'.

An event, we have said (Ch. II, Sect. 6), is a transition from one state of affairs to another, or from a state to a process, or from a process to a state; or it is a transformation of processes. The Logic of Change, which we sketched in the preceding chapter, is primarily a logic of events of the first type. Events of the second and third type are also called the beginning (commencing, starting) and the end (ceasing, stopping) of processes.

The events which are effected through action can be of any of the several types just mentioned. The acts of opening a window or of killing a person effect changes in states of affairs. Starting to run or stopping to talk may be acts which effect a change from a state to a process and from a process to a state respectively. But when a walking man starts to run, his action effects a transformation of processes.

The Logic of Action, which we are going to outline in the next chapter, will primarily be a logic of acts which effect changes among states of affairs. Other types of action will not be explicitly dealt with in our formal theory.

The examples of acts which we have here mentioned are examples of what I shall call *generic acts* or *act-categories*. There is an, in principle, unlimited number of cases of window-opening or of starting to run.

The several cases of generic acts I shall call *individual acts* or *act-individuals*. It is noteworthy that the word 'act' is used ambiguously in ordinary language to mean sometimes a generic and sometimes an individual act. It is, *e.g.*, correct to call murder an act; this is an act-category. It is also correct to call the murder of Caesar an act; this is an act-individual.

To the generic act of opening a window there answers the generic change of a window becoming open. To the individual act, which was the murder of Caesar, there answers the individual event of Caesar's death.

The logical difference between acts and events is a difference between 'activity' and 'passivity'. An act requires an agent. An individual event is the taking place or happening of some generic event on a specified *occasion*. An individual act again is the doing of a generic act on a specified occasion by a specified *agent*.

3. When we say that an individual event happens on a certain occasion we may regard this occasion for the happening of the event as constituted by two successive occasions for the obtaining of certain states of affairs (see above Ch. II, Sect. 6). Similarly, when we say that an individual act is done on a certain occasion we may regard this occasion for the doing of the act as constituted by the two successive occasions for the corresponding individual event.

Not every occasion (or pair of successive occasions) is an occasion on which just any individual event may happen or act be done. Thus, for example, only on an occasion when a certain window is closed *can* this window open or become opened. Generally speaking, only on an occasion on which the generic state of affairs described by *p* obtains, *can* the generic change described by *pT ~p* or that described by *pTp* take place or become effected ('at will').

We shall say that an occasion constitutes an *opportunity* for the happening of a certain generic event or for the doing of an act of a certain category, when the occasion has some generic feature which makes the happening of this event or the doing of this act (logically) possible on that occasion. For example: Only on an occasion when the window is closed, is there an opportunity for opening it.

Any opportunity for the doing of an act of a certain category is also an opportunity for the happening of the corresponding generic event, *i.e.* for the event effected through the act. The converse entailment, however, does not hold. Not every opportunity for the happening of a certain generic event is also an opportunity for the doing of a corresponding act. The occasion for the happening of the event has to satisfy additional conditions in order to constitute an opportunity for the doing of the corresponding act, *i.e.* the act of bringing about this event. Which these additional conditions are will be discussed later (Sect. 7).

4. The notion of an agent is essential to the distinction between acts and events. We shall here make only a few brief comments on this notion.

We may distinguish between *empirical* (natural) and *super-empirical* (super-natural) agents. An agent is empirical, I shall say, if the agent's existence is a contingent or empirical fact. Super-empirical agents have necessary existence. The difference between the two categories of agent can also be expressed by saying that an empirical agent is a 'perishable', a super-empirical agent an 'eternal' being.

The ideas of necessary existence and of super-empirical agents cannot be discussed within the limits of this work.

Agents who perform human action are empirical. But not all agents of human acts are human individuals.

We can distinguish between *personal* and *impersonal* agents. An impersonal agent is, for example, any so-called legal or juristic person (such as a corporation), a law court, a legislative assembly, or the state.

The action of impersonal agents is certainly 'human action' in some sense of the word. The question may be raised whether acts which we impute to juristic persons and other impersonal agents of human acts are 'logical constructions', *i.e.* could be defined (conceptually explicated) in terms of acts of some personal agents. This question, however, we shall not discuss.

Of what I here call personal agents we can further distinguish two kinds, *viz. individual* and *collective* agents.

When an act is performed by one man we shall say that it is performed by him *individually*.

Sometimes the performance of an act requires the joint acting of several men. The table may be too heavy to be removed from the room by one person alone, but two or more persons may do it by their joint efforts. We then say that the act of removing the table is performed by two or more men *collectively*.

That an act is performed by several agents collectively may also be described by saying that the *agent* who performs this act is a collectivity of men or a collective agent.

A collective agent must not be confused with an impersonal agent such as, say, a corporation or the state or some other juristic person. But the acts of a juristic person *may* entail the collective acting of some men.

Whenever several men perform an action collectively ('by joint efforts'), each man does something individually. The question may be raised whether acts attributed to collective agents could not be regarded as 'logical constructions' of acts of some individual agents. This is another problem which will not be discussed here.

5. To every act (of the kind which we are here considering) there corresponds a change or an event in the world. The terms 'change' and 'event' must then be understood in the broad, generalized sense, which covers both changes (events) and not-changes (not-events). This correspondence between act and change is an *intrinsic* or logical tie. The act is, as it were, 'defined' as the act of effecting such and such a change. For example: the act of opening a certain window is, logically, the act of changing or transforming a world in which this window is closed to a world in which it is open.

By the *result* of an act we can understand either the change corresponding to this act or, alternatively, the end-state (see Ch. II, Sect. 6) of this change. Thus, by the result of the act of opening a certain window we can understand either the fact that the window is opening (changes from closed to open) or the fact that it is open.

On either way of understanding the notion of a result of action the tie between the act and its result is intrinsic. The act cannot be truly described as being an act of the category in question unless it effects a change or ends in a state of affairs of the kind in question, which we call its result. An act cannot be truly called an act of opening the window unless it ends (results) in the window's being open—at least for a short time. *Trying* to open the window need not, of course, result in this.

When the world changes in a certain respect it may happen that it also, by virtue of so-called causal or natural necessity, becomes transformed in a certain other respect. We then say that the second transformation is a *consequence* of the first. If the first transformation is effected through action, is the result of an act, then the second is a consequence of action, is a consequence of this act.

For example: a consequence of the act of opening a window may be that the temperature in a certain room sinks (is subsequently lower than it was before).

Whether a certain transformation will cause a certain other transformation to take place or not will usually depend upon the presence or absence of a number of other features of the world *beside* the states associated with the two transformations themselves.

39

This is true also of human action. Whether the temperature in a room will sink or not as a consequence of opening a window will depend, among other things, upon the antecedent difference in outdoor and indoor temperature. Sometimes the temperature will not sink but rise.

Unlike the relation between an act and its result, the relation between an act and its consequences is *extrinsic* (causal).

Someone may wish to object to our terms 'result' and 'consequence' (of action) on the ground that what is here called a consequence is quite commonly in ordinary language spoken of as the result of an act, and vice versa. Thus, for example, we say that as a result of the window's being opened he caught a cold. The catching of the cold, however, was a consequence, to use our terminology, of the act whose result was that the window became open.

I am, of course, not anxious to correct the ordinary use of 'result' and 'consequence'. What matters are not the terms, but the conceptual distinction between such changes and states as have an intrinsic and such as have an extrinsic relation to a given act. This distinction is important to note, and it is somewhat unfortunate that no clear terminological indication of it in ordinary parlance should exist.

Perhaps this 'defect' of ordinary language is connected with the fact that the distinction between the result and the consequences of an act, although logically sharp, is at the same time in an important sense relative. What I mean by this can be explained as follows:

Consider again the act whose result we said was that a certain window is open (at a certain time and place). Could one not truthfully answer the question of what the person who opened the window *did*, by saying that he let cool air into the room (thus lowering the temperature)? Is not the cooling of the room the result, rather than the consequence? A consequence may be that someone in the room began to shiver and went out or subsequently caught a cold.

The answer is that we can certainly speak of an act of cooling the room, but that this is a *different* act from that of opening the window. The act of cooling the room requires *logically* that the temperature should go down, and *may* require *causally* that the window should be opened. The act of opening the window again requires *logically* that the window is opened, and *may* lead *causally* to the fact that the indoor temperature sinks.

Thus, one and the same change or state of affairs can be both the result and a consequence of an action. What makes it the one or the other depends upon the agent's *intention* in acting, and upon other circumstances which we shall not discuss in this work.

The act of opening a window and that of cooling a room are *logically distinct*, because of the nature of their results. But there is a sense in which the two acts may be said to 'look' exactly alike. The sense in which they look alike is that the *activity* involved in performing the two acts may be identical, *viz.* certain muscular contractions and movements of the agent's limbs.

6. We shall distinguish between *act* and *activity*. To close a window or to kill a person is to perform an act. To smoke or to run or to read is to be engaged in activity.

The distinction is obviously important, but philosophers have so far done very little to clarify it. Here I shall make only a few scattered observations on the topic.

As acts are related to *events*, so are activities related to *processes* (cf. Ch. II, Sect. 5). Events happen, processes go on. Acts effect the happening of events, activities keep processes going.

Activity is not internally related to changes and to states of affairs in the same manner in which acts are related to their results. Activity, however, may be externally or causally related to changes and states which are consequences of performing this activity. Running need not leave any 'imprint' on the world, but smoking may leave smoke. As a consequence of drinking a person may get drunk. Getting drunk is an event, and drunkenness a state.

The question may be raised whether activity is logically prior to acts, or vice versa.

In some sense activity seems to be prior. Action may be said to presuppose or require activity. The bodily movements which are a prerequisite of most human acts may be regarded as activity in which the agent has to engage in order to perform those acts. The changes and states which we call *results* of action may be viewed as *consequences* of such prerequisite activities.

Yet in another way action seems prior. Human activity has a beginning and an end. The beginning and the ending of activity have, sometimes at least, the character of acts. To *run* is an activity, but to *start* running or to *stop* running are acts of a kind. These acts, however, differ characteristically from acts which effect changes in states of affairs. The first of them implies a change or transition from a state to a process, the second again from a process to a state (cf. Ch. II, Sect. 6).

Beside the distinction between act and activity, we have to note a distinction between *acting* and *doing*. To do something is to perform an act. To be doing something is to be engaged in some activity. That which we have called the result of an act is that which any agent who (successfully) performs this act on a certain occasion *has done* on that occasion. When an act fails of its intended result the agent *has tried* to do something which, in fact, he failed to accomplish (do). Trying is thus a 'logically incomplete' mode of acting. It is not immediately clear whether trying should be counted as falling in the category of act or in that of activity (cf. below, Section 10).

7. We have previously (Ch. II, Sect. 7) introduced the notion of an *elementary change*. The four types of elementary change, we said, are the four types of change and not-change which are possible with regard to a given (atomic) state of affairs and a pair of successive occasions. As schematic descriptions of the four types of change we introduced pTp, $pT \sim p$, $\sim pTp$, and $\sim pT \sim p$.

We now introduce the notion of an *elementary act*. By an elementary act we shall understand an act the *result* (Section 5) of which is an elementary change. The correspondence between elementary act and elementary change is one to one.

We shall use the symbol d for acting. The schematic descriptions of the four types of elementary act shall be $d(pTp)$, $d(pT \sim p)$, $d(\sim pTp)$, and $d(\sim pT \sim p)$. It should be observed that $d(pTp)$, etc., are schematic representations of *sentences* which describe acts, just as pTp, etc., are schematic representations of sentences which describe changes, and p, etc., are schematic representations of sentences which describe (generic) states of affairs.

We shall now consider the nature of the four types of elementary act in turn. For purposes of illustration, let p represent the sentence 'The door is open'.

Take first $d(\sim pTp)$. It describes the act of changing or trans-forming a $\sim p$-world to a p-world. In terms of our illustration: it describes the act of opening the door. We could say that $d(\sim pTp)$ represents the sentence 'the door is being opened'. A way of reading the schema $d(\sim pTp)$ would be 'it is being done that p'. For purposes of convenience, however, we shall read it, though this is somewhat inaccurate, 'p is done' and call the act which the schema describes, 'the doing of p'. (A more accurate, but clumsier, name would be 'the doing so that p'.)

It is easy to see that the act described by $d(\sim pTp)$ *can* (logically) be done only provided two conditions are satisfied. The first condition is that the state described by $\sim p$ prevails on the first of the two successive occasions which jointly constitute an occasion for doing the act. Only when the door *is* closed *can* it become opened. One cannot open an open door. The second condition is that the change described by $\sim pTp$ does not happen, as we say, 'of itself', *i.e. independently of the action of an agent*, from the first to the second of the two occasions. If a door is so constructed that a spring or other mechanism pulls it open as soon as it has become closed, then there is no such *act* as the act of opening this door. (But there may be an act of closing it and of keeping it closed. See below.)

Consider next $d(pT\sim p)$. It describes the act of changing a p-world to a $\sim p$-world. If we call the act described by the schema $d(\sim pTp)$, 'the doing of p', we could call the act described by the schema $d(pT\sim p)$, 'the destroying of p'. If we apply the schema to our example it describes the act of closing the door.

The conditions for the doing of the act described by $d(pT\sim p)$ are as follows: The state described by p should prevail on the first of two successive occasions, *and* not 'of itself' change to its opposite from this occasion to the next. For example: A door can become closed as a result of action, only provided it is open and does not close 'of itself'. Here the words 'of itself' mean that the change is due to some 'natural' cause, such as, *e.g.*, the operation of a spring, and is independent of the action of an agent.

Which act does $d(pTp)$ describe? pTp means that the world does not change in the feature described by p on two successive occasions. Can this be a result of action? It certainly can. The world might change in a certain feature, unless there is some agent to prevent it from changing. This is the sort of action that $d(pTp)$ describes. We might call it 'the preserving of p'. This act can be done, provided that the state described by p initially obtains, and would change into its contradictory state unless the change were prevented through action. For example: It could happen that a door which is open will close, *e.g.*, under the influence of a spring-mechanism, unless somebody keeps it open.

$d(\sim pT \sim p)$, finally, describes the act of keeping the world unchanged in the feature described by $\sim p$. We could call this act 'the suppression of p'. This act can be done provided that the state described by $\sim p$ obtains, but would change into the state described by p unless prevented through action. For example: It could happen that a door which is closed will open, unless someone keeps it closed.

If by the result of an act we understand, not a change, but the end-state of a change, then the correspondence between act and result is not a one-to-one correspondence. The same state may be the result of more than one act. Thus, the state described by p can be the result both of the elementary act described by $d(pTp)$ and of the elementary act described by $d(\sim pTp)$. The fact that a certain window is open can be a result either of an act of opening it or of an act of keeping it open.

Each one of the four types of elementary act can be performed only provided a certain state of affairs obtains. The types of act described by $d(\sim pTp)$ and $d(pT \sim p)$, moreover, can be done only provided the change, which is their result, *does not* take place 'of itself', *i.e.* independently of action. The types of act described by $d(pTp)$ and $d(\sim pT \sim p)$ again can be done only provided that the changes described by $pT \sim p$ and $\sim pTp$ respectively would take place unless prevented by action. But this is the same as to say that the changes (not-changes) described by pTp and $\sim pT \sim p$, *i.e.* the changes which are the results of the respective acts, *do not* take place 'of themselves', *i.e.* independently of action.

The question may be raised what we shall say of the case when some *other agent* beside the agent in question effects the change, which must not happen 'of itself', if we are to say truly that the agent in question has *done* it. Shall we say, then, that neither agent does the act? Or shall we say that both do it? If a person shoots at another at the very moment when the latter dies of a stroke the first person cannot be rightly said to have killed the second. The second died, but was not killed. The first did not commit murder, although he may have attempted to do so. Suppose, however, that two persons at the same time shoot at a third, and that each

44

shot individually would have killed him. Obviously, we must say
that the third man was killed, *i.e.* that his death was a result of
action. But by whom was he killed? If the assumption is that each
shot individually would have killed him it is not correct to say
that the two murderers killed him 'jointly' or 'by joint efforts', and
that therefore the agent, technically speaking, was a collective
agent. The right thing to say is, in my opinion, that he was killed
by each one of the two murderers, *i.e.* that his death was the result
of an act of the one murderer *and* of an act of the other murderer.
Both did it, not 'jointly', but 'individually'.

We must thus think of the changes, the not-happening of which
are conditions for the performance (performability) of an act,
that they are changes *in nature*, *i.e.* such changes as happen
independently of the interference of agents. This explains the
meaning of the phrase 'of itself', which we have been using when
speaking of those changes.

8. Beside acts we have also to study their 'correlatives', *forbearances*. What is it to forbear (to do) something?

Forbearing is not the same as not-doing *simpliciter*. That one
forbears to produce through action the change described by
$\sim pTp$, or the state of affairs described by p, cannot be described
by $\sim d(\sim pTp)$. If, for example, a certain window is closed on a
certain occasion one *does not* close it on that occasion—but neither
does one *forbear* closing it then. Furthermore, things which are
beyond human capacity to do (*e.g.* to change the weather), one
does not do—but neither does one forbear doing them.

It is also clear that forbearing cannot be defined as the doing of
not-changes. $d(\sim pT \sim p)$ does not mean that an agent forbears to
produce the state of affairs described by p. It means that he
('actively') prevents this state from coming into existence—*e.g.*
keeps open a door which otherwise would close.

It seems that forbearing cannot be defined in terms of action
and change (and truth-functional notions) alone. But we can define
it in terms of action, change, and ability. We propose the following
definition:

An agent, on a given occasion, forbears the doing of a certain
thing if, and only if, he *can do* this thing, but *does* in fact *not do* it.

The notion of forbearing, thus defined, is the logically *weakest*
member of a series of progressively stronger notions of forbearing.

45

On our definition, forbearing to do something which one can do does not presuppose *awareness* of the opportunity. In a stronger sense of 'forbear', an agent forbears only such action as he knows he can perform on the occasion in question. In a still stronger sense, an agent forbears only such action as he knows he can perform but *decides* (chooses, prefers) to leave undone on the occasion in question. If, in addition, he feels an inclination or temptation to do the action, which he chooses not to do, then he is in a still stronger sense forbearing it. Of this strongest sense of 'forbear' we also use such words as 'abstain' or 'forsake'.

We shall introduce a special symbol f for forbearing.

$f(\sim pTp)$ shall mean that one forbears to change through action a $\sim p$-world to a p-world. We shall call this kind of action *forbearing to do*. The forbearance described by $f(\sim pTp)$ is possible only in a $\sim p$-world which does not, on the occasion in question, 'of itself' change into a p-world. For example: To forbear to close a door is possible only provided this door is open *and* does not close 'of itself'.

$f(pT\sim p)$ means that one *forbears to destroy* (annihilate, undo) the state described by p. This forbearance is possible only in a p-world, which does not, on the occasion in question, 'of itself' change into a $\sim p$-world.

$f(pTp)$ means that one *forbears to preserve* the state of affairs described by p. This is possible only in a p-world which will, on the occasion in question, change into a $\sim p$-world, unless the change is prevented through action.

$f(\sim pT\sim p)$, finally, means that one *forbears to suppress* the state of affairs described by p. This is possible only in a $\sim p$-world, which will, on the occasion in question, change into a p-world unless the change is prevented through action.

The modes of conduct which we have just been discussing we shall call the four types of *elementary forbearances*. It should be clear in which sense we can talk of 'corresponding' elementary acts and forbearances. To the elementary act described by $d(pTp)$ corresponds the elementary forbearance described by $f(pTp)$, and so forth.

Forbearing, just as much as acting, has results and consequences.

Primarily, the results of forbearing are that certain changes do *not* take place. Thus, the forbearance described by $f(\sim pTp)$ results in that the change described by $\sim pTp$ does not occur. And similarly for the other elementary types of forbearance.

46

There is a *prima facie* objection to this way of arguing, which has to be answered. The result of my forbearing to open a certain window, say, is that *I* do not open it. But what if somebody else opens it? Cannot, in spite of my forbearance, the change from 'window closed' to 'window open' take place as the result of some *other* agent's interference with the state of the world? The answer seems to me to be this:

At the very moment when another agent opens a window, which I have up to this moment forborne to open, the *opportunity* for (continued) forbearing gets lost. What I may forbear to do, when the window is being opened by another person, is to keep the window closed or to prevent the other person from opening it. But I *can* no longer forbear to open the window. Thus, my forbearance to do this will necessarily be 'reflected' in the fact that the window remains closed.

Using our generalized notion of change, which includes not-changes, we can also say that the results of forbearing are that certain changes *take* place. There is a certain convenience in this mode of expression.

Thus, instead of saying that the forbearance described by $f(\sim pTp)$ results in the fact that the change described by $\sim pTp$ does not take place, we can say that it results in the fact that the change described by $\sim pT\sim p$ takes place. For, if the state of affairs described by $\sim p$ obtains on a certain occasion and if the world does not change in this feature, then—by the laws of the Logic of Change—the world remains unchanged in this feature.

By similar argument we can say that the forbearances described by $f(pT\sim p)$, $f(pTp)$, and $f(\sim pT\sim p)$ respectively result in the changes described by pTp, $pT\sim p$ and, $\sim pTp$ respectively.

Instead of calling certain changes the results of forbearance, we can also call certain states of affairs the results of forbearance. These states are the *end*-states of the resulting changes. Unlike the correspondence between forbearances and changes as their results, the correspondence between forbearances and states is not one-to-one, but one-to-two. Thus, *e.g.*, the state of affairs described by p can be the result either of a forbearance to prevent it from coming into being or of a forbearance to destroy it. It can also, as will be remembered, be the result either of an act of doing or of an act of preserving it. Finally, this state can exist, without being the result of either an act or a forbearance.

47

It should now be clear what has to be understood by the *consequences* of forbearances—and also clear that forbearance can have consequences. The consequences of a certain forbearance are the consequences of the state or change which is the result of this forbearance. Thus, *e.g.*, if the state described by p is the result of a forbearance to prevent it from coming into being, then everything which is a consequence of the change described by $\sim pTp$ is a consequence of this forbearance. There is no difference 'in principle' between the consequences of acts and of forbearances. (This is a logical observation of some importance to a certain type of ethical theory.)

We can exhibit the correspondences between the elementary acts, forbearances, and changes, together with the conditions of acting and forbearing and the results of acts and forbearances, in a table. (See p. 49.)

In ordinary language, it seems, the words 'act' and 'action' are used pretty much as synonyms. The philosopher is free to give to the two words different meanings for the purpose of marking some conceptual distinction which he thinks important. Here I shall employ the term 'action' as a common name for acts and forbearances. Acts and forbearances, we could say, are two *modes of action*.[1]

9. From the discussion of *acts* (and forbearances) we now move to a discussion of *abilities* or the notion of 'can do'.

We have distinguished between generic and individual acts (Section 2), between the result and the consequences of an act (Section 5), and between act and activity (Section 6). These distinctions are relevant to the present discussion.

When do we say of an agent that he *can do* a certain thing—for example, can open a window, or can get up from his bed, or can tell a lie? This is a very complicated question. What is said about it here will be confined to a necessary minimum for our theory of norms.

To be able to do some act, we shall say, is to *know how* to do it. Sometimes we can also say that it is to master a certain technique. The mere fact that by some haphazard movements of my hands

---

[1] Sir David Ross, too, makes a distinction between act and action. The distinction for which he uses the two terms is quite different from the distinction for which they are used here. See *The Right and the Good* (1930), p. 7.

Condition of action	Act or forbearance	Result of action
$pT \sim p$ p is but vanishes, unless preserved	$d(pTp)$ p is preserved	pTp p remains
Same	$f(pTp)$ one lets p vanish	$pT \sim p$ p vanishes
pTp p is and remains, unless destroyed	$d(pT \sim p)$ p is destroyed	$pT \sim p$ p vanishes
Same	$f(pT \sim p)$ one lets p remain	pTp p remains
$\sim pT \sim p$ p is not and does not happen, unless produced	$d(\sim pTp)$ p is produced	$\sim pTp$ p happens
Same	$f(\sim pTp)$ one lets p remain absent	$\sim pT \sim p$ p remains absent
$\sim pTp$ p is not but happens, unless suppressed	$d(\sim pT \sim p)$ p is suppressed	$\sim pT \sim p$ p remains absent
Same	$f(\sim pT \sim p)$ one lets p happen	$\sim pTp$ p happens

and fingers I succeed in opening a door with a complicated lock-mechanism does not entitle me to say that I *can* open a door with this type of lock. But if normally, *i.e.* on most occasions, when I set myself to the task I succeed in opening the door without much trial and error, then I may be said to be able to do this sort of thing. I then *know how* to do it. I also master a certain technique.

Ability to do a certain act must be distinguished from ability to perform a certain activity, such as to walk, to run, or to speak. Of the ability to perform a certain activity we do not normally use the phrase 'know how'. A child who has learnt to walk or to speak is not ordinarily said to know how to walk or to speak. But ability to perform an activity can sometimes quite naturally be characterized as mastership of a technique; for example, when a child has learnt to handle knife and fork in eating.

The 'can do' which we are here discussing is the 'can do' of acts, and not the 'can do' of activities.

One can make a distinction between *ability* and *skill*, and relate it to a distinction between knowing how and having the mastership of a technique. The man who is able to do a certain thing knows how to do it. Only if the activity which is involved in doing the thing is of a complicated kind does this ability amount to mastership of a technique. When it does this we call such ability a skill.

We can also make a distinction between *ability* and *capacity*. Capacity often has the character of 'second order' ability. It is within a man's capacity to do a certain thing, we may say, when he *can* acquire the ability or skill needed for doing this thing, although he does not yet possess it.

On the view of ability which we are here adopting, a criterion for judging truly that a man can do a certain act is that normally, on most occasions for doing it, he should succeed. But is this not like saying that he *can do* something only if, on most occasions, he *can do* this? Are we not moving in a circle here?

I do not think that we have a circle here but a noteworthy shift in the meaning of certain words. That I 'can do' something has a different meaning when it refers to an act-individual and when it refers to an act-category. That on some occasion a certain state of affairs, say that a door is open, comes (came) into being as a *consequence* of some *activity* on my part, say some movements of my hands and fingers, is a necessary and sufficient condition for saying that I can (could) do this thing or produce this state *on that occasion*. The sole criterion of the 'can do' is here the success of certain efforts. Of this 'can do' no 'know how' and no reasonable assurance of success before the attempt is required. These are requirements of that 'can do' which refers to act-categories and which alone amounts to ability. It is, moreover, only when these requirements are satisfied that consequences of activity assume the character of *results* of *action*.

I shall call the 'can do' which refers to individual acts the *can do of success*, and that which refers to generic acts the *can do of ability*. The first 'can do' is always relative to an occasion for acting. The second is *independent* of occasions for acting. By this I mean that it makes no sense to say that we can do—in this sense of 'can do'—the thing on one occasion, but not on another—unless that other occasion belongs to a stage in our life-history which is either before we have learnt to do this thing or after we have forgotten how to do it.

Before we have acquired the ability, success and failure on the individual occasion for acting is the only sense in which we can or cannot do a certain thing. When the ability (or skill) has become acquired, however, we can also do things which we *sometimes* fail to accomplish in spite of efforts. We may fail because of some unforeseen obstacle, or because another agent interferes and prevents us from completing the act. When this happens we describe what we *did* on the occasion by saying that we *tried to do* something, but failed.

Yet, as already observed, we cannot be said to have the ability, unless *on most occasions*, when we set ourselves to do the act, we succeed in doing it. In this way success can be said to be the measure and criterion of ability, and yet the meaning of the 'can do' of ability be different from the meaning of the 'can do' of success.

10. It would be a mistake to think that whenever an agent has successfully accomplished an act he has also tried to accomplish it. A similar remark can be made of activity. Normally, when I shut a door or walk or read I cannot be said to *try*, successfully, to shut the door or to move my legs or to read out the words. To construe every act as a result or consequence of trying to act would be a distortion.

Although doing does not entail trying to do, it would seem that ability to do entails capacity for trying to do. If I *can do*, I also *can try*.

It would also be a mistake to think that, although one cannot *do* any given thing, one can at least *try to do* it. One cannot, for example, jump to the moon. But can one not *try* to jump to the moon? It is not clear what sort of behaviour we should describe as 'trying to jump to the moon'. Not until we have at least some idea of how to do a thing, can we try to do that thing. To 'have an idea' of how to do a thing again presupposes that we are not convinced that it is humanly impossible to do that thing. Since we *are* convinced that it is humanly impossible to jump to the moon, in the ordinary sense of 'jump', we can rightly say that we are unable even to try to perform this feat. To say 'I try, although I know that I shall fail' is to state a contradiction in terms.

There are also many things which I know are humanly possible and which I may learn or otherwise acquire the ability to do, but which at present I cannot even try to do, because of my ignorance.

The question may be raised: Is trying act or activity? In the course of trying to do something, one may perform various acts. But, basically, trying seems to me to belong to the category of activity. Trying to do something may, as we say, 'result' in the act's being successfully performed. But performing the act is not tied to trying to perform it in the same way as the resulting change is tied to the doing of the act. One is inclined to call the successful performance a consequence rather than a result, in our sense of the terms. It is *contingent* whether trying leads to result, but it is *necessary* that acting result in change.

When an agent *tries* to do something which he *can* do, but *fails* to accomplish the act, has he then forborne to do the thing in question? We are free to answer Yes or No, depending upon how we wish to mould the notion of forbearing. *Here* we shall understand 'forbear' in such a way that unsuccessful trying to do something which it is within the agent's *ability* to accomplish, counts as forbearing. 'Forbearing to do', in other words, will not be understood so as to entail 'forbearing to try'.

On this ruling, doing and forbearing are two *jointly exhaustive* modes of action. If an agent can do a certain thing, then, on any given occasion when there is an opportunity for him to do this thing, he will either do it or forbear doing it.

We could, however, also mould the notions in a way which would make unsuccessful trying a 'middle' between doing and forbearing. That which is *here* called 'forbearing' could then be called 'failing to do' or 'leaving undone'. Perhaps it would be more in accordance with ordinary usage to call the two jointly exhaustive and mutually exclusive modes of action 'doing' and 'failing to do' rather than 'doing' and 'forbearing'. But usage seems to be vacillating. The important thing is not whether we

should choose this or that terminology, but that it should be clear
how the terminology actually chosen is to be understood.

11. The notion of forbearing we have thus defined (see Section
8) that ability to do and ability to forbear doing the same thing are
reciprocal abilities.

It may appear more plausible to say that what an agent can do
he can also forbear doing than to say that what an agent can
forbear doing he can also do. It is inviting to think that it is
somehow 'easier' to forbear than to do, and that there are many
more things which we can forbear than things we can do.

The appearance of asymmetry between the abilities is partly, I
think, due to confusions and to neglect to observe certain conceptual distinctions.

First, the idea may be guilty of a confusion between *not-acting*
and *forbearing*. On an occasion which is not an *opportunity* (see
Section 3) for doing a certain act, an agent necessarily does not do
this act. Of course, we could so define 'forbear' that an agent is
said to forbear those acts also which he has not even an opportunity of doing. But this would be an odd use. We should then
have to say such things as that an agent who is in a room where
the window is open 'forbears' to *open* the window in that room.

Secondly, the impression that there are more things one can
forbear than things one can do may be due to a confusion between
doing and *trying to do*. Consider a man on the bank of a river, which
is, as a matter of fact, too wide for him to cross swimming. He
cannot cross it, but if he can swim and is not certain whether he
will reach the other shore he may *try* to cross it. If he can try he
can also forbear trying. He forbears trying by not plunging into
the water and setting out for the other shore. This is exactly the
same 'negative behaviour', by which our man would manifest his
forbearance to swim across the river, could he perform this feat.
But this does not mean that forbearing to swim across the river
and forbearing to try to swim across the river are one and the
same thing. They are different just because they are forbearances
relative to different modes of action.

In a sense, therefore, forbearing is precisely as 'difficult' as
doing. But in another sense, forbearing can quite rightly be said
to be, normally, *easier* than doing. That an agent can or is able to
do a certain thing shall mean, we have said (Section 9), that he

knows how to do this, has learnt it, sometimes that he has acquired mastership of a technique. However, in order to be able to forbear, an agent need not, normally, learn anything in addition to learning to *do* the thing in question. We could express this insight in several ways. 'Can do', we might say, is *prior* to 'can forbear', although the two 'cans' are reciprocal. There is no special 'know how' of forbearing.

Consider again the eight elementary acts and forbearances which answer to a given state of affairs.

An agent's abilities with regard to corresponding acts and forbearances, we have found, are reciprocal. That which an agent can effect as a result of his action he can also forbear to effect as a result of his action, and conversely.

An agent's abilities with regard to acts and/or forbearances of different types, but relative to the same state of affairs, are *not* reciprocal. They are, on the contrary, *logically independent* of one another. The fact that an agent can, through his action, destroy a state of affairs which exists and does not vanish 'of itself' is no guarantee that he can produce this same state of affairs, if it does not exist and does not come into being independently of his action. There are plenty of examples of this. To take a drastic but convincing one: Men can kill each other, but they cannot raise the dead. Generally speaking: that a man can or cannot do the act described by $d(\sim pTp)$ is logically independent of the proposition that he can or cannot do the act described by $d(pT\sim p)$.

The same seems to be true, 'in principle', of the pairs of acts described by $d(\sim pTp)$ and $d(pTp)$ and by $d(pT\sim p)$ and $d(\sim pT\sim p)$ respectively. That I can suppress something which happens unless it is suppressed does not entail that I can destroy it if it exists. Nor does the converse entailment hold. And that I can prevent from vanishing something which exists, does not entail that I can produce it if it does not exist, or vice versa.

12. There are two types of act which are of great importance to deontic logic and which relate to one agent's ability to interfere with the ability of another agent to perform a certain act. These are the types of act which we call *hindering* or *preventing* and *compelling* or *forcing*.

These two types of act are obviously interdefinable. Therefore

54

we can here limit the discussion to one of them. To compel an agent to do something is the same as to prevent him from forbearing this thing. And to hinder an agent from doing something is the same as to force him to forbear it.

To hinder an agent from doing something is to act in such a manner that it becomes impossible for that agent to do that thing. To hinder or prevent is to 'make impossible'. The result of the act of hindering an agent from doing a certain thing on a certain occasion is to change the world in such a way that the agent cannot do that thing on that occasion. But this result, be it observed, can be effected only on condition that the agent *can* do this thing. One cannot prevent people from doing that which they, in any case, cannot do. An act of preventing thus results in the fact that an agent, in some sense, cannot do that which he, in some sense, can do.

This may look like a paradox, though it certainly is not one. But it is an interesting illustration of the two senses of 'can do', which we distinguished and discussed in Section 9. The sense in which one must be able to do something in order to become prevented from doing this thing is that sense of 'can do' which refers to act-categories. The sense, again, in which one is not able to do that which one has become prevented from doing is the sense of 'can do' which refers to act-individuals. Preventing from doing does not annihilate ability to perform the generic act. Preventing, on the contrary, presupposes this ability, and destroys the successful exercise of it only on an individual occasion.

This, of course, is not to say that abilities could not become annihilated or destroyed as a result or consequence of action. By injuring a person I may temporarily or even permanently make him unable to perform a certain generic act, which before he could do. This, however, is not what we ordinarily call 'preventing'. We call it 'disabling'.

IV

THE LOGIC OF ACTION

1. BY an *elementary d-expression* we shall understand an expression which is formed of the letter *d* followed by an elementary *T*-expression (within brackets). The letter *f* followed by an elementary *T*-expression will be said to form an *elementary f-expression*.

By an *atomic d*-expression we shall understand an expression which is formed of the letter *d* followed by a (atomic or molecular) *T*-expression. The letter *f* followed by a *T*-expression will be said to form an *atomic f*-expression.

By *df-expressions*, finally, we shall understand atomic *d*- and atomic *f*-expressions and molecular complexes of atomic *d*- and/or *f*-expressions.

Examples: $d(qT \sim q)$ is an elementary *d*-expression. $f((p \mathbin{\&} \sim q) T (r \vee s) \vee \sim pTp)$ is an atomic *f*-expression. $d(pTp) \mathbin{\&} f(\sim qTq)$ is a *df*-expression.

Elementary *d*-expressions describe elementary acts, and elementary *f*-expressions, elementary forbearances. Generally speaking, a *df*-expression describes a certain (mode of) action which is performed by *one and the same* unspecified agent on *one and the same* unspecified occasion.

The logic of *df*-expressions or the *df*-calculus is a fragment of a (general) Logic of Action.

2. We shall in this section briefly discuss the logical relations between the eight elementary acts and forbearances, which answer to one given state of affairs.

Firstly, we note that corresponding elementary acts and forbearances are *mutually exclusive*. One and the same agent cannot both do and forbear the same thing on the same occasion. But one and the same agent can do something on some occasion and forbear doing the (generically) same thing on a different occasion.

Secondly, we note that any two of the four types of elementary act (relative to a given state of affairs) are mutually exclusive. Consider, for example, the acts described by $d(pTp)$ and by $d(\sim pTp)$. They cannot be both done by the same agent on the same occasion. This is a consequence of the fact that no occasion constitutes an opportunity for doing both acts. This again is so, because a given state and its contradictory state cannot both obtain on the same occasion. Or consider the acts described by $d(pTp)$ and by $d(pT\sim p)$. They, too, cannot both be done by the same agent on the same occasion. For a given state of affairs either changes or remains unchanged. If, independently of action, it would remain unchanged the agent may destroy it, but cannot preserve it. That is: there is then an opportunity for destroying it, but not for preserving it. If again, independently of action, the world would change in the feature under consideration the agent may preserve, but cannot destroy, this feature.

Thirdly, we note that any two of the four types of elementary forbearances are mutually exclusive. Since no state and its contradictory state can both obtain on the same occasion, no agent can, for example, both forbear to preserve and forbear to suppress a given state on a given occasion. And since a state which obtains either changes or remains unchanged independently of action, no agent can, for example, both forbear to preserve and forbear to destroy it on one and the same occasion.

From the above observations we may conclude that all the eight elementary acts and forbearances which answer to one given state of affairs are mutually exclusive.

The question may be raised: Are the eight elementary acts and forbearances *jointly exhaustive*? Let, for example, the state of affairs described by p be that a certain window is closed. Is it necessarily true, given an agent and an occasion, that this agent will on that occasion either close the window or leave it open, open the window or leave it closed, keep the window close or let it (become) open, or keep the window open or let it close?

I think we must, when answering this question, take into account considerations of human *ability*. Assume that the state of affairs is one which the agent can neither produce nor suppress, if it does not exist, nor destroy or preserve, if it exists. Then he can, of course, not be said truly to produce or suppress or destroy or preserve it. But neither can he be rightly said to *forbear* to produce or suppress or destroy or preserve it. For forbearing, as we understand it here, *makes sense* only when the act *can* be done. (See Ch. III, Sect. 8.)

There are many states towards whose production or suppression or destruction or preservation human beings can do nothing. Most states of the weather are of this kind, and states in remote parts of the universe. And there are states with which some agents cannot interfere in any way whatsoever, but with which other, more 'powerful', agents can interfere in some, if not in every, way. A child may have learnt to open a window, but not to close it.

The correct answer to the above question concerning the jointly exhaustive character of the eight elementary acts and forbearances, answering to a given state of affairs, therefore is as follows:

Only on condition that the agent *can* produce *and* suppress *and* destroy *and* preserve a given state of affairs, is it the case that he necessarily will, on any given occasion, either produce *or* forbear producing, suppress *or* forbear suppressing, destroy *or* forbear destroying, *or* preserve *or* forbear preserving this state of affairs.

In the subsequent discussion it will be assumed that this requirement as regards ability is satisfied and that consequently the eight types of elementary acts and forbearances may be treated as not only mutually exclusive but also jointly exhaustive.

3. Every *df*-expression expresses a truth-function of elementary *d*- and/or *f*-expressions. This is so because of the fact that the operators *d* and *f* have certain distributive properties. These properties are 'axiomatic' to the *df*-calculus: that is, they cannot be proved in the calculus. Their intuitive plausibility, however, can be made obvious from examples.

Consider an atomic *d*-expression. Let the *T*-expression in it be in the positive normal form (Ch. II, Sect. 9). It is then, normally, a disjunction of conjunctions of elementary *T*-expressions. The conjunctions describe mutually exclusive ways in which the world changes and/or remains unchanged. Obviously the proposition that some of these ways is effected through the action of some

58

unspecified agent on some unspecified occasion is equivalent to the proposition that the first of these ways is effected through the action of that agent on that occasion or . . . or the last of these ways is effected through the action of that agent on that occasion.

For example: $d(\sim pTp \text{ v } pT \sim p)$ says that some agent on some occasion either produces the state described by p or destroys it. The same thing is also expressed by $d(\sim pTp) \text{ v } d(pT \sim p)$.

Thanks to the disjunctive distributivity of the d-operator, every atomic d-expression may become replaced by a disjunction of atomic d-expressions, in which the d-operator stands in front of a change-description (Ch. II, Sect. 10).

Now consider for example the meaning of $d((pT \sim p) \text{ \& } (qT \sim q))$. An agent, on some occasion, through his action makes both of two states vanish. Does this not mean that he makes the one and makes the other state vanish, *i.e.* does the above expression not mean the same as $d(pT \sim p) \text{ \& } d(qT \sim q)$?

I shall answer in the affirmative and accept the identity of the expressions. I also think this answer accords best with ordinary usage. Be it observed, however, that ordinary usage is not perfectly unambiguous in cases of this type. To say that somebody through his action has become 'responsible' for two changes in the world *could* be taken to mean that he effected one of the two changes, whereas the other took place independently of his action. But to say that he effected or produced the two changes would not seem quite accurate, unless he actually produced the one and also produced the other. We must not, however, be pedantic about actual usage. But we must make the intended meaning of our symbolic expressions quite clear. Therefore we rule that the d-operator is conjunctively distributive in front of change-descriptions.

Consider an atomic f-expression. Is the f-operator too disjunctively distributive in front of a disjunction which describes some mutually exclusive alternative changes in the world? What does it mean to say that an agent forbears this *or* that? Since the changes (the 'this' and the 'that') are mutually exclusive, the occasion in question cannot afford an opportunity for forbearing to produce more than one of the changes. The agent therefore, on the occasion in question, either forbears to produce the first or . . . or forbears to produce the last of the mutually exclusive alternative changes in the world.

It is essential to this argument that the changes are *mutually exclusive*. To forbear this *or* that, when both things *can* be done on the same occasion, would, I think, ordinarily be understood to mean that the agent forbears both things, *i.e.* does neither the one nor the other.

Thus the *f*-operator too is disjunctively distributive in front of a *T*-expression in the perfect normal form. For example: $f((\sim pTp)$ v $(pT\sim p))$ means the same as $f(\sim pTp)$ v $f(pT\sim p)$.

Remains the case when the *f*-operator stands in front of a change-description. For example: $f((pT\sim p)$ & $(qT\sim q))$. What does the agent do, who, on some occasion, forbears to destroy two existing states? The question can be answered in more than one way. If, however, we stick to the view that forbearing is not-doing on an occasion for doing *and* accept the above interpretation of $d((pT\sim p)$ & $(qT\sim q))$, then we must answer the question as follows: To forbear to destroy two existing states is to forbear the destruction of at least one of them. $f((pT\sim p)$ & $(qT\sim q))$ thus equals $f(pT\sim p)$ v $f(qT\sim q)$. Generally speaking: the *f*-operator is *disjunctively* distributive in front of change-descriptions.

These four rules for the distributivity of the *d*- and *f*-operators secure that every atomic *d*- or *f*-expression expresses a truth-function of elementary *d*- or *f*-expressions. Since truth-function-ship is transitive, it follows *a fortiori* that every *df*-expression expresses a truth-function of elementary *d*- and/or *f*-expressions.

The elementary *d*- and/or *f*-expressions, of which a given *df*-expression expresses a truth-function, will be called the *df-constituents* of the *df*-expression. Which truth-function of its *df*-constituents a given *df*-expression expresses can be investigated and decided in a truth-table. The distribution of truth-values over the *df*-constituents in the table is subject to the limitations imposed by the mutually exclusive and jointly exhaustive nature of the eight types of elementary acts and forbearances (relative to the same state of affairs).

If a *df*-expression expresses the tautology of its *df*-constituents we shall call it a *df-tautology*. If it expresses their contradiction we call it a *df-contradiction*.

$d(pTp)$ & $f(pTp)$ is an example of a *df*-contradiction. Hence $\sim d(pTp)$ v $\sim f(pTp)$ is a *df*-tautology.

Assume that the *T*-expression in an atomic *d*- or *f*-expression is

60

a T-contradiction. Then the positive normal form of the T-expression is a 0-termed disjunction. We cannot use the distributivity of the d- and f-operators for transforming the atomic d- or f-expression into a molecular complex of elementary d- and/or f-expressions. A special rule has to be introduced for the case. The rule is simple: the atomic d- or f-expression in question is a df-contradiction. The intuitive meaning of this rule is obvious: If it is logically impossible that a certain change should happen, then it is also logically impossible to effect or leave uneffected this change through one's action.

4. On the assumption, which we are here making, that the eight types of elementary acts and forbearances are jointly exhaustive of 'logical space', every df-expression has what I propose to call a *positive normal form*. (Cf. Ch. II, Sect. 9.) It is a disjunction-sentence of conjunction-sentences of elementary d- and/or f-expressions. It is called 'positive', because it does not contain negation-sentences of elementary d- and/or f-expressions.

The positive normal form of a given df-expression is found as follows: The df-expression is first transformed into a molecular complex of elementary d- and/or f-expressions, according to the procedure described in Section 3. The new df-expression thus obtained is thereupon transformed into its perfect disjunctive normal form. This is a disjunction-sentence of conjunction-sentences of elementary d- and/or f-expressions and/or negation-sentences of elementary expressions. We replace each negation-sentence of an elementary d- or f-expression by a 7-termed disjunction-sentence of elementary expressions. The new df-expression thus obtained is transformed into its perfect disjunctive normal form. From the normal form we omit those conjunction-sentences, if there are any, which contain two or more different elementary d- or f-expressions of the same variable (p, q, etc.). What remains after these omissions is the perfect normal form of the original df-expression.

We give a simple example to illustrate this procedure:

Let the df-expression be $d(pTp)$ v $d(qTq)$. Its perfect disjunctive normal form is $d(pTp)$ & $d(qTq)$ v $d(pTp)$ & $\sim d(qTq)$ v $\sim d(pTp)$ & $d(qTq)$. We replace $\sim d(pTp)$ by the 7-termed disjunction-sentence $d(pT \sim p)$ v $d(\sim pTp)$ v $d(\sim pT \sim p)$ v $f(pTp)$ v $f(pT \sim p)$ v $f(\sim pTp)$ v $f(\sim pT \sim p)$, and $\sim d(qTq)$ by the 7-termed disjunction-sentence $d(qT\sim q)$ v $d(\sim qTq)$ v $d(\sim qT\sim q)$ v $f(qTq)$ v $f(qT\sim q)$ v $f(\sim qTq)$ v $f(\sim qT\sim q)$. After distribution we get the 15-termed disjunction-sentence of 2-termed conjunction-sentences $d(pTp)$ & $d(qTq)$ v $d(pTp)$ & $d(qT\sim q)$ v $d(pTp)$ & $d(\sim qTq)$ v $d(pTp)$ & $d(\sim qT\sim q)$ v $d(pTp)$ & $f(qTq)$ v $d(pTp)$ & $f(qT\sim q)$ v $f(\sim qTq)$ v $d(pTp)$ & $f(\sim qT\sim q)$ v $d(pT\sim p)$ & $d(qTq)$ v $d(\sim pTp)$ & $d(qTq)$ v $d(\sim pT\sim p)$ & $d(qTq)$ v $f(pTp)$ & $d(qTq)$ v $f(pT\sim p)$ & $d(qTq)$ v $f(\sim pTp)$ & $d(qTq)$ v $f(\sim pT\sim p)$ & $d(qTq)$. This is the positive normal form of the original df-expression. It is a complete enumeration of the 15 mutually exclusive generic modes of action, which are covered by the description $d(pTp)$ v $d(qTq)$.

5. We have previously (Ch. II, Sects. 3 and 10) introduced the notions of a state-description and a change-description. By analogy, we now introduce the notion of an *act-description*. An act-description is a conjunction-sentence of some n elementary d- and/or f-expressions of n different atomic variables. Thus, for example, $d(pTp)$ & $f(qT\sim q)$ is an act-description.

As we know, n atomic variables determine 2^n different possible state-descriptions and 2^{2n} different possible change-descriptions (cf. Ch. II, Sect. 10). An act-description is obtained from a given change-description through the insertion of the letter d or the letter f in front of each of the n T-expressions in the change-description. The insertion can take place in 2^n different ways. Consequently, the total number of act-descriptions which are determined by n atomic variables is $2^n \times 2^{2n}$ or 2^{3n}.

(pTp) & $(qT\sim q)$ is a change-description. To it answer four act-descriptions, *viz.* $d(pTp)$ & $d(qT\sim q)$ and $d(pTp)$ & $f(qT\sim q)$ and $f(pTp)$ & $d(qT\sim q)$ and $f(pTp)$ & $f(qT\sim q)$.

Given n atomic variables, we can list in a table the 2^n state-descriptions, the 2^{2n} change-descriptions, and the 2^{3n} act-descriptions, which these variables determine. On the next page there is a fragment of such a list for the case of two variables, p and q.

The positive normal form of a df-expression which contains n variables for states of affairs is a disjunction-sentence of (none or) one or two or . . . or 2^{3n} conjunction-sentences of n elementary d- and/or f-expressions. If the disjunction-sentence has no members the df-expression expresses a df-contradiction. If it has 2^{3n} members the df-expression expresses a df-tautology.

It is often convenient to regard the positive normal form of a

State-descriptions	Change-descriptions	Act-descriptions
p & q	(pTp) & (qTq)	$d(pTp)$ & $d(qTq)$ $d(pTp)$ & $f(qTq)$ $f(pTp)$ & $d(qTq)$ $f(pTp)$ & $f(qTq)$
	(pTp) & $(qT\sim q)$	
	$(pT\sim p)$ & (qTq)	
	$(pT\sim p)$ & $(qT\sim q)$	
4. $\sim p$ & $\sim q$	$(\sim pT\sim p)$ & $(\sim qT\sim q)$	
	$(\sim pT\sim p)$ & $(\sim qTq)$	
	$(\sim pTp)$ & $(\sim qT\sim q)$	
	16. $(\sim pTp)$ & $(\sim qTq)$	$d(\sim pTp)$ & $d(\sim qTq)$ $d(\sim pTp)$ & $f(\sim qTq)$ $f(\sim pTp)$ & $d(\sim qTq)$ 64. $f(\sim pTp)$ & $f(\sim qTq)$

df-expression as consisting of 'bits' or segments answering to the various conditions (change-descriptions), which constitute opportunities for doing the act in question. Thus, for example, the 15-termed disjunction-sentence, which is the positive normal form of the expression $d(pTp)$ v $d(qTq)$ (Section 4), may become divided into the following seven 'bits':

$d(pT\sim p)$ & $d(qTq)$ v $f(pT\sim p)$ & $d(qTq)$ answering to (pTp) & $(qT\sim q)$; $d(pTp)$ & $d(qT\sim q)$ v $d(pTp)$ & $f(qT\sim q)$ answering to $(pT\sim p)$ & (qTq); $d(pTp)$ & $d(qTq)$ v $d(pTp)$ & $f(qTq)$ v $f(pTp)$ & $d(qTq)$ answering to $(pT\sim p)$ & $(qT\sim q)$; $d(pTp)$ & $d(\sim qTq)$ v $d(pTp)$ & $f(\sim qTq)$ answering to $(pT\sim p)$ & $(\sim qT\sim q)$; $d(pTp)$ & $d(\sim qT\sim q)$ v $d(pTp)$ & $f(\sim qT\sim q)$ answering to $(pT\sim p)$ & $(\sim qTq)$; $d(\sim pTp)$ & $d(qTq)$ v $f(\sim pTp)$ & $d(qTq)$ answering to

$(\sim pT \sim p)$ & $(qT \sim q)$; and $d(\sim pT \sim p)$ & $d(qTq)$ v $f(\sim pT \sim p)$ & $d(qTq)$ answering to $(\sim pTp)$ & $(qT \sim q)$.

6. We shall distinguish between the *external* and the *internal* negation of a *df*-expression.

External negation is negation in the 'ordinary' sense. Its symbol is $\sim$. If the positive normal form of a given *df*-expression has *m* members (conjunction-sentences), then the positive normal form of the external negation of this *df*-expression has 2^{3n}-m members, *n* being the number of atomic variables of the expression. Thus, for example, the positive normal form of $\sim(d(pTp)$ v $d(qTq))$ is a disjunction-sentence of 49, *i.e.* of 64–15, conjunction-sentences of two elementary *df*-expressions. It is readily seen that this normal form has 16 'bits', of which the shortest is $f(pTp)$ & $f(qTq)$. The other segments are either 2-termed or 4-termed disjunction-sentences (of conjunction-sentences of two elementary *df*-expressions).

The internal negation of a given *df*-expression is obtained as follows: The expression is transformed into its positive normal form, and the normal form is divided up into segments. We form the disjunction-sentence of all those conjunction-sentences (of elementary *df*-expressions of the same atomic variables) which do *not* occur in the segments but answer to the same conditions for acting (change-descriptions) as the conjunction-sentences in the segments. The expression thus formed is the (positive normal form of the) internal negation of the given *df*-expression.

For example: The internal negation of $d(pTp)$ v $d(qTq)$ is the 13-termed disjunction-sentence $d(pT \sim p)$ & $f(qTq)$ v $f(pT \sim p)$ & $f(qTq)$ v $f(pTp)$ & $d(qT \sim q)$ v $f(pTp)$ & $f(qT \sim q)$ v $f(pTp)$ & $f(qTq)$ v $f(pTp)$ & $d(\sim qTq)$ v $f(pTp)$ & $f(\sim qTq)$ v $f(pTp)$ & $d(\sim qT \sim q)$ v $f(pTp)$ & $f(\sim qT \sim q)$ v $d(\sim pTp)$ & $f(qTq)$ v $f(\sim pTp)$ & $f(qTq)$ v $d(\sim pT \sim p)$ & $f(qTq)$ v $f(\sim pT \sim p)$ & $f(qTq)$.

The internal negation of $d(pTp)$ & $d(qTq)$ is the 3-termed disjunction-sentence $d(pTp)$ & $f(qTq)$ v $f(pTp)$ & $d(qTq)$ v $f(pTp)$ & $f(qTq)$. Its external negation is (in the normal form) a 63-termed disjunction-sentence.

The internal negation of $d(pTp)$ is $f(pTp)$. Generally speaking: *the internal negation of doing is forbearing*.

The external negation of $d(pTp)$ is, in the normal form, the

7-termed disjunction-sentence $d(pT \sim p)$ v $d(\sim pTp)$ v $d(\sim pT \sim p)$ v $f(pTp)$ v $f(pT \sim p)$ v $f(\sim pTp)$ v $f(\sim pT \sim p)$.

The external negation says that the action described by the expression in question is *not* done (by the agent in question on the occasion in question). The internal negation says that, under the same conditions of action, the 'opposite' of the action described by the expression in question *is* done (by the agent in question on the occasion in question).

An action and its external negation are incompatible (modes of action). This means: they cannot both be performed by the same agent on the same occasion. An action and its internal negation are also incompatible.

We can distinguish between external and internal incompatibility of actions (and of expressions for action). Two actions will be called externally incompatible when the proposition that the one has been performed (by some agent on some occasion) entails the proposition that the external negation of the other has been performed (by the same agent on the same occasion). Two actions will be called internally incompatible when the proposition that the one has been performed entails the proposition that the internal negation of the other has been performed.

For example: The actions described by $d(pTp)$ & $d(qTq)$ and by $d(pT \sim p)$ & $d(qT \sim q)$ are *externally* incompatible. The actions described by $d(pTp)$ & $d(qTq)$ and $d(pTp)$ & $f(qTq)$ are *internally* incompatible. Also: the actions described by $d(pTp)$ and $f(pT \sim p)$ are externally, the actions described by $d(pTp)$ and $f(pTp)$ internally incompatible.

It is readily seen that internal incompatibility entails external incompatibility, but not vice versa.

The notions of external and internal incompatibility can be generalized so as to become applicable to any number n of actions (and of descriptions of actions).

n actions are externally incompatible when they cannot be all performed by the same agent on the same occasion. n actions are internally incompatible when they are externally incompatible *and* the conditions under which each of them can be performed are the same.

Speaking of descriptions of action, we can say that n *df*-expressions are externally incompatible when their conjunction is a *df*-contradiction. They are internally incompatible when they are externally incompatible *and* answer to the same change-descriptions.

Three or more actions can be (externally or internally) incompatible, even though no two of them are incompatible. An example would be the three actions described by $d(pTp)$ & $d(qTq)$ v $d(pTp)$ & $f(qTq)$ and $d(pTp)$ & $f(qTq)$ v $f(pTp)$ & $d(qTq)$ and $d(pTp)$ & $d(qTq)$ v $f(pTp)$ & $d(qTq)$. Their incompatibility, moreover, is internal, since the condition under which each of them can be performed is the same, *viz.* $(pT \sim p)$ & $(qT \sim q)$.

7. We shall also distinguish between the external and the internal *consequences* of (the proposition expressed by) a given *df*-expression.

A *df*-expression entails (in the Logic of Action) another *df*-expression if, and only if, the implication-sentence whose antecedent is the first and whose consequent is the second *df*-expression is a *df*-tautology. When a *df*-expression entails another the second is called an external consequence of the first.

For example: $d(pTp)$ & $d(qTq)$ entails $d(pTp)$ & $d(qTq)$ v $d(pT \sim p)$ & $d(qT \sim q)$. 'If a person on some occasion continues both of two states, then, trivially, he either continues them both or destroys them both.' This entailment is valid already by virtue of the laws of the Logic of Propositions.

A *df*-expression is an internal consequence of another *df*-expression if, and only if, the first is a (external) consequence of the second *and* the two expressions answer to the same change-description (conditions of action).

For example: $d(pTp)$ & $d(qTq)$ v $f(pTp)$ & $f(qTq)$ is an internal consequence of $d(pTp)$ & $d(qTq)$. 'If an agent on some occasion continues both of two states, then, trivially, he either continues both or lets both vanish.'

8. Two or more *df*-expressions which contain exactly the same variables for states of affairs will be called *uniform* with regard to the variables. Expressions which are not uniform can be made uniform by a vacuous introduction of new variables into them.

If, *e.g.*, the variable p does not occur in a given *df*-expression, we can introduce it into the expression by forming the conjunction-sentence of the given *df*-expression and, *e.g.*, the *df*-expression $d(pTp)$ v $\sim d(pTp)$. In a similar manner, the variable p can be introduced into a given T-expression by conjoining the expression with (pTp) v $\sim(pTp)$, and into a given p-expression by conjoining it with p v $\sim p$.

Consider the T-expression pTp. If we want to introduce the variable q into it, we can form the conjunction-sentence (pTp) & $(qTq$ v $\sim(qTq))$ or the conjunction-sentence (pTp) & $(qTq$ v $qT\sim q$ v $\sim qTq$ v $\sim qT\sim q)$. But we can achieve the same by replacing p in the original expression by the conjunction-sentence p & $(q$ v $\sim q)$. The reader can easily satisfy himself that the two operations lead to the same result, *i.e.* that after the appropriate transformations we reach in the end the same T-expression. Because of this fact we say that T-expressions are *extensional* with regard to p-expressions. This means, generally speaking, that if for some p-expression which occurs in a T-expression we substitute a (in the p-calculus) tautologously equivalent p-expression the new T-expression which we get through the substitution is (in the T-calculus) tautologously equivalent to the original T-expression.

df-expressions, be it observed, are *not* extensional with regard to p-expressions, nor with regard to T-expressions. If for some p-expression which occurs in a *df*-expression we substitute a (in the p-calculus) tautologously equivalent p-expression the new *df*-expression is not necessarily (in the *df*-calculus) tautologously equivalent to the first. And similarly, if for some T-expression which occurs in a *df*-expression we substitute a (in the T-calculus) tautologously equivalent T-expression. In the said respect *df*-expressions may be said to be *intensional* and the *df*-calculus may be called an intensional calculus.

Consider some elementary d-expression, *e.g.*, $d(pTp)$. As known from the Logic of Propositions, p is tautologously equivalent to p & q v p & $\sim q$. Consider now the atomic d-expression $d((p$ & q v p & $\sim q)$ T $(p$ & q v p & $\sim q))$. According to the laws of the Logic of Change, $(p$ & q v p & $\sim q)$ T $(p$ & q v p & $\sim q)$ is tautologously equivalent to pTp & $(qTq$ v $qT\sim q$ v $\sim qTq$ v $\sim qT\sim q)$. Consider next the atomic d-expression $d(pTp$ & $(qTq$ v $qT\sim q$ v $\sim qTq$ v $\sim qT\sim q))$. According to the Logic of Action, this is tautologously equivalent to the molecular d-expression $d(pTp)$ & $d(qTq$ v $qT\sim q$ v $\sim qTq$ v $\sim qT\sim q)$, which in its turn is equivalent to $d(pTp)$ & $(d(qTq)$ v $d(qT\sim q)$ v $d(\sim qTq)$ v $d(\sim qT\sim q))$.

Let us compare the first and the last of our above d-expressions. Do the two mean the same? The first says that a certain agent on a certain occasion through his action preserves a certain state of affairs, *e.g.*, keeps a certain door open. The second says that a certain agent on a certain occasion does this same thing and also another thing in addition to it. This additional thing is that he, through his action, either preserves or destroys or produces or suppresses a certain state of affairs, *e.g.*, the state of affairs that a car is parked in the front of his house. It is plain that, even if it were (which it need not be) possible for the agent to do the first thing *and* one of the mutually exclusive four other things on one and the same occasion it is not necessary that he should do any of the four other things on an occasion when he does the first. Hence, the meaning of $d(pTp)$ is *not* the same as the meaning of $d(pTp)$ & $(d(qTq) \vee d(qT \sim q) \vee d(\sim qTq) \vee d(\sim qT \sim q))$.

That the two meanings must be different is not at all difficult to understand. The disjunction of changes described by $qTq \vee qT \sim q \vee \sim qTq \vee \sim qT \sim q$ is a tautology, something which necessarily *happens* on any occasion. But neither the disjunctive act, described by $d(qTq \vee qT \sim q \vee \sim qTq \vee \sim qT \sim q)$, nor the equivalent disjunction of acts described by $d(qTq) \vee d(qT \sim q) \vee d(\sim qTq) \vee d(\sim qT \sim q)$ is a tautology, *i.e.* something which will necessarily be *done* on every occasion. If, for example, an agent forbears to do one of the four acts, then he does not do any of them. And if, for some reason or other, he *cannot* do any of them, then he neither does nor forbears any of them on a given occasion.

Though it is easy to see that the two expressions have different meanings, it may yet appear as something of a paradox that there should be this difference—considering how the two expressions are related to each other 'formally'. We reached the last from the first through a series of substitutions of tautologously equivalent expressions and of a series of transformations of expressions into tautologously equivalent forms. We have no reason to deny or to doubt any of these equivalences. What we have to do, then, is to reject some of the substitutions (as not leading from one expression to another, which is tautologously equivalent to the first). The substitution which we reject is the first. The *act* described by $d(pTp)$ is not the same as the act described by $d((p \,\&\, q \vee p \,\&\, \sim q) T (p \,\&\, q \vee p \,\&\, \sim q))$—although the *change* described by $(p \,\&\, q \vee p \,\&\, \sim q) T (p \,\&\, q \vee p \,\&\, \sim q)$ is the same as the change described by pTp and the *state* described by p & q v p & $\sim q$ is the same as the state described by p.

When *df*-expressions are uniform with regard to the variables and in the positive normal form it can instantly be seen from the 'look' of the expressions whether they are compatible or not. They are compatible if, and only if, the normal forms have at least one disjunct in common.

When *df*-expressions are uniform with regard to the variables and in the positive normal form it can also instantly be seen from the 'look' of the expressions whether the one entails (or is a consequence of) the other. The one entails the other if, and only if, the normal form of the first is a part of the normal form of the other.

V

THE ANALYSIS OF NORMS

1. IT is convenient to distinguish between the following six 'components' or 'ingredients' or 'parts' of norms which are prescriptions: the character, the content, the condition of application, the authority, the subject(s), and the occasion.

From a complete statement to the effect that such and such a prescription has been given it should also be clear which are its six above-mentioned components.

There are two more things which essentially belong to every prescription without, however, being 'components' of prescriptions in the same sense as the above six. These two we call *promulgation* and *sanction*.

The character, the content, and the condition of application constitute what I propose to call the *norm-kernel*. The norm-kernel is a logical structure which prescriptions have in common with other types of norm. There may, however, exist specific differences between the kernels of norms of different types. Here we are directly concerned with the kernels of prescriptions only.

The authority, the subject(s), and the occasion seems to be specific characteristics of prescriptions which do not belong to the other types of norm.

The formal theory of norms or Deontic Logic, which we are going to develop in later chapters of this work, is essentially a theory of norm-kernels. Since the kernels are the common ingredients of all, or nearly all, types of norm, this formal theory may, with some caution, be regarded as a 'basic logic' of norms in general.

70

2. The *character* of a norm depends upon whether the norm is to the effect that something ought to or may or must not be or be done.

For the 'ought'-character of norms we shall introduce the symbol O, and for the 'may'-character the symbol P. Norms of the 'ought'-character can also be called *obligation*-norms, and norms of the 'may'-character *permissive* norms. We shall also speak of the O-character and the P-character of norms, and of O-norms and P-norms.

Later in this chapter we shall discuss in some detail the mutual relations between the three norm-characters. It will be seen that the 'ought'-character and the 'must not'-character are interdefinable. This is the reason why we have not introduced a special symbol for the second. It may be suggested that the 'may'-character and the 'must not'-character are interdefinable too. The question is open to debate, and we shall not attempt to decide it. This is the reason why we retain a special symbol for the permissive norm-character.

If a *prescription* is to the effect that something ought to be done we often call it a *command* or *order*. If it is to the effect that something may be done we call it a *permission*. If, finally, it is to the effect that something must not be done we call it a *prohibition*.

Advice, counsel, prayer, recommendation, request, warning are related categories to command, permission, and prohibition. We shall not, however, call *them* prescriptions or norms. We restrict the field of meaning of 'prescription' and 'norm' to things of the O-character or P-character. This seems in good accord with ordinary usage.

3. By the *content* of a norm we mean, roughly speaking, *that which* ought to or may or must not be or be done. The content of a prescription, in particular, is thus the prescribed (commanded, permitted, prohibited) thing.

From the point of view of their content, norms (other than ideal rules) can be divided into two main groups, *viz.* norms concerning *action* (acts and forbearances) and norms concerning *activity*. Both types of norm are common and important. 'Close the door' orders an act to be done. 'Smoking allowed' permits an activity. 'If the dog barks, don't run' prohibits an activity.

It seems that prescriptions (and maybe other norms too)

71

concerning activity are in an important sense *secondary* to prescriptions (norms) concerning action. Let us ask: What does the regulation 'Smoking prohibited' require us to *do*? The answer is: If we are engaged in the activity of smoking the regulation orders the *act* of ceasing to smoke (*e.g.*, by throwing the cigarette away); and if we are not smoking it prohibits the *act* of starting to smoke (*e.g.*, by lighting a cigarette). Similarly, the command not to run, if the dog barks, orders the act of stopping, should we happen to be running, and prohibits the act of starting to run, should we be walking or standing still.

Thus, at least in some cases, prescriptions (norms) concerning activity may become 'translated' into prescriptions (norms) concerning action. Whether this is always possible we shall not discuss.

4. The norm-contents with which we shall be concerned in our Deontic Logic are the meanings of *df*-expressions. *df*-expressions, it will be remembered, are molecular compounds of atomic *d*- and/or *f*-expressions, *i.e.* of sentences which describe generic acts and/or forbearances (Ch. IV, Sect. 1).

It is convenient to divide norms into *positive* and *negative*, depending upon whether their content is an act or a forbearance, or strictly speaking: whether their content is the meaning of a molecular compound of atomic *d*-expressions or of atomic *f*-expressions. But it should be remembered that this division is not exhaustive. A norm whose content is the meaning of a *df*-expression, with both atomic *d*- and atomic *f*-expressions among its constituents, falls in neither category. Such norms might be called (norms of) *mixed* (content).

'One must not open the window, nor shut the door' enunciates a positive prohibition. 'The door may be left open' has the form of a negative permission, 'open the door' that of a positive command. 'Close the window, but leave the door open' illustrates a mixed prescription.

By an *elementary* norm we shall understand a norm whose content is an elementary act or forbearance.

As we know, there correspond to one given state of affairs four elementary types of change and eight elementary types of act or forbearance (Ch. III, Sects. 7 and 8).

Every one of the eight elementary types of act or forbearance can be the content of a O-norm or of a P-norm. The total number of types of elementary norm which correspond to one given state of affairs is therefore *sixteen*.

By an *elementary O-expression* we shall understand an expression formed of the letter O followed by an elementary d- or f-expression.

By an *elementary P-expression* we understand an expression formed of the letter P followed by an elementary d- or f-expression.

By an *atomic* O-expression we understand an expression formed of the letter O followed by a df-expression (elementary, atomic, or molecular).

By an *atomic* P-expression we understand an expression formed of the letter P followed by a df-expression.

By an OP-expression, finally, we understand a molecular compound of atomic O-expressions and/or P-expressions.

p-expressions, T-expressions, and df-expressions, we have said, are sentential symbols or sentence-schemas. They express propositions. They describe generic states of affairs, changes, and acts or forbearances respectively.

OP-expressions too may be regarded as schematic representations of sentences. Whether these sentences, or 'norm-formulations' as we shall call them (see Chapter VI), express propositions is, however, a question which will have to be discussed later.

5. The condition which must be satisfied if there is to be an opportunity for doing the thing which is the content of a given norm (other than an ideal rule), will be called a *condition of application* of the norm. As will be seen presently, this can be the sole condition of application of a given norm. But it need not be the sole condition (Section 6).

The conditions of application of elementary norms are simply the conditions for performing the corresponding elementary acts. Let p describe a state of affairs. Consider an occasion on which this state neither obtains nor comes into being independently of action. This constitutes an opportunity for effecting or leaving uneffected through action the elementary change described by $\sim pTp$. Effecting this change can be ordered or permitted. Leaving it uneffected can similarly be ordered or permitted. The symbolic expressions for these four elementary prescriptions are: $Od\ (\sim pTp)$, $Pd(\sim pTp)$, $Of(\sim pTp)$, and $Pf(\sim pTp)$ respectively.

As the reader will easily realize, there are four elementary types of norm whose conditions of application are that a given state of affairs does not obtain, but comes into being unless prevented through action; four elementary types of norm whose conditions of application are that a given state of affairs obtains and does not vanish independently of action; and four elementary types of norm whose conditions of application are that a given state of affairs obtains but vanishes unless prevented through action.

Every norm-content or, strictly speaking, proposition expressed by a *df*-expression, is a truth-function of elementary acts and/or forbearances or, strictly speaking, of the propositions expressed by the *df*-constituents of this *df*-expression. The condition for doing the thing which is described by a given *df*-expression is a truth-function of the conditions for doing the things of which the proposition expressed by the *df*-expression is a truth-function. The condition for doing this thing, moreover, is *the same* truth-function of the conditions of the elementary acts and/or forbearances as is this thing itself of the corresponding elementary acts and/or forbearances.

Let p mean that the door is closed and q that the window is open. $O(d(\sim pTp)$ & $f(qT\sim q))$ then is a symbolic expression of the command to close the door but leave the window open. The condition of application of this command is that both the door and the window are open and do not close 'of themselves', *i.e.* independently of action. If the window closes of itself, but the condition otherwise remains the same, a command which aims at the same result as the first would have to be formulated 'close the door and *keep* the window open'.

6. From the point of view of their conditions of application norms can be divided into *categorical* and *hypothetical*.

We shall call a norm (other than an ideal rule) categorical if its condition of application is the condition which must be satisfied if there is going to be an opportunity for doing the thing which is its content, *and no further condition*.

We shall call a norm (other than an ideal rule) hypothetical if its condition of application is the condition which must be satisfied if there is going to be an opportunity for doing the thing which is its content, *and some further condition*.

If a norm is categorical its condition of application is given with its content. From knowing its content we know which its condition of application is. For this reason, special mention of the condition is not necessary in a formulation of the norm. It is, for example, understood from an order to shut a window that it applies to a situation when a certain window is open.

If a norm is hypothetical its condition of application cannot be concluded from its content alone—if 'content' is defined as we have done here. Mention of the (additional) condition must therefore be made in its formulation. An example would be an order to shut a certain window, *if* it starts raining.

As previously (Ch. I, Sect. 7) stated, it is important not to confuse *hypothetical* and *technical* norms. How the two types of norm shall be distinguished is not, however, quite easy to tell. We shall return to this question in Ch. IX, Sects. 2 and 3.

Our symbolic notation is, so far, adequate only for expressing the norm-kernels of categorical norms. For dealing with hypothetical norms we shall have to make use of an embellished symbolism. The embellishment will not, however, be made until later, in Ch. IX.

7. By the *authority* of a prescription I understand the agent who gives or issues the prescription. The authority orders, permits, or prohibits certain subjects to do certain things on certain occasions.

By calling the authority of a prescription an agent we indicate that prescriptions come into being as a result of action. For the peculiar mode of action, which results in the existence of prescriptions, we coin the name *normative action*.

Prescriptions which are thought to flow from a super-empirical agent as their authority we call *theonomous*. They are also called the commands or the law of God. We shall not here discuss the problems connected with theonomous norms. We need not even take it for granted that the notion of a super-empirical agent itself makes sense or that there are any theonomous norms. It seems to me that the idea of theonomous prescriptions is an analogical or secondary notion which is modelled on the pattern of norms which flow from human agents as their sources. We cannot therefore understand the concept of theonomous rules of human action until we have a clear understanding of the primary concept of human rules of human action.

Prescriptions the authorities of which are empirical agents may be called *positive*. The authority of some positive norms is a personal agent, the authority of others an impersonal agent. (On the types of agent see Ch. III, Sect. 4.)

The laws of the state, the by-laws of a magistrate, the statutes of a corporation are examples of positive prescriptions, which are (normally) issued by an impersonal authority. It may be thought that impersonal authorities of positive prescriptions are but 'logical constructions' of human beings acting, individually or collectively, as norm-authorities. If this view is correct there would be ground for saying that the concept of a positive norm with an impersonal norm-authority, unlike the concept of a theonomous norm, is *not* an analogical idea.

The concept of an impersonal norm-authority is intimately connected with the concept of an *office*. This again is, partly at least, a normative notion. An office confers upon its holder certain rights and/or duties, *e.g.*, rights and/or duties to make laws and issue regulations for others. We shall not here discuss the concept of an office in detail. Some remarks bearing on the notion will be made in Chapter X.

A personal norm-authority can be either a human individual or a human collectivity. The latter case is by no means uncommon. Within a group of 'equals', prescriptions of the form 'We command . . .' (addressed, *e.g.*, to a member who is unwilling to participate in the work for a common end) are probably more common than prescriptions of the form 'I command . . .'. When an adult human individual issues a command or gives a permission to another adult he is usually either acting in the capacity of holder of some office (*e.g.*, as officer in the army or as policeman) or speaking in the name of a group of men. There are some reasons why this should be so. They are connected with the nature of normative activity. We shall examine them in some detail in Chapter VII.

8. The concept of a norm-authority has some bearing on the well-known division of norms into *heteronomous* and *autonomous*.

The concept of a heteronomous norm is relatively unproblematic. A prescription is heteronomous, we shall say, if it is given by somebody to somebody *else*. Heteronomous prescriptions have different authority and subject(s).

The idea of an autonomous norm is more problematic. One way of understanding the idea is to regard those norms, or *some* of those norms, as being autonomous, which are not given or issued by any authority at all. Perhaps moral principles could be regarded as autonomous norms in this way. We shall not discuss the question here.

Another way of understanding the idea of autonomous norms is to call those prescriptions autonomous which are given by some agent *to himself*. On this view, autonomous norms are self-commands, self-permissions, and self-prohibitions.

The question may be raised: *Can* an agent give prescriptions (commands, permissions, prohibitions) to himself? That is: Is this *logically* possible? It must not be taken for granted that the answer is affirmative. My view is that an agent can sometimes correctly be said to command or give permissions to himself, *but only in an analogical or secondary sense*. The attribute 'autonomous', moreover, does not seem to me ill-suited for such self-reflexive prescriptions.

If only norms which lack a norm-authority are called autonomous, then no prescription can be autonomous. If norms with identical authority and subject are called autonomous, and if such cases are possible, then some prescriptions are autonomous. My view is that, in a primary sense, prescriptions are heteronomous. Only in a secondary sense (of 'prescription') are there autonomous prescriptions.

9. By the *subject* (or subjects) of a prescription I understand the agent (or agents), to whom the prescription is addressed or given. The subjects are commanded or permitted or forbidden by the authority to do and/or forbear certain things.

There are as many kinds of norm-subject as there are kinds of agents who are capable of human action. If acts of impersonal agents are 'reducible' to acts of personal agents, and collective action to the action of individuals, then prescriptions whose subjects are individual men hold a basic position relative to all other prescriptions. As said earlier (Ch. III, Sect. 4), whether such a reduction is possible will not be investigated in this work. Here we shall consider only individual men as subjects of prescriptions.

We shall say that a prescription is *particular* with regard to its subject when it is addressed to *one* specified human individual. This is the case, for example, with the command addressed to N.N. to open the window.

(The prescription can also be given to several, *i.e.* a finite number of, specified subjects. This case will not receive special attention here. I shall regard it as being resolvable into a plurality of cases of the first kind mentioned.)

We shall say that a prescription is *general* with regard to its subjects when it is addressed either to *all* men unrestrictedly or to *all* men who satisfy a certain description.

The laws of the state, to the extent that they are concerned with the conduct of individuals, provide examples of prescriptions which are given to men of a certain description. The laws are made for the citizens of the state and not for all mankind. Prescriptions of the type 'Children under 12 must not work the lift' are also addressed to agents satisfying a certain description.

The question may be raised whether there are (can be) prescriptions which are given to all men unrestrictedly. 'Thou shalt not kill', 'Never tell a lie', 'Love your neighbour as yourself'—are not these examples of such prescriptions? We can regard the three sentences as formulations of moral principles. The principles surely 'apply to' or 'concern' all men unrestrictedly. This kind of generality may, moreover, be regarded as a characteristic of moral principles. But this does not show that they are *prescriptions* for all men without restriction. If moral principles are prescriptions (on our understanding of the term) we should be able to answer the question '*Who gave* the moral law?' Some think that God gave the moral law. The formulation of moral principles by means of sentences in the imperative mood may be said to 'hint at' this conception of morality. If, however, we do not subscribe to this conception we cannot instance moral principles as examples of prescriptions addressed to all men unrestrictedly. Our doubts about the possibility of such prescriptions have to do with considerations of the nature of normative action and of relationships of power or strength between norm-authority and norm-subject(s). We shall return to these questions in a later chapter.

Consider a captain's command to the passengers 'Someone ought to leave the boat'. To whom is it addressed? The answer could be: to *all* the passengers. Yet it would not be true to say that *every* passenger has been ordered to leave the boat. In fact, no *one* passenger has been commanded to do this. The passengers are 'disjunctively' under an obligation to do something. How shall this be understood?

The captain counts the passengers, he knows that the vessel cannot carry them all safely to the destination, and says to himself, 'Someone ought to leave the boat.' If this is an order at all it is one which the captain addresses, as it were, to himself, and not to the passengers 'disjunctively'. The self-command, as it were, emerges as the conclusion of an argument: 'If there are as many people as this on board, the passage will not be safe; therefore I must see to it that someone disembarks before we travel.' Having reached this conclusion, the captain may turn to *some one* (or several) of the passengers and order *him* (or them) to leave the boat. In this case there is no obligation imposed on the passengers 'disjunctively'. But he may also turn to *all* the passengers and order them to see to it that *one* of them leaves the boat. If this is what the captain does I shall say that the order is addressed to the passengers *collectively* or that the subject of the prescription is not individual men but the *collectivity* of passengers. This collective agent has been ordered to perform an act which results in one of the members of the collectivity leaving the boat. The passengers may, for example, discuss the situation among themselves and agree that the heaviest of them must leave, or the one who embarked last. This decision may be construed as a prescription addressed by the collectivity to a particular one of its members.

Thus, on our suggested analysis, a prescription which addresses (commands, permits, or forbids) all agents of a certain description disjunctively is not a prescription which is general with regard to its subjects. The prescription is particular with regard to its subject, this subject being *a collective agent*.

10. The contents of prescriptions, which we here study, are certain generic acts and/or forbearances. These contents the norm-subjects are commanded or permitted by the norm-authorities to realize in individual acts and/or forbearances *on certain occasions*.

Mention of the component, which we call 'occasion' in the formulation of a prescription, is usually mention of a location, *i.e.* place or span, in time. 'Now', 'next Monday', 'within a week', 'once every second year', 'sometime(s)', 'always' are words and phrases which may be used to make clear the occasion(s) for which the prescriptions are made (given).

A prescription which is for *one* specified occasion only we shall call *particular* with regard to the occasion. 'Open the window now' is an example. 'If it starts raining, shut the window immediately' is another.

A prescription which is for a finite number of specified occasions we also call particular. This case is not of independent interest.

A prescription which is for an unlimited number of occasions we shall call *general* with regard to the occasion.

A prescription is *conjunctively* general with regard to the occasion if it orders or permits the realization of its norm-content on *all* (every one) of this unlimited number of occasions. 'Shut the window whenever it starts raining' would be an example.

That a prescription is *disjunctively* general with regard to the occasion will mean that it orders or permits the realization of its norm-content on *some* (at least one) of this unlimited number of occasions. As in the case of generality with regard to subject, the question may be raised whether prescriptions can be genuinely disjunctively general with regard to the occasion.

Sometimes the temporal specification of the occasion is such that several occasions for realizing the norm-content may arise within the time specified. For example: The stranger who on arriving in a country is asked to report to the police within a week can comply with this requirement either to-day or to-morrow or . . . If he chooses to report to-morrow he can do so either in the morning or . . .

The question may be raised whether there can be an unlimited number of occasions for doing a certain act within a limited time-span, such as a day or a week or a year. If the answer is affirmative it may be thought that an order or permission to do a certain thing within such a time-span is disjunctively general with regard to the occasion.

It may, however, also be thought that, even if there can be an unlimited number of occasions for doing a certain act within a limited time-span, an order or a permission to do a certain thing within such a time-span is *particular* with regard to the occasion. We then regard the time-span in question as *one* occasion. This one occasion is, so to speak, 'disjunctively constituted' of a (finite or infinite) number of occasions of a shorter duration. The conception of the time-span as one occasion is somewhat similar to the conception of a collectivity of men as one agent.

I shall accept the view that a command or permission to do a certain thing within a limited time-span is particular with regard to the occasion. An order to me to do something, say, within the present year is particular, and not disjunctively general with regard to the occasion, even if it could be truly said that there are an unlimited number of occasions within the time specified for doing the thing in question. An order to do something once every year, *e.g.*, to make an income-tax return, is general with regard to the occasion—but 'conjunctively' and not 'disjunctively' general.

11. As noted in the two preceding sections, considerations relating to subject and occasion lead to a classification of prescriptions as *particular* or *general*.

We shall call a prescription *particular* if it is particular with regard both to subject *and* to occasion.

'N.N., open the window now' enunciates a particular prescription.

We shall call a prescription *general* if it is general with regard to subject *or* to occasion (or both). If it is general with regard both to subject *and* to occasion we shall call it *eminently general*.

As noted in Section 9, a prescription which is general with regard to subject, and the subjects of which are human individuals, need not be addressed to all men unrestrictedly. Its subjects can be all men who satisfy a certain description, *e.g.*, that they are British citizens.

We raised some doubts as to whether there *can* be prescriptions which are addressed to all men unrestrictedly. These doubts, be it observed, do not concern the possibility of prescriptions that are eminently general. A regulation which concerns all British citizens but no others can be eminently general.

The question may be raised whether a prescription which is addressed to all men of a certain description could not be regarded as a *hypothetical* prescription, which is addressed to all men unrestrictedly. For example: Could not a regulation which concerns all British citizens be regarded as a prescription which orders or permits all men unrestrictedly to do a certain thing *if* (in case) they happen to be British citizens?

No doubt, we can so define 'hypothetical prescription' that prescriptions whose subjects are agents satisfying a certain description may be called 'hypothetical'. But then we must distinguish between prescriptions which are hypothetical in the sense that their subjects are restricted to agents satisfying a certain description (such as 'British citizen'), and prescriptions whose conditions of application are restricted to certain contingencies (such as 'if it starts raining').

We shall decide *not* to enlarge the scope of the term 'hypothetical prescription' in such a way that it covers also prescriptions whose class of subjects is restricted to agents of a certain description.

Laws of the state, we have said before (Ch. I, Sect. 5), are a species of prescriptions. It may be thought to be of the 'essence' of a law that it must be a general and cannot be a particular prescription.

If we accept the view that laws must be general we may raise the further question whether they must be eminently general or whether generality with regard to subject *or* with regard to occasion is sufficient.

This question recalls a difference of opinion between two famous names in jurisprudence, Blackstone and Austin, concerning the meaning of 'law' or 'rule'. Blackstone seems to have held that a law is distinguished from a particular command by being general with regard to its *subjects*. A law obliges generally the members of a given community or the persons of a given class (description). Austin again saw the distinguishing feature of laws in the generality of the *occasions* for which they are issued or made.

On Austin's view, an order may address all citizens of a given state and yet not deserve the name of a rule. 'Suppose,' Austin says, 'the sovereign to issue an order, enforced by penalties, for a general mourning, on occasion of a public calamity. Now, though it is addressed to the community at large, the order is scarcely a rule, in the usual acceptation of the term. For, though it obliges generally the members of the entire community, it obliges to acts which it assigns specifically, instead of obliging generally to acts or forbearances of a class.'[1]

On the other hand, an order may, according to Austin, be given

[1] *The Province of Jurisprudence Determined* (1832), Lecture One, in the section called '*Laws* or *rules* distinguished from commands which are *occasional* or *particular*'.

to one specified agent only and yet deserve the name of a rule, because of the generality of occasions for which it is given. 'A father may set a *rule* to his child or children; a guardian, to his ward; a master, to his slave or servant.'[1] 'If you command your servant . . . to rise at such and such an hour on such and such a morning . . . the command is occasional or particular. . . . But if you command him *simply* to rise at that hour, or to rise at that hour *always*, or to rise at that hour *till further orders*, it may be said, with propriety, that you lay down a *rule* for the guidance of your servant's conduct.'[2]

Most of the laws of the state, Austin thought,[3] are what we have here called eminently general, *i.e.* general both with regard to subject and with regard to occasion.

As far as the *term* 'rule' is concerned, it seems to me that Austin was right in thinking that generality with regard to occasion, and not generality with regard to subject, is the distinguishing mark of prescriptions which deserve to be called rules.[4]

As far as the *term* 'law' is concerned, the dispute between Austin and Blackstone seems uninteresting. It could nevertheless be an interesting question of political philosophy and the philosophy of jurisprudence, whether it is not of the essence of law (or of the state) that laws of the state are general. The question would then have to be related to ideas concerning the purpose of laws and the *raison d'être* of a state.

12. In the remaining sections of this chapter we shall discuss the various norm-*characters*. We begin with a discussion of the relation between the 'ought'-character and the 'must not'-character. Speaking of prescriptions, the question concerns the relation between command and prohibition.

It is obvious that the two characters in question are interdefinable (cf. Section 2). That which ought to be done is that which must not be left undone, and vice versa. That which ought to be left undone is that which must not be done, and vice versa. Every positive norm of 'ought'-character is identical with a negative

---

[1] *Op. cit.*
[2] *Ibid.*   [3] *Ibid.*
[4] The use of 'rule' to cover a class of prescriptions must be distinguished from other uses of the word to cover norms which are not 'prescriptions' in our sense of the term. Cf. Ch. I, Sect. 4.

norm of 'must not'-character, and conversely. Every negative norm of 'ought'-character again is identical with a positive norm of 'must not'-character, and conversely. Speaking of prescriptions: a command to do (positive command) is a prohibition to forbear (negative prohibition), and vice versa; and a command to forbear (negative command) is a prohibition to do (positive prohibition), and vice versa.

We shall list these identities below for the eight types of elementary O-norms:

$Od(pTp)$ says that the state of affairs described by p ought to be preserved, or, which means the same, that one must not let it vanish.

$Of(pTp)$ says that the state of affairs described by p must not be prevented from vanishing, or, which means the same, that one ought to let it vanish.

$Od(pT \sim p)$ says that the state of affairs described by p ought to be destroyed, or, which means the same, that one must not let it continue.

$Of(pT \sim p)$ says that the state of affairs described by p must not be destroyed, or, which means the same, that one ought to let it continue.

$Od(\sim pTp)$ says that the state of affairs described by p ought to be produced, or, which means the same, that one must not let it continue to be absent.

$Of(\sim pTp)$ says that the state of affairs described by p must not be produced, or, which means the same, that one ought to let it continue to be absent.

$Od(\sim pT \sim p)$ says that the state of affairs described by p ought to be suppressed, or, which means the same, that one must not let it come into being.

$Of(\sim pT \sim p)$, finally, says that the state of affairs described by p must not be suppressed, or, which means the same, that one ought to let it come into being.

Although 'ought to' and 'must not' are interdefinable, it is convenient to retain the use of both phrases, and also to retain the use of both terms 'command' and 'prohibition'. But there is no point in having different symbols for the two norm-characters in our formalism (cf. Section 2).

When the content of a prescription is *mixed*, a compound of acts and forbearances (cf. Section 4), it is usually not more natural to call the prescription a 'command' than to call it a 'prohibition'. Such prescriptions can be said to be both commands and prohibitions, or partly the one and partly the other. Does, for example, 'Close the window or leave the door open' enunciate a command or a prohibition? It does not matter what we call it. But it is interesting to note that the same prescription which we expressed by a sentence in the imperative mood could also have been expressed by the 'ought'-sentence 'You *ought to* close the window *or* leave the door open' and by the 'must not'-sentence 'You *must not* leave the window open *and* close the door'.

13. We have distinguished (Section 2) between obligation-norms or O-norms and permissive norms or P-norms. When the norms concerned are prescriptions obligation-norms are, broadly speaking, commands or prohibitions. Permissive prescriptions are also simply called 'permissions'.

The independent status of permissive norms is open to debate. The problems in this region are, it seems, more urgent to a theory of prescriptions than to a theory of other types of norm. Therefore these problems are also more relevant to legal and political philosophy than to moral philosophy.

We here limit our discussion of permissive norms to a discussion of 'permissions', *i.e.* permissive prescriptions. The main problem before us is this: Are permissions an independent category of prescriptions? Or can they be defined in terms of command and prohibition? Strictly speaking: Can prescriptions of the P-character be defined in terms of prescriptions of the O-character?

There are two ways in which it has been attempted to deny the independent status of permissions. The one is to regard permissions as nothing but the absence or non-existence of 'corresponding' prohibitions. The other is to regard permissions as a peculiar kind of prohibitions, *viz.* prohibitions to interfere with an agent's freedom in a certain respect. These two views of permissions must be sharply distinguished and kept apart.

The view that a permission to do a certain thing is the same as the absence or lack of a prohibition to do this thing is common. I have accepted it myself in previous publications. It seems to me, however, that this view is in serious error, for a variety of reasons. Here I shall state *one* reason only.

One cannot make an inventory of all conceivable (generic) acts. New kinds of act come into existence as the skills of man develop and the institutions and ways of life change. A man *could not* get drunk before it had been discovered how to distil alcohol. In a promiscuous society there *is* no such thing as committing adultery.

As new kinds of act originate, the authorities of norms may feel a need for considering whether to order or to permit or to prohibit them to subjects. The authority or law-giver may, for example, consider whether the use of alcohol or tobacco should be permitted. In the case of every authority, personal or impersonal, there will always be a great many acts about the normative status of which he never cares.

It is therefore reasonable, given an authority of norms, to divide human acts into two main groups, *viz.* acts which are and acts which are not (not yet) subject to norm by this authority. Of those acts which are subject to norm, some are permitted, some prohibited, some commanded. Those acts which are not subject to norm are *ipso facto* not forbidden. If an agent does such an act the law-giver cannot accuse him of trespassing against the law. *In that sense* such an act can be said to be 'permitted'.

If we accept this division of acts into two main groups—relative to a given authority of norms—and if we decide to call acts permitted simply by virtue of the fact that they are not forbidden, then it becomes sensible to distinguish between two kinds of permission. These I shall call *strong* and *weak* permission respectively. An act will be said to be permitted in the weak sense if it is not forbidden; and it will be said to be permitted in the strong sense if it is not forbidden but subject to norm. Acts which are strongly permitted are thus also weakly permitted, but not necessarily vice versa.

Roughly speaking, an act is permitted in the strong sense if the authority has considered its normative status and decided to permit it. But this must not be understood to mean that the authority is necessarily aware of having permitted the act. The permission may also be a *logical consequence* of other norms which he has issued. What this means will be explained later.

Weak permission is not an independent norm-character. Weak permissions are not prescriptions or norms at all. Strong permission only is a norm-character. Whether it is an independent norm-character remains to be discussed. We return to the question in Section 16.

14. Here a few words must be said about the famous principle *nullum crimen sine lege*. Can this principle be quoted in support of the idea that permission consists in mere absence of prohibition?

The principle in question can, I think, be sensibly interpreted in two different ways, neither of which, however, supports the view mentioned about the nature of permission.

According to the one interpretation, the principle lays down a rule, not about the subject's *freedom to act*, but about the authority's *right to punish*. The principle, under this interpretation, is also often worded *nulla poena sine lege*.

According to the second interpretation, the principle is to the effect that anything which is not forbidden within a certain normative order (system, hierarchy), *i.e.* within a totality of prescriptions which flow from one and the same supreme authority, is permitted within this order. (The concepts of normative order and supreme authority will be discussed in Ch. X.) This is not a definition of the concept of permission, but a permissive norm with a peculiar content. Its content is, so to speak, the 'sum total' of all acts and forbearances which are not already forbidden.

A *nullum crimen* rule permitting all not-forbidden acts and forbearances may or may not occur within a given normative order. If it occurs within a normative order, then, relative to this order, all human acts are subject to norm. Such an order without 'gaps' we shall call *closed*.[1] Normative orders which are not closed will be called *open*.

The question may be raised whether a normative order could not also be closed by means of a ruling to the effect that anything which is not permitted within the order is forbidden?[2]

[1] Kelsen seems to me to be in error when he argues that the legal order *cannot* have any gaps. See, *e.g.*, his *General Theory of Law and State* (1949), pp. 146–149. Kelsen's argument hinges on the assumption that anything which the law does not prohibit it *ipso facto* leaves the citizens free to do. There is an interesting discussion of these problems from the standpoint both of deontic logic and of legal theory in the work by Amedeo G. Conte, *Saggio sulla completezza degli ordinamenti giuridici* (1962).

[2] Aristotle seems to have had this possibility in mind in *Ethica Nicomachea* 1138ª 6–8.

Consider a possible result of action such that there is no prescription in the normative order in question which permits the doing of this thing (result), nor any prescription which permits the forbearing of it. Then, by the suggested 'converse' of the *nullum crimen* principle, both the doing and the forbearing of this thing would be forbidden. But this—as we shall see presently—is a logical impossibility. Therefore a normative order cannot be closed by means of a norm prohibiting all not-permitted acts and forbearances, unless there is in the order, for any possible result of action, a permission to achieve this result or to forbear achieving it. If it is thought that a complete inventory of all human acts is not possible (cf. Section 13), then this condition cannot be satisfied. And then the suggested way of closing a normative order must be rejected as absurd.

It would, however, be logically possible to close a normative order by means of some weakened form of the principle that anything which is not permitted is forbidden. The closing principle could, for example, be that any *act*, the doing of which is not permitted, is forbidden. It would then, by virtue of the laws of deontic logic, follow that it is also permitted to *forbear* anything the doing of which is not permitted. An alternative way of closing an order would be by means of a principle to the effect that any *forbearance* which is not permitted is forbidden. Of such an order it would hold true that it is also permitted to *do* anything the forbearance of which is not permitted.

Closing a normative order by means of the *nullum crimen* principle faces no such difficulties and is subject to no such restrictions as closing it by means of the suggested 'converse' principle. The reason for this is that, whereas both the doing and the forbearing of one and the same thing cannot be forbidden (or commanded) without contradiction, both things can perfectly well be permitted without contradiction. The closing of a normative order by means of an unrestricted *nullum crimen* principle, moreover, does not presuppose a complete inventory of human acts.

15. It seems possible to distinguish between various kinds of strong permission—permissions, as it were, of increasing degree of strength.

In permitting an act the authority may only be declaring that he is going to *tolerate* it. The authority 'does not care' whether the subject does the act or not. The authority is determined not to interfere with the subject's behaviour as far as this act is concerned, but he does not undertake to protect the subject from possible interferences with his behaviour on the part of other agents.

Any (strong) permission is at least a toleration, but it may be more than this. If a permission to do something is combined with a *prohibition to hinder or prevent* the holder of the permission from doing the permitted thing, then we shall say that the subject of the permissive norm has a *right* relatively to the subjects of the prohibition. In granting a right to some subjects, the authority declares his toleration of a certain act (or forbearance) and his intolerance of certain other acts.

To prevent an agent from doing (or forbearing) a certain thing is to act in a way which makes the doing (or forbearing) of this thing impossible to this agent. Preventing from forbearing is also called *compelling* or *forcing* to do.

We ought to distinguish between *not* making an act *im*possible (for someone to perform) and *making* an act *possible*. The second is also called *enabling* (someone to do something). It is the stronger notion. Enabling entails not-hindering, but not-hindering does not necessarily amount to enabling.

If a permission to do something is combined with a *command to enable* the holder of the permission to do the permitted thing, then we shall say that the subject of the permissive norm has a *claim* relatively to the subjects of the command. It is understood that any claim in this sense is also a right, but not conversely.

Assume that it is part of a country's constitution that every citizen has a 'right to work'. Assume that no employer has a job for Mr. X. They cannot be accused of hindering Mr. X from taking up an employment. But Mr. X nevertheless cannot exercise his right. It may then be argued that the constitutionally granted right is 'empty' if it is not a right in the stronger sense of a claim. The claim could, for example, be instituted in the form of a command addressed to all employers disjunctively (or collectively, cf. the discussion in Section 9) to take care that a job is provided for anyone who wants to work.

For the sake of avoiding misunderstanding it must be mentioned that what is here being said about rights and claims does

89

not pretend to be a complete analysis of the notions of *legal* rights and *legal* claims. We use 'right' and 'claim' in a technical sense, adapted to our purposes. I think, however, that our concepts of rights and claims are relevantly related to the legal notions; that the former catch hold of essential, though not exhaustive, logical features of the latter.

Rights and claims, unlike tolerations, are not concerned with the individual permission-holder only, but also with the normative status of his relations to his fellow creatures. Rights and claims are thus *social* in a sense in which mere toleration is not.

It may be suggested that it is inherent in the nature of permissions to entail rights and/or claims.[1] If this is accepted we should have to say that 'mere' toleration does not yet amount to a 'full' permission. It may also be suggested that the only sense in which laws of the state are permissive is by prohibiting interference with the behaviour of agents in certain respects.[2]

16. We shall now return to the question, raised in Section 13, whether the norm-character of permission can be defined in terms of the (mutually interdefinable) characters of prohibition and/or command.

We have, in the previous section, seen that the specific characteristics of the two species of (strong) permission, which we called rights and claims, can be accounted for in terms of prohibition and/or command. It follows from this that if there is an element in permissions which is not reducible to the other norm-characters this element is identical with what we called *toleration*. Thus, what is characteristically 'permissive' about permissions would be the norm-authority's declaration of his toleration of a certain behaviour on the part of the norm-subject(s). 'Permissions are essentially tolerations', we could say.

In order to see whether permission is an irreducible norm-character or not, we must thus examine the notion of toleration. It seems to me that a declaration of toleration can be understood in two different ways:

---

[1] This position has been argued by Professor K. E. Tranøy. See his paper 'An Important Aspect of Humanism' in *Theoria*, 23, 1957.

[2] This appears to be the position, *e.g.*, of Kelsen, *op. cit.*, p. 77: 'The legal order gives somebody a permission, confers on somebody a right, only by imposing a duty upon somebody else.'

A declaration of toleration can be a *declaration of intention* on the part of the permission-giver not to interfere with the permission-holder's freedom in a certain respect. Or it can be a *promise* of not-interference.

It may now be suggested that a declaration of intention is not a normative concept at all, whereas a promise obviously is. If this is accepted, permissions as 'mere' declarations of intention not to interfere would not be regarded as norms at all. Only permissions as promises of not-interference would be norms. Then the question whether permission is definable in terms of the other norm-characters would be reducible to the question whether the normative character of a promise (or at least of a promise of non-interference) can be accounted for in terms of 'ought' and 'must not'.

That the answer to the last question is affirmative would probably be universally conceded. I shall myself accept the view that permission as a species of promise can be defined in terms of the other norm-characters. If, when permitting something to somebody, the norm-authority has promised not to interfere with the norm-subject's freedom in a certain respect, then the authority *must not* interfere with this freedom.

If, however, permissions which are tolerations are regarded as a peculiar kind of promise the question will arise whether such permissions are norms of the kind which we have here called 'prescriptions'. Prescriptions, we have said, require an authority and a subject; they are someone's prescriptions to someone. The mere fact that permissions are given by someone to someone does not ensure, however, that permissions are prescriptions. For if the normative element in the permission is a prohibition to interfere, then, although the norm-authority of the permissive norm is the giver of the permission, the norm-subject is *not* the receiver of the permission. The norm-subject is the receiver of the prohibition. This is the norm-authority itself.

Thus, on the view of permissions as promises, permissions would be self-reflexive prescriptions, *viz*. self-prohibitions. But the question whether there are (can be) self-reflexive prescriptions is open to debate (cf. Section 8). If we think that such prescriptions cannot exist we should have to conclude that permissions are not prescriptions.

What kind of norm shall we then say that permissions are?

That is: What kind of norm is it that says that promises ought to be kept, or that this or that ought to be done on account of its having been promised? That promises ought to be kept would ordinarily be thought of as a typically *moral* norm, and the obligation to do this or that because one has promised to do it would be called a moral obligation. The status of moral norms is problematic (see Ch. I, Sect. 8). Some think they are a kind of prescription, *viz.* the commands and prohibitions of God to men. (On this view, if permissions are a sort of promise, it is God who has prohibited that the givers of permissions subsequently interfere with the receiver's freedom.) Others think of moral norms as related to technical norms concerning means to ends.

Thus, the conception of permissions as promises would give to permissions a peculiar *moral* flavour.

The conception of declarations of toleration as promises can be said to *supplement* the conception of rights as prohibitions to a third party. In granting somebody a right, the norm-authority issues a prohibition to any third party to interfere with the right-holder's freedom in a certain respect (see Section 15). By at the same time promising to respect (tolerate) this freedom he, as it were, prohibits himself too to interfere with it.

On the question whether permission is or is not an independent norm-character, I shall not here take a definite stand. The view that (all) permission is mere absence of prohibition I reject. The view that it can become defined in terms of prohibitions of non-interference with a person's freedom in a certain respect I find attractive. But I do not know exactly which form this view should take and how certain objections to it should be met.

In the Logic of Norms, which we are here going to develop, we shall therefore retain permission as an independent norm-character.

VI

NORMS, LANGUAGE, AND
TRUTH

1. WE shall distinguish between *norm* and *norm-formulation*. The norm-formulation is the sign or symbol (the words) used in enunciating (formulating) the norm.

When the norm is a prescription formulating it in language is sometimes called the *promulgation* of the norm.

Norm-formulations belong to language. 'Language' must then be understood in a wide sense. A traffic-light, for example, normally serves as a norm-formulation. A gesture or a look, even when accompanied by no words, sometimes expresses a command.

The distinction between norm and norm-formulation is reminiscent of the distinction between *proposition* and *sentence*. We do not, however, suggest that the former distinction be regarded as a special case of the latter. Under a sufficiently comprehensive use of the term any norm-formulation could perhaps be called a 'sentence'. But whether any norms can be called 'propositions' is debatable, and that some (types of) norms cannot be so called is obvious (see below Section 8).

It is common to distinguish between the two 'semantic dimensions' of *sense* (connotation, meaning) and *reference* (denotation) (cf. Ch. II, Sect. 2). It is plausible to say that the sense of a descriptive sentence (Ch. II, Sect. 2) is the proposition which it expresses. Some logicians and philosophers would wish to say that the reference of a descriptive sentence is the *truth-value* of the proposition which it expresses. It seems to me more plausible to say that the reference is the *fact* which makes the proposition, expressed by the sentence, true (cf. Ch. II, Sect. 5). In this terminology we would have to say that only sentences which express true propositions have reference. Sentences which express false propositions lack reference. But they do not lack sense.

As far as I can see, it would be misleading to conceive throughout of the relation between norms and their expressions in language on the pattern of the above two 'semantic dimensions'. At least norms which are prescriptions must be called neither the reference nor even the sense (meaning) of the corresponding norm-formulations. The semantics of prescriptive discourse is characteristically different from the semantics of descriptive discourse. It must not be thought that the conceptual tools for dealing with the latter can as a matter of course be applied to a study of the former type of discourse as well.

What, then, is the relation between norm-formulation and norm if the second is neither the sense nor the reference of the first? We shall not discuss this question in detail. The following observation on the relationship under consideration will suffice:

When the norm is a prescription, the promulgation of the norm, *i.e.* the making of its character, content, and conditions of application (see Ch. V, Sects. 2–6) known to the norm-subjects, is an essential link in (or part of) the process through which this norm originates or comes into existence (being). The use of words for giving prescriptions is similar to the use of words for giving promises (cf. Ch. VII, Sect. 8). Both uses can be called *performatory* uses of language. The verbal performance, moreover, is necessary for the establishment of the relation of norm-authority to norm-subject and of promisor to promisee.

For the reason just mentioned, prescriptions can be called *language-dependent*. The existence of prescriptions necessarily presupposes the use of language in norm-formulations. This is not in conflict with the fact that prescriptions which have not been overtly formulated may sometimes become deduced as logical consequences of other prescriptions. What such deduction means will be discussed in Chapter VIII.

2. Are all norms language-dependent? Can there, for example, exist rules of a game which are never formulated in language and which are not logical consequences of formulated rules? One can

learn to play a game without being told (all) its rules—*e.g.*, by watching it. But this does not prove that the rules need not have been, at some stage, formulated. It is, on the contrary, reasonable to think that norms which are rules are language-dependent too. But the way in which rules are language-dependent is not exactly the same as the way in which prescriptions are language-dependent. The formulation of rules of a game is not a 'performatory use of language', at least not in the same sense in which the giving of orders or promises is so.

Can technical norms, *i.e.* norms concerning the necessary means to given ends, exist without being formulated in language? It can, of course, be 'objectively' the case that some agent ought to do a certain thing in order to attain a certain end of his, but that neither he nor anybody else is aware of the necessary connexion. The connexion is not, for its existence, dependent upon a formulation in words. But the anankastic relationship is not the same as the technical norm (see Ch. I, Sect. 7). Therefore one cannot from the language-independent character of the former conclude to the language-independent nature of the latter.

Customs, we have said (Ch. I, Sect. 6), exert a 'normative pressure' on the members of a community. Customs, it seems, are largely adopted through a process of *imitation*. In this they differ characteristically from norms, which are prescriptions (laws, regulations, orders). Customs are not 'laid down' in the way rules (of a game) normally are; nor are they 'promulgated' as are laws and other prescriptions. Thus, in the origination of customs language plays no prominent or typical role. Of all the things which may reasonably become included under the heading 'norms', customs are probably the least language-dependent. It is a question of some interest whether it should be regarded as essential to customs that they can exist only within communities with a language or whether one can speak of customs proper in animal communities too; *i.e.* the discussion of this question may contribute interestingly to the formation of the *concept* of a custom. We shall not, however, discuss it here.

Even if one cannot maintain the language-dependent character of norms without qualification and restriction, it is obvious that there is a characteristic difference between norms and values in their respective relationship to language. Perhaps there are also types of valuation which are language-dependent in the sense that they are not logically possible among beings who do not master a language. But it is also obvious that there are reactions, deserving to be called valuations, on a pre-language level—among animals and infants. Roughly speaking: valuation is, conceptually, on a level with pleasure and want; norms are, conceptually, on a higher level. Norms can, I think, be said to presuppose logically valuations—but valuations can exist independently of norms. And that which, substantially, marks norms as conceptually higher than values is the dependence of the former upon language.

3. We shall here disregard norm-formulations, such as gestures or signposts, which are not 'language' in a narrower sense of this term. Disregarding them, there are *two* grammatical types of sentence which are of particular importance to the language of norms. The one type is sentences in the *imperative mood*. The other is sentences which contain what I propose to call *deontic* auxiliary verbs. The principal deontic verbs are 'ought', 'may', and 'must not'. We shall call the first type imperative sentences and the second type deontic sentences.

It is useful to raise separately the following two questions concerning the relation of imperative sentences to norms:

(*a*) Are imperative sentences used chiefly, or even exclusively, as norm-formulations?

(*b*) Can all norms be formulated by means of imperative sentences?

'Imperative' means in origin the same as 'commanding'. From this it does not follow, however, that all uses of the imperative mood are for commanding. There are several typical uses of it which are not for this purpose. *One* is in prayers. 'Give us this day our daily bread', 'Look upon us in mercy'. To say that these sentences express commands would not only be to depart grossly from ordinary usage; it would also be to ignore important features of logic. (The logic of prayer is different from the logic of command.) Prayers are not norms of the kind which we call prescriptions, nor of any of the other kinds which we have distinguished. As we know, the meaning of the term 'norm' is vague and flexible. There is no good ground, however, why prayers should be called norms.

Other typical uses of the imperative mood which are not for

96

commanding are in requests ('Please, give me . . .') and warnings ('Don't trust him'). Requests and warnings are not norms of any of the kinds which we have distinguished. They could perhaps be called *norm-like* categories. They are more like norms than are prayers.

Consider also such forms of expression as 'Don't be afraid', 'Take it easy', 'Let us assume that . . .'. These are common and typical uses of the imperative mood. But only under a strained use of the term 'norm' could we call the sentences in question norm-formulations.

The answer to the first of the above two questions is thus in the negative.

The answer to the question whether every norm can be enunciated in the imperative mood is complicated by the fact that the morphological character of the imperative mood in most languages seems to be rather indistinct. Whether a verb is said to be in the imperative mood often depends upon how the context in which it occurs is understood. 'You take it easy.' Is 'take' in the indicative or in the imperative mood? The question cannot be answered on the basis of considerations of grammatical form alone.

Imperative sentences which are used as norm-formulations are mainly used to enunciate prescriptions. There is some plausibility in thinking that every prescription of the O-character, *i.e.* command and prohibition, can be expressed by means of a sentence in the imperative mood—although part of the plausibility springs from our inclination to make the meaning of the sentence a criterion for *calling* its mood imperative. But permissive prescriptions or prescriptions of the P-character are ordinarily expressed by means of deontic sentences, using the verb 'may' in combination with the verb for doing the permitted thing. If we take the view that permissions are prohibitions addressed to a 'third party' we could argue that they can be formulated obliquely in the terms of imperatives ('Don't interfere . . .', 'Let him do . . .'). But even then the fact would remain that permissions, when addressed directly to the permission-holder, are normally expressed by means of 'may'-sentences.

There is, however, a kind of imperative sentence whose normal function seems to be to enunciate permissions. I am thinking of the form 'Do so-and-so, if you want to' or 'Do so-and-so, if you please'.

97

Occasionally, imperative-sentences of the categorical form 'Do so-and-so' also express permissions, and not commands or prohibitions. If when walking along the pavement I arrive at a street corner and the traffic light reads 'Cross now' the norm (prescription) addressed to me with these words is a permission to cross the street and not a command to do so.[1]

To say that the permission is incorrectly formulated because it is in the imperative mood would be sheer pedantry. But it seems plausible to regard imperative sentences of the categorical form 'Do so-and-so', when used for enunciating permissions, as abbreviated or elliptic forms of hypothetical imperative sentences 'Do so-and-so, if you wish'. Thus, the traffic light 'Cross now', addressed to pedestrians, is short for 'Cross now, if you wish'.

Although imperative sentences, as norm-formulations, are *mainly* used for enunciating norms which we call prescriptions, it would be a mistake to think that they are, as norm-formulations, used *exclusively* for that purpose. To say 'If you want to make the hut habitable, then heat it' is grammatically no less correct than to say 'If you want to make the hut habitable, then you ought to heat it'. Both sentences would ordinarily be understood to mean the same. It would not be right to say that with the first sentence a command is given and with the second sentence a rule concerning means to an end. The function of the imperative mood in 'If you want to make the hut habitable, then heat it' and in 'If it starts raining, then shut the window' is different. The first imperative sentence expresses a technical norm, the second a hypothetical prescription (command, order).

4. There is a prominent tendency in contemporary philosophy, including moral philosophy, to lay strong emphasis on language. 'Ethics,' a recent writer says,[2] 'is the logical study of the language of morals.' And moral language, he thinks, is 'prescriptive language',[3] so therefore 'the study of imperatives is by far the best introduction to the study of ethics'.[4] He is aware of the fact that imperatives 'are a mixed bunch',[5] but nevertheless decides 'to follow the grammarians and use the single term "command"

---

[1] I am indebted to Professor Tranøy for drawing my attention to this clear-cut case of a 'permissive imperative'.

[2] R. M. Hare, *The Language of Morals* (1952), Preface, p. v.

[3] *Op. cit.*, p. 1.   [4] *Op. cit.*, p. 2.   [5] *Op. cit.*, p. 4.

to cover all these sorts of things that sentences in the imperative mood express'.[1] This is done because the author is interested 'in features that are common to all, or nearly all, these types of sentence'.[2] That there are such features he seems to take for granted, and also that his readers are 'no doubt familiar enough' with the differences between the various kinds of imperative.[3]

I doubt the usefulness of the suggestion that philosophical ethics should start from a logical study of language in the imperative mood. I hope that some of my reasons for disagreeing with this view are plain from the above brief observations (in Section 3) on imperative sentences and their meanings. Neither as a morphological nor as a semantic category is the notion of the 'imperative mood' clear and homogeneous enough to make even a provisional identification of norms with the meanings of sentences in this mood plausible.

To characterize the language of norms as 'prescriptive' would not be unplausible. It would, however, imply either a much broader use of the term 'prescriptive' or a much narrower use of the term 'norm' than we are making here. Prescribing and prescriptions, in our use of the words, certainly play an important role in the moral life of man. But, unless we take a theonomous view of morality, moral norms (principles) can hardly be regarded as prescriptions in our sense of the word. And regardless of whether we *call* moral norms 'prescriptions' or not, it is doubtful whether moral norms can be formulated in the imperative mood. Consider, for example, the principle that promises ought to be kept. We can, and often do, urge people to keep their promises by addressing them with 'Keep your word' and similar imperative sentences. One can, using such sentences, command people to keep their word and prohibit people from breaking their word. This is prescriptive use of language. It is use of language for moral purposes, and in this sense 'moral language'. But the moral norm (principle) that promises ought to be kept is hardly the same as the command (or prohibition) which 'Keep your word' and similar imperative sentences may be used to enunciate. The proper linguistic medium for formulating moral principles is *not* language in the imperative mood.

Ethics, moreover, is concerned with values as well as with norms. To characterize the language of valuations as 'prescriptive'

[1] *Op. cit.*, p. 4.   [2] *Op. cit.*, p. 4.   [3] *Op. cit.*, p. 4.

seems to me rather misleading.[1] And therefore to base the philosophical study of values on a logical study of imperatives would be misleading too.

There is a sector of linguistic forms which may be said to bear to value-judgments a relation which is somewhat analogous to the relation which norms bear to sentences in the imperative mood. These are the part of speech and the syntactical category called *interjections*. Very roughly speaking: To value is more like exclaiming than like prescribing. To say this is not to deny that evaluative and prescriptive discourse are logically closely related. Nor is it to suggest that the study of interjections is the best, or even a good, introduction to the study of value.

5. The two questions which we raised in Section 3 concerning the relation of imperative sentences to norms, can be raised *mutatis mutandis* also for deontic sentences:

> (*a*) Are deontic sentences used chiefly, or even exclusively, as norm-formulations?
>
> (*b*) Can all norms be formulated in terms of deontic sentences?

In answering the questions we have to make allowance both for the unsharp nature of the concept of a deontic sentence and for the unsharp nature of the concept of a norm.

It is reasonable to think that the answer to the second of the above questions is affirmative. One could make it a partial definition of 'norm' that every norm is to the effect that something ought to or may or must not be or be done. It would then follow, trivially, that every norm can become expressed in a deontic sentence.

Quite apart from the question of definition of 'norm', however,

---

[1] Hare (*op. cit.*, p. 3) classifies imperatives and value-judgments under the common heading 'Prescriptive Language'. This tends to obscure the conceptual (logical) difference between norms and valuations. A 'classical' example of how distinctions may become blurred in this region is the following quotation from the writings of a distinguished contemporary philosopher: 'It is easy to see that it is merely a difference of formulation, whether we state a norm or a value-judgment. A norm or rule has an imperative form . . . actually a value statement is nothing else than a command in a misleading grammatical form.' For an early criticism of these confusions see the paper by Torgny T. Segerstedt, 'Imperative Propositions and Judgments of Value' in *Theoria*, 11, 1945.

it is obvious that deontic sentences have a much richer *semantic capacity* as norm-formulations than imperative sentences. This is so for two main reasons. One is the absence of a peculiar form of 'permissive imperative' corresponding to the deontic word 'may'; the other is that the imperative form, when used in norm-formulations, is used typically for expressing norms which are prescriptions. Deontic sentences, it seems, have no such alliance with one particular type of norm.

The answer to the first of the above two questions is without doubt negative. Besides the use of deontic sentences as norm-formulations there are two other equally common and typical uses of them.

The one is the use of deontic sentences to state *anankastic* (see Ch. I, Sect. 7) *relationships*. 'If the hut is to be habitable, it ought to be heated' does not express a norm, but states a fact about necessary connexions in nature. It is, on the loose definition we have given, to be counted as a deontic sentence.

Although sentences which state necessary connexions often use the word 'ought' to express the necessity, they can also be formulated using the word 'must'. For example: 'If the hut is to be habitable, it must be heated.' It may be thought that the 'must'-sentence is a more adequate expression of the anankastic relationship than the 'ought'-sentence. In any case it seems always possible to replace an 'ought'-sentence which is used to state an anankastic relationship by a 'must'-sentence. But it would certainly be contrary to common usage if we suggested that 'ought'-sentences which are used as norm-formulations can always be replaced by 'must'-sentences. 'Must' is typically an anankastic word. 'Ought' is anankastic *or* deontic.

Another typical use of deontic sentences, other than their use as norm-formulations, is for making what I propose to call *normative statements*. What is meant by a normative statement will be explained later (see below Section 9).

6. It must not be thought that imperative and deontic sentences are the *only* grammatical types of sentence which are used as norm-formulations. Indicative sentences, other than deontic sentences, are also quite commonly used for expressing norms.

When the norm is a prescription and its expression in words is an (ordinary) indicative sentence the future tense is often used.

101

'You will be leaving the room' does not necessarily express a prediction. It may just as well express a command—and be synonymous with the imperative sentence 'Leave the room' and the deontic sentence 'You ought to leave the room'.

In legal codes norm-formulations in the indicative mood, either in the present or in the future tense, seem particularly common. When, for example, in the Finnish constitution we read: 'The President of the Republic assumes office on 1 March next after the election' this is not meant as a description of what the president habitually *does*, but as a prescription for what he *ought to do*.—I have noted that in Swedish criminal law the indicative form answering to 'is punished' or 'will be punished' and the subjunctive form answering to 'be punished' are used indiscriminately to express norms to the effect that so and so ought to take place. The Swiss penal code, I understand, consistently uses the indicative form throughout.[1]

7. I hope that the observations on the language of norms in the preceding sections will have made it clear that norm-formulations, linguistically, are a very varied bunch. They cut across several grammatical types of sentence without including or being included in any one type. One must therefore warn against the idea of basing the conceptual study of norms on a logical study of certain linguistic forms of discourse. Deontic logic, *i.e.* the logic of norms, is not the logic of imperative sentences or of deontic sentences or of both categories jointly—just as propositional logic is not the logic of indicative sentences.

Whether a given sentence is a norm-formulation or not can never be decided on 'morphic' grounds, *i.e.* seen from the *sign* alone. This would be true even if it were the case that there existed a grammatically (morphologically and syntactically) sharply delineated class of linguistic expressions whose 'normal' or 'proper' function is to enunciate norms. For even then it would be the *use* of the expression, and not its 'look', which determines whether it is a norm-formulation or something else.

When we say that it is the use and not the look of the expression which shows whether it is a norm-formulation we are in fact saying that the notion of a norm is primary to the notion of a

[1] Cf. O. Brusiin, *Über das juristische Denken* (Soc. Sci. Fenn. Comm. Hum. Litt. XVII 5, 1951), p. 51.

norm-formulation. For the use to which we refer is itself defined as *use to enunciate a norm*. We thus rely upon the notion of a norm for determining whether an expression is used as norm-formulation or not.

8. It is appropriate to say something here about the relation of norms to truth. Are norms true or false? Or shall we think, on the contrary, that norms lack truth-value, that norms 'fall outside the category of truth'?

The question has been the object of much dispute. It is useful to raise it separately for the various types of norm which there are. Maybe the answer is not the same for all types. Here we shall consider it very briefly for some main types of norm only.

Have rules, *e.g.*, of a game, a truth-value? Of rules of a game we have said (Ch. I, Sect. 4) that they determine a concept. Chess, *e.g.*, is 'by definition' the game which is played according to such and such rules. That a rule of a game cannot be false seems plain. We may be mistaken in thinking that there is a rule to such and such effect, or that, according to the rules, such and such a move is or is not permitted in a certain game. What is false is then a proposition *about* the rules. The false proposition is not itself a rule—not even a false one.

Since rules of a game obviously *cannot* be false, does it follow that they *must* be true? Some would, I think, call them analytic (or necessary) truths. I would myself not call them truths at all; and I should be inclined to take the same attitude to rules generally. It is not necessary, however, to argue the point in detail here.

Are technical norms true or false? For example, that if I want to be at the station in time for the train I ought to break up the party now? What is certainly true or false, depending upon anankastic relationships in nature, is the proposition that, unless I break up the party now, I shall not be at the station in time. What is also true or false, depending upon my present condition, is the proposition that I want to be at the station in time for the train. The technical norm, however, is not the same as the anankastic proposition. Nor is it the conjunction of the two propositions about necessary relations and wants respectively. The relation of the technical norm to these two propositions is not clear to me, nor is therefore the relation of the technical norm to truth and falsehood.

The status of moral norms (principles and ideals) in relation to truth and falsehood we shall not discuss in this work at all.

That prescriptions lack truth-value we can, I think, safely accept. Or would anyone wish to maintain that the *permission*, given by the words 'You may park your car in front of my house', or the *command* formulated 'Open the door', or the *prohibition* 'No through traffic', are true or false?

Those philosophers who have defended the view that norms generally lack truth-value have sometimes, it seems, implicitly identified norms with prescriptions. If by 'prescription' we understand commands and permissions which are *given* by some norm-authority to some norm-subject(s), the identification of norms with prescriptions must appear much too narrowing. If again we understand 'prescription' in some wider sense it may become doubtful whether the thesis that prescriptions lack truth-value can be upheld.

To accept the view that prescriptions, and perhaps other types of norm too, *lack truth-value* does not of course constitute a hindrance to saying truly that norm-formulations, of prescriptions and other types of norm, *have meaning* or that they *make sense*.[1] Whether we shall say that the sense or meaning of a norm-formulation *is* the norm which it enunciates, is quite another matter. A full discussion of the question would raise problems of philosophical semantics which we cannot treat within the scope of the present work. Some comments on the topic were made in Section 1.

9. Suppose I say to someone, for example in reply to a question: 'You may park your car in front of my house.' Is this a norm-formulation? It is easy to see that there are two possibilities to be considered here.

In replying with those words I might actually have been *giving permission* to the questioner to park his car in front of my house. In this case the sentence was (used as) a norm-formulation. It did not say anything which was true or false.

[1] Yet there was a time not long ago when it was seriously maintained in some philosophic circles that norm-formulations actually are 'meaningless' because removed from truth and falsehood. This illustrates the power of philosophic dogmas—in this case the so-called verificationist theory of meaning—of perverting the philosopher's use of language.

But the same words might also have been used for *giving information* to the questioner concerning existing regulations about the parking of cars. In this case the sentence was a descriptive sentence. It was used to make a, true or false, statement. I shall call this type of statement a *normative statement*.

The very same words may thus be used to enunciate a norm (give a prescription) and to make a normative statement. This ambiguity, moreover, seems to be characteristic of deontic sentences generally (cf. above Section 5).

Which use is in question in the individual case may not be instantly clear. Sometimes both uses are involved at the same time. One and the same token of an 'ought'-sentence, for example, may be used both to remind the receiver of an order of the fact that he has been given this order *and* to give new emphasis to (reissue) the order itself. The possibility, however, that the meanings thus mix does not entail that they could not be logically sharply distinguished.

The systematic ambiguity of deontic sentences was, as far as I know, first clearly noted and emphasized by the Swedish philosopher Ingemar Hedenius.[1] He coined for (an aspect of) the distinction between the two uses the terms 'genuine' and 'spurious' legal sentence. Genuine legal sentences are used to formulate the legal norms themselves. Spurious ones are used to make existential statements about legal norms (normative statements).

10. A normative statement, schematically speaking, is a statement to the effect that something or other ought to or may or must not be done (by some agent or agents, on some occasion or generally, unconditionally or provided certain conditions are satisfied). The term 'statement' is here used in that which I propose to call its 'strict' sense. A statement in the strict sense is either true or false. (The sentence which is used in making the statement expresses a proposition.)

By the *truth-ground* of a given normative statement I understand a truthful answer to the question *why* the thing in question ought to or may or must not be done.

Let the normative statement be, for example, that I may park my car in front of your house. Why may I do this? The answer

[1] In his book *Om rätt och moral* ('On Law and Morals', 1941). See especially *op. cit.*, pp. 65 f.

could be that there is a regulation according to which I am permitted to do this. The existence of this regulation (norm, prescription, permission) is the truth-ground of the normative statement.

Also with a view to the *norm* (permission) that I may park my car in front of your house, the question, 'Why?' may be raised. The proper answer to this question 'Why' is not that there *is* this norm (permission). The answer tells us why this norm (permission) *has been given*. The answer thus makes reference to the aims and ends (motives) of the authority who granted the permission.

Generally speaking, the truth-ground of a normative statement is the existence of a norm. This holds good, as far as I can see, not only for prescriptions, but for the other types of norm as well. Why is it that, in chess, a pawn which has reached the last line may become exchanged for a queen? Because there is a rule which gives this 'right' to the players. Why is it that I ought to break up the party now? The answer could be that I want to be at the station in time for the train and that, unless I leave now, I shall be late. Here, the existence of a technical norm is the truth-ground of the normative statement.

The proposition that such and such a norm exists, I shall call a *norm-proposition*. For example: that there is a regulation permitting me to park my car in front of this house is a norm-proposition. The norm-proposition is true or false, depending upon whether the norm in question exists or not.

The existence of a norm is a *fact*. The truth-grounds of normative statements and of norm-propositions are thus certain facts. In the facts which make such statements and propositions true lies the *reality* of norms. The problem of the nature of these facts can therefore conveniently be called the *ontological problem of norms*. Some aspects of this problem will be discussed in the next chapter.

VII

NORMS AND EXISTENCE

1. THE ontological problem of norms is essentially the question what it means to say that there *is* (exists) a norm to such and such effect.

It is reasonable to think that the logical nature of the facts which make norm-propositions true will be different for the different types (kinds, species) of norm which there are. For most types of norm, however, these facts are *contingent* (empirical). It is a contingent fact that there are such and such customs in a community or laws of a state. In one sense, it is contingent that chess is played according to such and such rules. For it is a contingent fact that there should exist the *game* which we call 'chess'. But in another sense it is necessary that chess is played according to *these* rules. For a game with different rules would not be *chess*.

Are there norms which have necessary existence? The question is complicated by the fact that the very notion of necessary existence is problematic. Some may think that moral norms have necessary existence, if they are theonomous, *i.e.* the commandments (law) of God. Others may hold that moral norms have necessary existence as a 'law of nature'. That moral norms are not contingent in the same way (sense) as customs and prescriptions exist contingently seems fairly obvious. But it does not follow from this that we must attribute necessary existence to them. The question will not be discussed further in the present work.

We shall here limit the discussion of the ontological problem of norms principally to prescriptions. Our main question will thus be: What does it mean to say that a prescription (command, permission, prohibition) to such and such effect exists?

We shall attack this problem in a somewhat roundabout way. The point of departure of the discussion will be the idea, associated chiefly with the ethics of Kant, that Ought entails Can. The justification of this procedure will be plain, I hope, from the answer which we are going to propose to our main problem under discussion.

2. The idea that Ought entails Can has been the subject matter of much discussion in recent times also. We may raise the question what Kant meant by it. This we shall not discuss at all. We may also ask what different things *could be meant* by it. And one may discuss whether the idea, when understood in a certain way, *is true* or not.

In our discussion of the principle we shall in turn focus attention on each of the three words contained in its formulation, *viz*. 'ought', 'entails', and 'can'.

Since 'ought to' and 'must not' are interdefinable (Ch. V, Sect. 12), it is fairly obvious that the principle must be regarded as applying to norms which prohibit action, just as much as to norms which enjoin action. What does the principle say when formulated explicitly for prohibitions? This is not quite clear. One suggestion would be this: If there is something which one must not do, then one can *forbear* this. If, however, 'can' here refers to the generic ability (Ch. III, Sects. 9 and 11) the above suggestion would be equivalent to: If there is something which one must not do, then one can *do* this. The formulation of the principle for norms which prohibit, thus challenges the question how the 'can' should be understood. We shall return to this question presently.

Does the principle apply to permissive norms? Does May too entail Can?

It is obvious that the answer to this question depends upon what we think of the nature of the permissive norm-character and of its relation to obligation (cf. Ch. V, Sects. 13–16).

If we accept the view that permission is mere absence or lack of prohibition, then it is clear that there are any number of things which one is permitted to do but which one cannot do. In fact, anything which an agent cannot do, he would then be permitted to do.

If we define permission in terms of prohibitions to a third party, then it would follow from the principle that Ought entails Can that if something is permitted to an agent, then other agents can prevent him from doing this thing. But since one can prevent an agent from doing only such things as he can (in the generic sense) do, it would follow *a fortiori* that, if something is permitted to an agent, then this agent can do this thing. May too would then entail Can.

If, finally, we regard permission as an independent norm-character we cannot deduce from Ought entails Can that May entails Can. A decision is called for. We make this decision as follows: In the same sense of 'entail' and 'can' that we accept the principle that Ought entails Can we shall accept the principle that May entails Can.

We can formulate the principle for prescriptions in the following way: *That something is the content of a prescription entails that the subject of the prescription can do this thing.*

3. What is the meaning of 'entails' or 'implies' in the principle under discussion? Is the alleged connexion between norm and ability a *logical* (conceptual) or a *physical* (causal) connexion?

This last question we shall answer by saying that the connexion is logical. The tie between norm and ability which the principle envisages is a conceptual tie.

'Entails' will thus mean 'logically entails' and 'implies' will mean 'logically implies'. The question may be raised, however, whether there is not a better name for the logical relation in question than either 'entails' or 'implies'. We shall return to this point presently.

The idea that Ought entails Can has sometimes been thought to constitute a counter-argument against the well-known view, associated chiefly with the name of Hume, that there is a sharp distinction between norm and fact, between Ought and Is. Those who wish to maintain a sharp distinction between the two, it is said, may be right in thinking that one cannot from the fact that this or that *is* the case conclude that something or other *ought to be* the case. But, if it is admitted that duty entails ability, then one may *modo tollente* from the fact that something can *not* be done

109

conclude that there *is not* a duty to do this thing either. And, although the duty to do a certain thing does not entail that this thing *is* done, it nevertheless entails another factual conclusion, *viz.* that this thing *can* be done.

Instead of using Kant's principle as an argument against Hume's view, we may wish to make the assumed sharp distinction between Is and Ought a ground for refuting the view that a norm could entail factual consequences about human ability.

I think that both ways of arguing here—with Kant against Hume, and with Hume against Kant—are wrong, and that the conflict between the Kantian and the Humean viewpoints is apparent only. Those who think that the viewpoints conflict are guilty of a confusion between *norms* and *norm-propositions*. If I am right this shows the importance of keeping this distinction clear.

The principle that Ought entails Can, as I understand it, does not affirm a relation of entailment between a *norm* and a *proposition*. The entailment is between (true or false) norm-propositions, on the one hand, and propositions about human ability, on the other hand. The antecedent (premiss) is to the effect that there is a norm of such and such character and content. The consequent (conclusion) is to the effect that the enjoined or permitted thing, which is the content of the norm, can be done. On this interpretation, the Kantian principle that Ought entails Can is in no conflict with the Humean idea of the logical independence of Ought and Is.

There is a sense in which facts about human ability can be said to be *prior* to facts about the existence of norms. Whether a man can or cannot do certain things can normally be decided independently of considerations as to whether the acts or forbearances in question are subject to norm. But, on our interpretation of the principle that Ought entails Can, whether there is or is not a norm to such and such effect *cannot* be decided without first consulting facts about human ability. The existence of a norm depends logically on facts about ability. This is how we here understand the principle that Ought entails Can.

Considering what has been said about logical priority, it would seem more to the point to replace the words '(logically) entails' in our formulation of the principle under discussion by 'logically presupposes'. Ability to act is a *presupposition* of norms. Norms cannot exist, or better: cannot come into existence, unless certain conditions about human ability are (already) satisfied.

For norms which are prescriptions, we now get the following formulation of the Kantian principle:

That there is a prescription which enjoins or permits a certain thing, presupposes that the subject(s) of the prescription can do the enjoined or permitted thing.

4. In Ch. III, Sect. 9 we distinguished two meanings of 'can do'. We called them the 'can do' of *ability* and the 'can do' of *success*. The distinction is connected with that between generic and individual acts, events, and states of affairs.

The question may be raised: When 'can' in the shorthand formulation 'Ought entails Can' means 'can do', does it then refer to ability or to success? Does 'can', in other words, mean that the agent or agents in question can do the *kind* of thing which the norm enjoins or permits—or does it mean that the agent or agents in question can, *on such and such occasions*, do the thing enjoined or permitted?

If the principle that Ought entails Can is interpreted as laying down a (logical) condition for the existence of norms, then it seems fairly obvious that the 'can' which is involved in it must be the 'can' of ability, *i.e.* of generic acts. If we accepted the alternative interpretation of 'can' we should run into the following 'paradox':

Consider a person who has been commanded to do a certain thing on a certain occasion. He tries to do this thing, but fails. We should then, since he could not do the thing in question, have to say that, strictly speaking, he was not even commanded to do it. Whenever a person unsuccessfully tried to follow a prescription there would be no prescription (for him). Failure to obey the norm would annihilate the norm. But this is certainly not how we wish to shape our notion of a prescription or norm. Therefore, if we wish to make the principle that Ought entails Can an ingredient of our concept of a norm we must understand its 'can' in a sense which is compatible with the 'cannot' of failure. That is to say, we must understand 'can do' to imply ability, but not to imply success in each individual case.

Compelling and preventing is an annihilation of power to do or forbear. The power thus annihilated, however, is the 'can do' which refers to act-individuals, and not the 'can do' which refers to act-categories (cf. Ch. III, Sect. 12). This observation has the following consequence for the principle that Ought entails Can:

When we say that only such things can be commanded or permitted or prohibited to an agent as this agent *can do*, we need not qualify this by the phrase 'unless he is prevented from doing them'. For the ability to which the principle that Ought entails Can refers, as understood by us, is the generic ability, and this does not pass out of existence when the agent is prevented from exercising it.

5. In Ch. I, Sect. 9, we distinguished between norms concerning that which ought to, may, or must not *be* and norms concerning that which ought to, may, or must not *be done*. The first we also call ideals (ideal rules).

The question may be raised whether the principle that Ought entails Can applies to ideals also. Ideal rules, as was observed, are largely concerned with so-called states of character. They say that a man ought to be brave, temperate, truthful, etc. Would an application of the principle that Ought entails Can to ideal rules mean, for example, that if a man ought to be brave, then he can be brave? And would it then follow that if a man is a notorious coward and incapable of showing bravery the ideal rule does not apply to his case?

I think that the answer to the last question is in the negative. It does not follow, however, that the principle that Ought entails Can does not apply to ideal rules. But it follows that it cannot be interpreted as saying, strictly, that what *ought to be* also *can be*. My suggestion is that, when applied to ideals, the principle should be understood to mean that, if a man *ought to be* such and such, then he *can become* such and such—unless he already is this.

A man, as he is now, may not be able to live up to the ideal. His character may be undeveloped or corrupt. But the ideal may nevertheless apply to his case too. It does this if, or as long as, his case is not 'hopeless', *i.e.* if, or as long as, it is true to say that he *may become* like the ideal.

This application of the principle that Ought entails Can to ideal rules raises interesting problems of moral philosophy. How shall the 'may (can) become' be understood? Does it refer only to that which a man may become as a consequence of his own efforts and training? Does it include that which may befall him as a consequence of natural causality, *e.g.*, processes affecting his bodily and mental development? Or is the suggestion that whether a man can become like the ideal or not depends neither on his own efforts nor on causality in nature alone, but also on the grace of God?

Since this is not a treatise on ethics, we shall not discuss these questions. But it may be useful to see their connexion with the more elementary problems which occupy us here.

6. I hope that the discussion in the preceding sections has made clear the *sense* in which we here understand the principle that Ought entails Can. The question may now be raised, what grounds there are for thinking that the principle as understood by us is *true*.

This question of truth must not be misunderstood. It is a question neither of empirical verification nor of logical proof. The adoption of the principle is rather a matter of decision. The purpose of the principle, as I see it, is to help to mould or shape the concept of a norm. The question of the truth of the principle is essentially a question of how well it serves the philosopher's purposes. It should perhaps rather be called a question of 'acceptability' or of 'plausibility' than a question of 'truth'.

It must not be taken for granted that the adoption of the principle is equally plausible for every kind or type of norm.

Shall we, for example, regard the principle as being valid for norms of the kind we call *rules*? We shall not attempt to answer the question. The first reaction to it is, I think, that it is not quite clear how the principle *applies* to rules. Consider, *e.g.*, the rules of a game. Obviously the existence of the rules of a game is independent of whether individual men master the moves of the game. But what shall we say of the case when there is a contradiction in the rules, so that a situation may arise when no player could possibly comply with the demands of the rules? One thing which could be said is that the game 'collapses' if its rules put contradictory demands on the players. It ceases to be a 'proper' game. It is a logical requirement of rules of a game that it must not be impossible to satisfy the requirements which the rules make on the players. *This* would be a way of applying the principle that Ought entails Can to rules (of a game).

Of more interest to the discussion of norms in the present work is the application of the principle that Ought entails Can to technical norms.

Let the norm be that, if I want to attain a certain end e, I ought to do a certain act a. Can I not want to attain this end independently of whether I can or cannot do any act which is necessary for its attainment? The answer to this question is not as obvious as may at first appear.

That e is something I want can mean several things. It can mean, for example, that e is something which I would 'welcome' if it happened to me—as a grace of fate or thanks to the action of some other agent. In this sense, e can be a thing wanted by me, even though I cannot do that which is necessary for its attainment. Or that e is something I want can mean that I *wish* that e would happen to me. This, too, I can do without being able to use the necessary means for the attainment of e. But to want something can also mean to pursue it *as an end of action*. This is neither the same as to wish for it nor as to welcome it if it happens. It may be argued that pursuit of something as an end of action is not independent of my abilities, but that, on the contrary, it requires or presupposes that I *know how* to attain the end, *can do* the things which are necessary for its attainment. I may, of course, fail to attain an end which I pursue, although this requirement on my ability is satisfied. For, as we know, ability to do something is no infallible guarantee of success in the individual case.

I shall accept the view that pursuing something as an end of action presupposes ability to do the things which are necessary for the attainment of the end. This conceptual connexion between the pursuit of ends and ability to do things will turn out to have important consequences for the application of Kant's principle to norms which are prescriptions.

7. When applied to prescriptions, Kant's principle, as already observed (Sections 3 and 4), states that the existence of a prescription enjoining or permitting a certain thing presupposes ability on the part of the norm-subject(s) to do the kind of thing enjoined or permitted. Is this an acceptable view of the relation between prescription and ability? We shall consider the question in the light of an example.

An officer orders a soldier to swim across a river. The soldier refuses to plunge into the water. He gives as an excuse that he cannot cross the river swimming. Must we not, however, say that he was commanded to swim across the river, irrespective of whether his excuse is truthful or not? How can we say that he *refused* to do something, if he cannot truly be said to have been *asked* to do this?

Assume that our soldier is court-martialled and charged with disobedience. If he cannot substantiate his claim not to be able to swim across the river, then clearly he can be sentenced and punished for disobedience. But if he *can* substantiate his claim, can he then *not* be sentenced and punished? The soldier can, of course, be treated in the way which is characteristic of punishment and which involves the infliction on him of some kind of pain or disagreeable thing. This treatment may even rightly be described as punishment. It would be punishment for the manner in which he answered the officer, or punishment because he did not, on the spot, prove that he could not perform the required act, *e.g.*, by plunging into the water and letting the officer thus test his ability. Or he may be punished because he had not learnt to swim, although he was supposed to have learnt to do so in the course of his training. But whatever he is being punished for must—if his lot is to be called punishment as distinct from mere maltreatment—be something which he *could* have done but neglected to do. And since, on our assumption, the soldier cannot do that thing which the order to swim across the river requires, he cannot be *punished* for having disobeyed *this* order. He cannot have *disobeyed* it, for there is 'room' for disobedience only where obedience is possible. And obedience is possible only when there is *ability* to do the required thing.

An attempt to describe the case of the officer and the 'disobedient' soldier reveals conflicting conceptual tendencies. On the one hand, there is an inclination to say that, since he could not do the required thing, he could not even be commanded to do it. On the other hand, there is an inclination to say that there was a command, since he obviously was required to do something. How shall these two inclinations be reconciled?

One possibility of reconciliation would be by means of a distinction between the *giving* of prescriptions and the *receiving* (taking) of prescriptions. One can give an order to somebody, it might be argued, irrespective of whether that person can carry it into effect or not—but one cannot *take* an order from anyone, unless one has the ability to comply with it. Similarly, it may be argued that a permission can be given to an agent, irrespective of

115

his abilities, but that one cannot *have* ('enjoy') a permission, unless one can do the thing permitted.

How does this splitting up of prescriptions into a giving- and a receiving-aspect affect the question of the *existence* of prescriptions? It would be tempting to say that this existence depends upon the giving-aspect *alone*. Then it would appear that ability to do the prescribed things is *not* a logical precondition of the existence of prescriptions.

I shall try to show, however, that, even if the existence of a prescription depends upon its giving alone, the conclusion that this existence is independent of the abilities of its receiver does not necessarily follow.

8. Prescriptions originate, come into existence, through a peculiar mode of human action. For this mode of action, the giving of prescriptions (orders, permissions, prohibitions), we have earlier coined the name *normative action* (see Ch. V, Sect. 7).

We have distinguished between act and activity, and between the result and the consequences of action (see Ch. III, Sects. 5 and 6). The questions may now be raised, whether the giving of a prescription is an act or an activity, and whether the existence of a prescription is the result or a consequence of normative action. I propose to answer these questions as follows:

The giving of a prescription is an *act*, the successful performance of which *results* in the existence of a prescription. The *consequences* of normative acts, broadly speaking, are the effects which (the giving of) prescriptions may have on the conduct of those to whom the prescriptions are given.

In acts, we have said (Ch. III, Sect. 6), activity is usually involved, *e.g.*, in the form of muscular activity and movements of limbs. The activity which is characteristic of normative acts is *verbal* activity. It consists in the use of norm-formulations to enunciate, or as we also say *promulgate* the norm (prescription) to the appropriate subjects.

We thus distinguish between the act of giving a prescription and the verbal activity which is involved in the act. The point of making this distinction can perhaps best be illustrated through an analogy between the giving of prescriptions and the giving of promises:

To promising, as to prescribing, the use of language is essential.

The giver of a promise usually utters a certain form of words, 'I promise to . . .'. The uttering of these words is activity.

The mere fact that somebody utters a promise-sentence does not entail that a promise has been *given*. If a small child says to me 'I promise to give you a thousand pounds to-morrow', or if I say to a friend 'I promise to make you Emperor of China', or if an actor says on the stage 'I promise to revenge my father', nothing has been promised. The child was talking unwittingly, I was joking, the actor was acting a role. This is trivial—but it shows that whether the uttering of a promise-sentence 'constitutes' an act of promising depends upon other factors beside the verbal activity which is essential to the act. The same holds true of prescriptions. Mere uttering of imperative sentences and use of other forms of prescriptive language does not establish that a command, permission, or prohibition has been *given*, does not by itself 'constitute' an act of commanding or permitting or prohibiting.

What, then, is required, in addition to the verbal performance, to constitute normative action ? For answering this question also, the comparison between promises and prescriptions is illuminating.

When the uttering of a promise-sentence 'constitutes' an act of promising or 'results' in a promise having been given, there exists henceforth and for a time a relationship between the giver and the receiver of the promise, the promiser and the promisee. The promiser is, as we say, under an obligation to fulfil his promise, *i.e.* to do the thing which he has promised to do. It is natural to call this a 'normative relationship' between the two parties. It would not be quite right to 'identify' the promise with this normative relationship. But it is certainly right to say that, when the uttering of a promise-sentence leads to or results in the establishment of this normative relationship, then a promise has been given.

Similarly, when the uttering of a command-sentence 'constitutes' an act of commanding, there exists henceforth and for a time a relationship between the giver and the receiver of the command, the commander and the commanded. We could call this too a 'normative relationship' between the two parties. I shall prefer to call it a 'relationship under norm' between them. Again, as in the case of promises, it would not be right to identify the command with this relationship under norm. But it is right to say

117

that, when use of prescriptive language leads to or results in the establishment of this relationship between a norm-authority and some norm-subject(s), then the prescription has been given, the normative act successfully performed, and the norm has come into existence.

Prescriptions do not only come into being; they also pass out of existence. Prescriptions cease to be, when the relationships under norm, which the giving of the prescriptions established, dissolve. The life-span of a prescription is thus the duration of a relationship between a norm-authority and one or several norm-subjects. As long as this relationship lasts, the prescription is said to be *in force*. The existence of a prescription is not the fact, as such, that it has been given, but the fact that it is in force.

9. Let the question be raised: *Why* does a certain agent command (order) another agent to do or forbear a certain action?

Sometimes an order is given because the giver of the order has, in his turn, been ordered to give it.

When a prescription is given because there is an order to give it, then the normative act is itself subject to, *i.e.* the content of, a norm. This is a common and important type of case. Some logical problems connected with it will be discussed later, in Chapter X. For present purposes we can, however, ignore it. For it only removes the question 'Why?', in which we are here interested, to the 'second order' normative act through which the order to perform the 'first order' normative act came into existence.

When the normative act of giving an order is not itself the content of a norm the common type of answer to our question appears to follow this general pattern:

The giver of the order *wants* the result of the prescribed act *to happen*. Therefore he *wants* the subject of the prescription *to do* the act in question, *i.e.* to make the wanted change happen. By commanding the subject he may *make him do* the act. Therefore he gives the order. The normative act is a *means* to the norm-authority's *ends*. It is a means to making the norm-subject do something, and this in turn is a means to making a certain thing happen. If we wish to say, as we are, I think, free to do, that wanting to attain an end entails wanting to use the means which are actually used for the sake of attaining this end, then we may also say that the norm-authority *wants to command* the norm-

118

subject and that he *wants to make* the subject *do* the prescribed act.

When we say that the norm-authority wants a certain thing to happen, and therefore wants the norm-subject to do this thing (make it happen), we *ground* the second want on the first. One can distinguish between necessary and sufficient grounds. In the case under consideration the first want is a sufficient, and *not* a necessary, ground of the second want. This means: wanting an agent to do a certain thing does not (logically) presuppose that I want this thing to happen. I may, for example, want somebody to do a certain thing merely because I want to put him in motion and not because I am interested in the result of his act. But it is probably right to say that *normally* we order people to do things because we are anxious to have those things done.

Wanting an agent to do something is obviously a sufficient ground for wanting to make him do that thing. As far as I can see, the first want is here also a necessary ground of the second. This means: One cannot (logically) want to make a person do a certain thing unless one wants him to do that thing.

Wanting to make an agent do a certain thing is a sufficient, but certainly *not* a necessary, ground for wanting to command him. Commanding is only one among several means of moving people to action.

These observations will suffice on the mutual relations of the four cases of 'want', which we distinguished in connexion with the normative act.

I do not wish to maintain that *always*, when the normative act is not itself the content of a norm, the question why it is done can be answered with a reference to wants according to the above pattern. Orders are sometimes given 'for no particular reason'. This, however, does not necessarily mean that the giver of the order could not be truly said to want the receiver of the order to do a certain thing. It need only mean that there is no particular reason for his wanting *this*. Yet I shall not deny that an order could be given 'for absolutely no reason'. This, however, would be a most uncommon case, 'conceptually alien' to the institution of commanding. One could perhaps call it a 'misuse' or a 'parasitic use' of this institution.

10. What has been said in the last section of commands applies, *mutatis mutandis*, to prohibitions as well. The giver of a prohibition

normally wants the receiver of the prohibition to forbear something and also wants to make him forbear this by prohibiting him.

The giver of a permission cannot normally be said to *want* the receiver of the permission to do the permitted action. To permit is to *let* somebody do something. The question can be raised: What does the agent *do*, who *lets* another do a certain thing?

This is but to raise afresh the question of the nature of permissions, which we discussed briefly in Sections 13–16 of Chapter V. —A person can be said to let another do a certain thing when he has not prohibited the doing of that thing to that person and is perhaps not even aware of his doing it. This use of 'let' would correspond to the view of permission as mere absence of prohibition. Letting another do a certain thing can, however, also mean that one tolerates this act by that person and is aware of the possibility that he will do it even if not of his actual doing of it. This use of 'let' answers to the view of permission as toleration. I shall call the first form of 'letting do' *passive* and the second *active*.

If we take the view that a permission is a toleration in combination with a prohibition of non-interference, then to give a permission to somebody is actively to *let* this other person do a certain act and to *want* others to forbear a certain other act, *viz.* the act of making the first act impossible to the permission-holder. If, finally, we take the view that only the prohibition of non-interference is essential to the permissive norm, then giving permission is wanting others to behave in a certain way and wanting to make them behave thus by commanding them.

Passively to let another person do a certain thing does not involve any kind of wanting on the part of the letting agent. But if a person actively lets another do a certain thing, *i.e.* is aware of the possibility that he will do it and tolerates this, then the first agent can also be said to want to leave the second agent free to do this. *Wanting to leave* an agent *free to do* something corresponds, in the case of permissions, to *wanting to make* an agent *do* something in the case of commands.

11. With the remarks in the last two sections on the intention and reasons involved in normative action we have arrived in the neighbourhood of a well-known 'classical' theory of the nature of norms. We can call it the *will-theory* of norms. According to it,

approximately speaking, norms are the expressions or manifestations of the will of some norm-authority with regard to the conduct of some norm-subject(s).

The will-theory of norms has a primary application only to norms which are prescriptions. For it is essential to this theory that norms should emanate from an authority. Historically, the will-theory of norms is known, above all, as a theory of (the nature of) the law of the state. Laws, on this view, are sometimes said to express the will of the state. As a theory of legal philosophy, the will-theory of norms may be said to challenge the question of the nature of the authority behind the legal norms, and ultimately the question of the nature of the state.

As a theory of the ontological status of prescriptions generally, the will-theory of norms appears to me substantially correct. As a theory of legal norms in particular, its acceptance need not, so far as I can see, commit one to an anthropomorphic or theomorphic conception of the state as a being endowed with a will.

If one had to give a brief characterization of the will, of which *commands* are manifestations, one should call it, I think, a will to make agents (norm-subjects) do and/or forbear things. For short we could call it *a will to make do or forbear*. This will is seldom a will to make do or forbear 'for its own sake', but has some ulterior end in view. As observed in the last section, the authority normally wants to *make* the subject do something, because he wants him to *do* this. And he wants him to do this, because he wants the thing done to *happen*. It is a major problem of political philosophy, how these ulterior ends of the state as the authority of the legal norms are (or should be) related to the ends of the citizens of the state as the subjects of these norms.

The will which permissions manifest can be called *a will to tolerate*.

12. The art of commanding, we could say, consists in ability to make agents do or forbear things which we want them to do or forbear.

It is clear that ability to command does not presuppose that the giver of the order can make its receiver perform an individual act which results in the wanted thing. He may succeed with his order to make the subject do this act, but he may also fail. When he succeeds, we say that the subject has *obeyed* the order. When he

121

fails, we do not necessarily say that the subject has disobeyed. There are at least three different types of reason why commanding may fail of its aim on the individual occasion:

One reason is that the subject *disobeys*. That the subject disobeys will mean that he understands the order and can do the kind of thing ordered, but forbears and does not even try to do it on the occasion in question.

Another reason why commanding may fail of its aim is that although the subject *tries* to do it and can do the kind of thing ordered, he *fails* to accomplish the act. He could not do it on the occasion in question, because prevented by 'physical obstacles' or the interference of other agents. This we do not call disobedience. But there is no sharp border in the individual case between disobedience and this type of failure to comply with an order.

A third reason, finally, is that the subject *cannot do* the kind of thing which he is ordered to do. Then he can neither obey nor disobey the order. In such circumstances it is natural to say that he cannot 'receive' the order at all. The subject is incapable of entering into the 'normative relationship' with the authority which the normative act of commanding aims at establishing. This incapacity, of course, lasts only as long as the subject has not learnt to perform acts of the category in question.

Does this third type of failure of a normative act mean that the authority *cannot command* the subject? Ability on the part of the authority to command, we have said, is an ability to make the subject do the kind of thing which is commanded. If the subject cannot do the kind of thing in question, neither can he be made to do it by being commanded. (The subject may, of course, be taught to do it or learn to do it, and then, on some other occasion, be made to do it by being commanded.) And if he cannot be made to do this kind of thing the authority does not possess the ability which, on our view of the matter, is logically required for commanding *this* subject to do that kind of thing. The answer to our question above is thus affirmative.

It follows from what has been said in this section that a necessary condition of the existence of a command from some authority to some subject to do or forbear a certain thing is that the subject of the command *can do* this kind of thing. It should now be clear in which sense and for which reasons the principle that Ought entails Can may be said to lay down a minimum condition of the existence of commands (and prohibitions).

To give permission, we said, is 'actively to let' an agent do or forbear a certain thing. If 'active letting' is defined as the toleration of some action in the power of some agent, then it follows trivially that one can permit an agent to do or forbear only such things as that agent can do. On this view of permitting, May entails Can also.

13. The 'art of commanding' admits of several degrees of generality, so to speak. To say that an agent 'can command' may mean no more than that he can command *somebody* to do *something*, some kind of thing. This is ability to command in the most general and extenuated sense. From it must be distinguished ability to command *a certain* agent to do *something*, ability to command *somebody* to do *a certain* thing, and ability to command *a certain* agent to do *a certain* thing.

Let there be a norm-authority *a*, a norm-subject *s*, and a norm-content *c*. We can then make a table of corresponding abilities of various degrees of generality to command and be commanded:

a can command somebody to do something	*s* can be commanded by somebody to do something
a can command somebody to do *c*	*s* can be commanded by somebody to do *c*
a can command *s* to do something	*s* can be commanded by *a* to do something
a can command *s* to do *c*	*s* can be commanded by *a* to do *c*

The two first pairs of abilities listed in the table consist of logically independent members. The two last pairs consist of logically identical members.

On the view which we take here, there can exist a command from *a* to *s* to do *c* if, and only if, the ability of *a* to command and of *s* to be commanded match as in the fourth of the above pairs. When the abilities of *a* and *s* match as in the first, second, or third of the above pairs it is possible but not certain that *a* can command *s* to do *c*. When *a* can command *s* to do something it is plausible to say that he can also *try* to command *s* to do *c*, irrespective of whether he actually can command *s* to do *c* or not. Similarly, when *a* can command somebody to do *c* it is plausible to think that he also can (at least) *try* to command *s* to do *c*, irrespective of whether he actually can do this or not. It is more doubtful whether the mere fact that *a* can command somebody to do something should be said to entail that he can try to command *s* to do something, try to command somebody to do *c*, and/or try to command *s* to do *c*. The notion of trying to command is not, in itself, precise enough to make a decision possible. The notion has to be moulded. We could distinguish between several concepts (senses) of trying to command, depending upon which of the above requirements as regards ability are satisfied.

Trying to command is compatible with but does not presuppose ability on the part of the agent whom we try to command to do the thing which we try to command him to do.

One must distinguish between *trying to command* and *commanding to try*. Commanding a person to do a certain thing presupposes, I shall say, that the commanded agent can try to do this kind of thing. As observed earlier (Ch. III, Sect. 10), it is not the case that one can try to do just anything. One may even argue that one can try to do, on an individual occasion, only such things as one can do generically. But this requirement may appear too strong. Perhaps we should say that some things which one cannot do in the generic sense of 'can do', one can yet try to do. But this notion of 'can try' presupposes that one at least 'has some idea' of how to do the thing in question. When there is no such idea present one cannot even try. One does not *know how* to try.

Thus, from the fact that *a* can try to command *s* to do *c* it does *not* follow that *a* can command *s* to try to do *c*. But, accepting what was said above about trying to command, from the fact that *a* can command *s* to try to do *c* it *does* follow logically that *a* can try to command *s* to do *c*.

The distinction between commanding and trying to command is of importance for the problem of the existence of commands and for the interpretation of the principle that Ought entails Can. Trying to command nearly always results at least in the production of the words or symbols which we called the norm-formulation.

124

Now the norm-formulation is the perhaps most 'conspicuous' feature in which the existence of a norm shows itself. For this reason it is tempting to say that already when a person is *trying to command* another a command comes into existence. This is how we often and naturally express ourselves. It is not the philosopher's business to correct language here. His task is to note the conceptual differences between cases—even when the cases are such that ordinary language blurs the differences.

One chief reason for laying down the conditions of existence in a manner which presupposes the validity of the principle that Ought entails Can is that this keeps the distinction between commanding and trying to command clear.

14. Wherein does ability to make agents do or forbear things by commanding them consist? In order to get a firmer grasp of this question, let us ask first: What does the agent who gives commands do?

With one aspect of what he does we are already familiar. This is the aspect which we called *promulgation*. It consists, broadly speaking, in making known to the norm-subjects, by means of language or other symbols, *what* the norm-authority wants them to do or forbear.

Promulgation is necessary, but not by itself sufficient, to the establishment of normative relationships among agents. Beside promulgation, there is also a second component involved in normative action. I shall refer to it by using another term from legal philosophy, *viz. sanction*.

Sanction may, for present purposes, be defined as an explicit, or implicit, *threat of punishment for disobedience* to the norm.

The existence of a threat of punishment is not, by itself, a motive for obedience. *Fear* of punishment, however, is. When threat of punishment constitutes fear of punishment I shall speak of an *effective* threat or sanction.

Fear of punishment need not be the *sole* motive for obedience to the norm. It may even be regarded as being of the essence of some types of prescriptions, *e.g.*, of laws of the state, that there should be other motives beside fear for obeying them. It is probably right to say that normally, when action conforms to prescriptions, the motive is *not* fear of punishment or of other unpleasant consequences. The function of sanction is to constitute a motive for obedience to the norm in the absence of other motives for obedience and in the presence of motives for disobedience. When the subject is tempted to disobey, fear of punishment is *one* of the things which may 'call him to order'. In extreme cases it is the *only* thing with this appeal on him.

The existence of the motive for obedience which fear of punishment is, does not entail that it is strong enough to overcome, in the individual case, motives for a contrary conduct. Effective sanction is compatible with disobedience to the norm. But disobedience must be occasional, must be the exception and not the rule. If disobedience is habitual rather than exceptional sanction is ineffective, punishment not (seriously) feared.

The meaning of 'exceptional' and 'habitual' (dis)obedience calls for a comment. If the command or prohibition is what we have (Ch. V, Sect. 11) called *eminently general*, disobedience to the norm is exceptional when most subjects on most occasions obey the norm. If the command or prohibition is general with regard to the occasion but addressed to a particular subject disobedience is exceptional when this subject on most occasions obeys the norm. Similarly, if the prescription is general with regard to subject, but for a particular occasion only, disobedience is exceptional when most subjects on this occasion obey the norm.

If, however, the prescription is (completely) *particular* it does not make sense to speak of exceptional and/or habitual disobedience to this norm. Shall we, then, say that disobedience proves that sanction was ineffective? We could say this. But we could also in such cases make the question of the efficacy of sanction depend on the subject's reaction to repeated prescriptions of the same content by the same authority. The two tests answer to slightly different notions of an effective threat. For present purposes we need a notion of efficacy which relies upon a test of the second kind.

We can now answer the question what the agent who gives commands does, as follows: He promulgates the norm and attaches to it an effective sanction or threat of punishment for disobedience. When this has been done a normative relationship between authority and subject has been established. The normative act has been successfully performed. As a result of its successful performance a prescription exists, *i.e.* has been given and is in force.

15. It is by no means trivially the case that any man can effectively threaten any other man to visit him with evil. The mere use of threatening words does not constitute an effective threat.

Occasionally a threat can constitute a motive for obedience to an order, even though the authority could not actually have carried his threat into effect. The subject may have overestimated the authority's power to make his threat effective.

A necessary condition that a threat shall be effective is that the person who is being threatened believes that the evil with which he is threatened will befall him if he disobeys. Instead of 'believes' we could also say 'estimates that there is a considerable risk'.

The subject can, of course, be mistaken in this belief. He may later find out that he need not have feared punishment, because the authority could not have punished him, even if he had wanted to. But it is probably right to say that normally such a belief is not mistaken. It usually has some 'ground' or 'foundation', *e.g.*, in what has happened in past cases of disobedience.

When the commander can actually punish (visit with evil) the commanded in case of disobedience I shall say that the first is, in the relevant respect, *stronger* than the second. Normally, a threat of punishment will be effective only if the person who threatens can carry his threat into effect. Normally, in other words, commanding is possible only when the authority of the commands is, in the relevant respect, stronger than the subject(s) of the commands. Ability to command is thus logically founded on a superior strength of the commander over the commanded. Occasionally, genuine commanding is possible even when this presupposition is not fulfilled. This happens when the subject mistakenly believes in the superior strength of the authority.

It is, of course, quite possible that a person who is well aware of the fact that another could not harm him with punitive measures, yet *does* as that other person asks him to do. There may be plenty of motives for such conformity to the will of another person. But then he has not been effectively commanded, and his conduct is *not* rightly called 'obedience to a command'.

The superior strength on which ability to command is logically founded can be either *accidental* or *essential*.

A person may accidentally be in a position to make another person behave according to his orders. He knows, *e.g.*, of some 'secret' which, if made public, would damage that other person's reputation and social position. *Blackmail* is a species of commanding which is based upon accidental superiorities of strength in the relationships among persons.

Adults may be said to enjoy a natural superiority of strength over children. That is why adults can command children. When the children grow up and come of age there is a natural end to this superiority. When the superiority of strength vanishes, commanding ceases too. Counsel and warning take the place of command and prohibition in the relations between adults and their offspring.

Adult people are among themselves approximate equals in strength, *i.e.* they have roughly the same power to do (good and) bad to each other. This explains why adults do not under normal circumstances issue commands to each other.

Officers command soldiers, and officers of superior rank command officers of inferior rank. Does this mean that the officers are stronger than the soldiers? 'In a state of nature' the individual officer need not be stronger than the individual soldier. The chances are that they are approximate equals. But *as officer*, the officer *is* stronger. He can, normally, carry into effect the threats by which he threatens recalcitrant subordinates. That he can do this is a consequence of the fact that he can command other soldiers to punish the recalcitrants. That he can command these other men is in its turn founded on his powers to threaten them with punishment for disobedience. This fabric of commanding powers is, in the last resort, dependent upon the fact that men in the army on the whole obey orders. Occasionally the fabric collapses. Subordinates no longer fear punishment for insubordination. Orders are not obeyed. The officers 'lose command' of the army, *can* no longer command.

The superior strength of the commander over the commanded is also the factual basis on which the legal order of the state is founded. The existence of a legal order is the existence of normative relationships between the authorities and the citizens. It is essential that the authorities should be able to back their prescriptions to the citizens with effective threats of punishment in case of disobedience. When this condition is not fulfilled the legal order collapses or dissolves, as when there is a successful revolution.

VIII

DEONTIC LOGIC:
CATEGORICAL NORMS

1. IN this and the next chapter we shall present the fundamentals of a formal Logic of Norms or Deontic Logic.

The 'substructure' of this logic has three layers, *viz.* the ('classical') Logic of Propositions, the Logic of Change, which we sketched in Chapter II, and the Logic of Action, which we sketched in Chapter IV. The formal set-up and the principles of these three logics are incorporated and presupposed in our Logic of Norms.

The Logic of Propositions is a formal study of *p*-expressions, our Logic of Change a formal study of *T*-expressions, and our Logic of Action a formal study of *df*-expressions. The formalism of the Logic of Change employs, in addition to the symbols of the Logic of Propositions, one new symbol *T*. The formalism of the Logic of Action employs, in addition to the symbols of the Logic of Propositions and the Logic of Change, two new symbols, *d* and *f*. An embellishment of the formalism of the Logic of Action with one further symbol will be made in Chapter IX.

In Chapter V we introduced the notion of the *norm-kernel*. The norm-kernel consists of the three components or parts of a norm, which we call the character, the content, and the condition of application. As symbols for the two norm-characters we introduced the letters *O* and *P*. The symbols for norm-contents are *df*-expressions.

One of the several ways of dividing norms into classes, which we mentioned in Chapter V, is their division into *categorical* and *hypothetical* norms. The conditions of application of categorical norms, we said (Ch. V, Sect. 6), can be 'read off' from their contents. No new symbol is needed for stating the conditions of application of categorical norms. The conditions of application of hypothetical norms, however, cannot be 'read off' from their contents; a new symbol is needed for stating them. This new symbol is the embellishment of the formalism of the Logic of Action to which we referred above and which will be introduced in the next chapter.

The symbols of the norm-kernels of categorical norms are the atomic *O*- and *P*-expressions, which we defined in Section 4 of Chapter V. A generalized notion of (atomic) *O*- and *P*-expressions will be defined in the next chapter in connexion with the introduction of a symbolism for the conditions of application of hypothetical norms.

The Logic of Norms, which we are going to outline, is a formal study of that 'part' of norms only which we call the norm-kernels (cf. Ch. V, Sect. 1). This is a limitation of our Logic of Norms which future research into the subject ought to remove.

The norm-kernels, we said in Section 1 of Chapter V, may be regarded as the common parts of norms of all types. The Logic of Norms, which we are here sketching, is primarily conceived of as a logical theory of the norm-kernels of *prescriptions*. No explicit claim will be made on behalf of its validity for the kernels of other types of norm.

The Logic of Norms we also call Deontic Logic. The Greek verb δέομαι means in English *to bind*. Related to it is the impersonal verb δεῖν, which may be translated by *ought* or *to be necessary*. A noun form of this impersonal verb is τό δέον, which means that which ought to be or is duty or obligatory. The adverb δεόντως roughly means *duly* or *as it should be*.

2. The first problem confronting our attempt to build a logic of norms is whether the so-called truth-connectives or the symbols for negation, conjunction, disjunction, etc. can be used for forming molecular complexes of (atomic) *O*- and *P*-expressions. It is important that we should see quite clearly the nature of the problem before us. For it is, no doubt, a somewhat confusing problem.

130

The ideas of negation, conjunction, etc., are primarily at home in descriptive discourse. In it sentences are used for making statements which express propositions. To say that the sentence 'It is not raining' is the negation (-sentence) of 'It is raining', is to say some such thing as this: The sentence 'It is not raining' expresses a proposition which is true if the proposition expressed by the sentence 'It is raining' is false, and false if the proposition expressed by the sentence 'It is raining' is true.

That the truth-connectives can be used for forming molecular complexes of T-expressions and of d- and f-expressions is no more problematic than that they can be used for forming molecular complexes of p-expressions. For p- and T- and df-expressions all belong to (formalized) descriptive discourse. They are schematic forms of sentences which express propositions. As schematic forms of sentences which are used for giving prescriptions, O- and P-expressions belong to prescriptive discourse. It is not clear that truth-connectives have a meaningful use in prescriptive discourse at all.

The *words* for truth-connectives in ordinary language are 'not', 'and', 'or', and a number of others. It is easy to note that these words have a use in prescriptive discourse too. 'Shut the window *and* open the door', 'You may *not* park here', 'Stop smoking *or* leave the room'.

The mere fact, however, that the words 'not', 'and', etc., are used in prescriptive discourse does not settle the question whether truth-connectives can be used for forming molecular complexes of O- and P-expressions. Of course, we can use the *signs* $\sim$, &, v, etc., for forming complexes of O- and P-expressions. But such use would challenge the question what the complexes, thus formed, mean, and whether the meaning of $\sim$, &, etc., in prescriptive language is sufficiently like their meaning in descriptive language to warrant the use of the same symbols.

It is here relevant to point out that norms, at least of the kind we call prescriptions, are neither true nor false. If O- and P-expressions are schematic forms of sentences which are used for giving prescriptions, then molecular complexes of such expressions would not express *truth-functions* of their constituent parts. This alone would mark them as logically different from molecular complexes of p-, T-, and df-expressions.

O- and P-expressions can be regarded as the 'formalized'

131

equivalents of *deontic sentences* (*O*-expressions also as formalizations of imperative sentences). As we know (Ch. VI, Sect. 9), deontic sentences in ordinary usage exhibit a characteristic ambiguity. Sometimes they are used as norm-formulations. We shall call this their prescriptive use. Sometimes they are used for making what we called normative statements. We call this their descriptive use. When used descriptively, deontic sentences express what we called norm-propositions. If the norms are prescriptions, norm-propositions are to the effect that such and such prescriptions 'exist', *i.e.* have been given and are in force (see Ch. VII, Sect. 8).

In view of this ambiguity, the question may be raised whether *O*- and *P*-expressions should be regarded as formalized norm-formulations or as formalized sentences expressing norm-propositions.

One way of answering the question would be to decide that *O*- and *P*-expressions shall be consistently understood prescriptively as norm-formulations. Then we should have to introduce, if needed, a special symbolism for sentences which express norm-propositions.

Another way of answering the question would be to let *O*- and *P*-expressions retain the same ambiguity as deontic sentences in ordinary language. Retaining the ambiguity, needless to say, must not lead to confusion. We should then have, not *two symbolisms*, but *two interpretations* of the same symbolism. I shall call them the *prescriptive* and the *descriptive* interpretation of *O*- and *P*-expressions. Prescriptively interpreted, these expressions are (formalized) norm-formulations. Descriptively interpreted, they are (formalized) sentences which express norm-propositions.

I shall here decide in favour of the second answer. It will save us the trouble of doubling our symbolism.

That truth-connectives can be used for forming molecular complexes of *descriptively interpreted O*- and *P*-expressions is clear and uncontroversial. The molecular complexes express truth-functions of the norm-propositions expressed by the atomic *O*- and *P*-expressions which occur in the complexes.

The question open to debate is, whether truth-connectives can be used for forming molecular complexes of *prescriptively interpreted O*- and *P*-expressions.

We can settle this question in the affirmative only at the cost of introducing an ambiguity in the meanings of the truth-connectives.

We should have to distinguish between a descriptive or *truth-functional* meaning of the signs ∼, &, etc., and a prescriptive or *non-truth-functional* meaning of them.

This distinction would be thoroughly sensible. The words of ordinary language 'not', 'and', etc., sometimes have a truth-functional meaning, as, *e.g.*, in 'The window is shut *and* the door is open'. Sometimes they have a non-truth-functional meaning, as, *e.g.*, in 'Shut the window *and* open the door'. If someone prefers to speak of 'function' or 'use' instead of 'meaning' I shall not object. One must not break one's head over the question whether 'and' means the same thing or not in the two sentences which we cited. But it is important to note that the first sentence, constructed by means of the word 'and' from two other sentences, expresses a truth-function of the propositions expressed by those other sentences, whereas the second sentence, constructed by means of 'and', does not do this.

We shall here decide to use ∼, &, etc., only in the truth-functional way. This means that we settle the above question in the negative. Truth-connectives cannot (will not) be used for forming molecular complexes of prescriptively interpreted *O*- and *P*-expressions. In other words: molecular complexes of *O*- and/or *P*-expressions will always be interpreted descriptively, as schematic forms of sentences expressing norm-propositions.

The question may be raised whether this is a practical decision. Since we have decided to retain in the formalism the ambiguity of deontic sentences in ordinary usage, why not retain in the formalism also the ambiguity of using the connectives, sometimes truth-functionally, sometimes non-truth-functionally? The practicality of the decision will have to show itself in the sequel. Be it only observed in this place that, although we shall study also non-truth-functional uses of the connectives, it will not be necessary for our purposes to duplicate the symbolism for the connectives.

The decision which we have taken answers (settles) the question which we raised at the beginning of the present section. But it also raises a number of new questions.

One such question is, whether the Logic of Norms which we are building is a logical study and theory of descriptively or of prescriptively interpreted *O*- and *P*-expressions. I do not myself know what is the best answer to this question. The 'fully developed' system of Deontic Logic is a theory of descriptively interpreted expressions. But the laws (principles, rules), which are peculiar to this logic, concern logical properties of the *norms* themselves, which are then reflected in logical properties of norm-propositions. Thus, in a sense, the 'basis' of Deontic Logic is a logical theory of prescriptively interpreted *O*- and *P*-expressions.

Another question is, what relevance to the logic of norms the prescriptive use of the connectives 'not', 'and', etc., may possess. This, too, is a question which I do not know how to answer in straightforward terms. That the prescriptive use of the connectives *is* relevant will, however, be plain from the subsequent discussion.

3. We introduce the notion of a *(self-)consistent* norm. *A norm will be called (self-)consistent if, and only if, the norm-content is consistent.* Conversely, a norm will be called *inconsistent* if, and only if, its content is inconsistent.

The conditions of consistency (and inconsistency) of *df*-expressions we have investigated earlier (Ch. IV, Sects. 3 and 4). A handy way of laying down the conditions is to say that a *df*-expression is consistent if, and only if, it has a (not-vanishing) positive normal form. Atomic *O*- and *P*-expressions are thus consistent if, and only if, the *df*-expression which follows after the letter *O* or *P* is consistent.

The ontological significance of this notion of a consistent norm is not clear in itself. That a *p*-expression (formula of propositional logic) is consistent means ('ontologically') that the state of affairs which it describes *can obtain*. Or, strictly speaking: it means that the state can obtain so far as the principles of the Logic of Propositions are concerned. There may, however, be other reasons of logic why the described state is impossible. Similarly, that a *T*-expression is self-consistent means that the change which it describes *can happen* (take place)—as far as the principles of the Logic of Change are concerned. That a *df*-expression is self-consistent means that the action, which it describes, *can be performed*—as far as the principles of the Logic of Action are concerned.

Could the self-consistency of *O*- and *P*-expressions mean anything analogous to this? As norm-formulations (of prescriptions) such expressions do not *describe* anything. They *prescribe*, *i.e.* order or permit, certain actions. It is not clear by itself why a prescription should be called consistent if the prescribed action can be performed and inconsistent if it cannot be performed.

It is clear that it is logically impossible for one and the same agent to do and forbear the same thing on the same occasion. But is it logically impossible to *command* or *permit* an agent to do and forbear the same thing on the same occasion? If commanding and permitting consisted just in shouting out certain words to him, then this would not be impossible. Surely I can address somebody with the words, *e.g.*, 'Shut the window and leave it open', and even threaten him with punishment if he does not obey. But does this mean that I have commanded him? The answer depends upon what we think that commanding is—wherein the giving of commands consists. The answer, in other words, depends upon the solution to what we called the ontological problem of norms (prescriptions).

We discussed this problem in the last chapter. We now begin to see the relevance of this discussion to the problems of formal logic with which we are dealing in this chapter.

We took the view that a prescription of O-character expresses or manifests a will to *make* agents do or forbear certain things, and a prescription of P-character a will to *let* agents do or forbear certain things. We also took the view that the normative relationship, in the existence of which the existence of the prescription consists, cannot materialize unless the subject(s) of the prescription *can* do or forbear those things which the authority of the prescription wants to make or let him (them) do or forbear. If, for reasons of logic, these things cannot be done (and forborne) one cannot make or let agents do or forbear them. Therefore, neither can one command or permit or prohibit them to agents. Such prescriptions cannot 'exist'.

Our definitions of consistent and inconsistent prescriptions thus amount to saying that, accepting a certain view of the ontology of norms, consistent prescriptions are such as *can exist* and inconsistent prescriptions such as cannot exist—as far as logic is concerned.

4. It is a function of the word 'not' in descriptive language to negate, *i.e.* to express propositions of the opposite truth-value to the propositions expressed by those sentences to which the word

135

is being attached or added. This is not the *only* function of 'not' in descriptive language, but it is perhaps its most important function.

In order to find an analogue to negation in prescriptive language we have to study how the word 'not', when attached to or inserted in sentences used for enunciating prescriptions, affects or changes the meaning of the original sentence. In particular, we have to consider whether the relationship between the meaning of a norm-formulation *with* and the meaning of a 'corresponding' norm-formulation *without* the word 'not' in it is sufficiently like the relation between a proposition and its negation to justify us in speaking about a prescription (norm) and *its* negation. That 'not' is used in prescriptive language as well as in descriptive language is easy to note. But from this alone it does not follow that the function of 'not' in prescriptive language is to negate, nor is it at all clear what 'negating' *means* in prescriptive contexts.

Consider the atomic O-expression $Od(\sim pTp)$. We can think of it as enunciating a command to open a window. In ordinary language this command could be expressed in an imperative sentence 'Open the window' or in a deontic sentence 'The window ought to be opened' ('You ought to open the window').

What *could* be the meaning of the expression not-$Od(\sim pTp)$? The only meaningful insertion of a negation into the imperative sentence 'Open the window' is to form of it the sentence 'Don't open the window'. It expresses a prohibition to open the window. It thus answers to the symbolic form $Of(\sim pTp)$. Shall we say that the 'negation' of an order to do a certain thing is an order to forbear this same thing? It is soon seen on reflexion that, even if $Of(\sim pTp)$ is a possible interpretation of not-$Od(\sim pTp)$, it is not the only possible interpretation of it, and hardly the most plausible one.

The insertion of 'not' into the above deontic sentences yields 'You ought not to open the window' and 'The window ought not to be opened'. They admit, *as norm-formulations*, of two interpretations. One is to understand them as expressing a prohibition to open the window. Then they answer to the symbolic form $Of(\sim pTp)$. The other is to understand them as expressing a permission to leave the window closed. Then they answer to the symbolic form $Pf(\sim pTp)$. Here we have a second candidate for the position of 'negation' of our original expression $Od(\sim pTp)$.

There is, however, still a third possibility to be considered.

'You ought not to open the window' could be understood to mean that you have not been ordered to open the window, that no such command (prescription, norm) has been given to you. When thus understood the deontic sentence with the 'not' in it is not a norm-formulation. It is a descriptive sentence, which expresses a norm-proposition.

Consider next the atomic P-expression $Pd(\sim pTp)$. An instantiation of it could be a permission to open a window. In ordinary language the permission could be expressed in the words 'You may open the window' or 'You are allowed to open the window'.

What *could* not-$Pd(\sim pTp)$ mean? In order to find an answer, consider how we should understand the sentences 'You may not open the window' or 'You are not allowed to open the window'.

It is obvious that there are two possible interpretations. The first is to regard the sentences with 'not' in them as enunciating a prohibition to open the window. The words 'may not' then mean the same as 'must not'. The meaning of the negated formula could also be expressed by $Of(\sim pTp)$.

On the second interpretation the sentences with 'not' in them are not prescriptive, but descriptive. They say that *there is* not a permission to open the window, that no such permission has been given and is in force. Generally speaking, not-$Pd(\sim pTp)$ then expresses a norm-proposition to the effect that there does not exist a permission to transform a $\sim p$-world to a p-world.

By similar arguments, we easily see that there are three candidates for the position of 'negation' of the atomic O-sentence $Of(\sim pTp)$ and two for the position of 'negation' of the atomic P-sentence $Pf(\sim pTp)$. The three possible meanings of not-$Of(\sim pTp)$ are given by the sentences 'p ought to be done', 'p may be done', and 'There is no prohibition to the effect that p must not be done'. The two possible meanings of not-$Pf(\sim pTp)$ again are expressed by 'p ought to be done' and 'There is no permission to the effect that p may be left undone'.

As we notice, the role of negation in prescriptive language is bewildering. Sentences which originate from norm-formulations thanks to the insertion of the word 'not' in them are grammatically correct and well known from ordinary discourse. But their meaning is unclear. Or rather: the sentences exhibit characteristic ambiguities. Several 'candidates', as we have said, for the position of the negation (of the meanings) of atomic O- and P-expressions emerge. We shall have to make a choice between them. Then the question, what justifies the choice, will arise. This question is but a special case of the general question of the criteria for calling one entity the 'negation' of another.

We cannot here discuss the problem of negation in general. As already observed in Section 2, the concept of negation is primarily at home in descriptive discourse and the realm of propositions. Even here it is a controversial notion. *One* way of defining it would be to lay down the following five requirements, which the negation of a given proposition has to satisfy:

(i) The negation of a given proposition shall be a proposition.

(ii) Negation shall be unique, *i.e.* there shall be one and only one negation of a given proposition.

(iii) Negation shall be reciprocal, *i.e.* if a second proposition is the negation of a first proposition, then the first is the negation of the second.

(iv) A given proposition and its negation shall be mutually exclusive, *i.e.* it must not be the case that they are both true or both false.

(v) A given proposition and its negation shall be jointly exhaustive, *i.e.* it must be the case that one or the other of the two is true.

(Logicians of the so-called intuitionist school would dispute that a proposition and its negation need be jointly exhaustive.)

If we apply, *mutatis mutandis*, these four requirements to the notion of the negation of a norm the first would say that the negation of a norm shall be a norm. And this would at once disqualify the interpretations of not-$Od(\sim pTp)$, etc., as expressing norm-propositions as possible candidates for the position of negations of the norms expressed by $Od(\sim pTp)$, etc.

The proposition expressed by the sentence 'There is not an order to the effect that p ought to be done' can correctly be said to be the *negation* of the *proposition* expressed by the sentence 'There is an order to the effect that p ought to be done'. But we shall *not* call it the negation of the *prescription* (norm) expressed in the words 'p ought to be done'. When not-$Od(\sim pTp)$ is interpreted descriptively, as expressing a norm-proposition, the part $Od(\sim pTp)$ in it must be interpreted descriptively too.

As indicated in Section 2, for the *descriptive* interpretation of

138

not-$Od(\sim pTp)$, and for it only, we shall use the symbol $\sim Od(\sim pTp)$.

For the *prescriptive* interpretation of not-$Od(\sim pTp)$ we need no new symbols. The reason why we need no special symbol for 'not' in prescriptive language may be gathered from our discussion above of the possible prescriptive meanings of not-$Od(\sim pTp)$, etc. When not-$Od(\sim pTp)$, etc., were not interpreted as sentences expressing norm-propositions they were interpreted as identical in meaning with certain *atomic* O- and P-expressions.

We now return to the question of selecting 'candidates' for the position of a 'negation' of a *norm* (prescription).

Of the two candidates for the negation of the norm expressed by $Od(\sim pTp)$ we dismiss $Of(\sim pTp)$, and of the two candidates for the negation of $Of(\sim pTp)$ we dismiss $Od(\sim pTp)$. After these rejections the remaining candidate for the negation of the norm expressed by $Od(\sim pTp)$ is $Pf(\sim pTp)$, for the negation of $Pd(\sim pTp)$ it is $Of(\sim pTp)$, for the negation of the norm expressed by $Of(\sim pTp)$ it is $Pd(\sim pTp)$, and for the negation of the norm expressed by $Pf(\sim pTp)$ it is $Od(\sim pTp)$.

The reason for the rejections is that we want negation to satisfy the requirements of uniqueness and reciprocity ((ii) and (iii) above). The requirement that the negation of a norm shall be a norm, we satisfy through a decision to stick to the prescriptive interpretation of the atomic O- and P-expressions throughout.

Now consider the two pairs:

$$Od(\sim pTp) \text{ and } Pf(\sim pTp)$$
$$\text{and } Of(\sim pTp) \text{ and } Pd(\sim pTp).$$

Our suggestion is that the norms which the members of each pair of norm-formulations express are related to one another as a norm and its 'negation'. On our suggestion the negation of a positive command is thus a negative permission and conversely, and the negation of a negative command is a positive permission and conversely. In still other words: a command to do and a permission to forbear are related to one another as negations, and so are a command to forbear and a permission to do.

This notion of a norm and its negation-norm can be generalized. We previously introduced the notions of external and internal negations of *df*-expressions, *i.e.* of possible norm-contents (see Ch. IV, Sect. 6). It is readily seen that the contents of the members of each pair of norms above are related to one another as *internal* negations. Their characters are 'opposite', *i.e.* one has the O-character and the other the P-character. Our generalized definition of the notion of a negation-norm now runs as follows:

A norm is the negation-norm of another norm if, and only if, the two norms have opposite character and their contents are the internal negations of each other.

Consider, for example, the norm expressed by $O(d(\sim pTp)$ v $f(\sim pT \sim p))$. It says that one ought to produce the state of affairs described by p or let it happen, depending upon the nature of the occasion. Its negation-norm is expressed by $P(f(\sim pTp)$ v $d(\sim pT \sim p))$. It says that one may leave the state of affairs described by p unproduced or suppress it.

Similarly, the negation of the norm expressed by $O(d(\sim pTp)$ & $d(\sim qTq))$ is the norm expressed by $P(d(\sim pTp)$ & $f(\sim qTq)$ v $f(\sim pTp)$ & $d(\sim qTq)$ v $f(\sim pTp)$ & $f(\sim qTq))$. The first orders the production of two states of affairs. The second permits the leaving of at least one of the two states unproduced.

Does the concept of a negation-norm satisfy, *mutatis mutandis*, the requirements (iv) and (v) above? Are a given norm and its negation-norm mutually exclusive and jointly exhaustive?

Before we can answer these questions it ought to be made clear what, *mutatis mutandis*, should be understood by mutual exclusiveness and joint exhaustiveness in prescriptive discourse. It is near at hand to define the notions in a manner which is analogous to our definition in Section 3 of consistency. A proposition is consistent if it can be true, a norm, we said, if it can exist. Similarly, we could say that two norms are mutually exclusive if they cannot both exist, *i.e.* co-exist, and jointly exhaustive if at least one of the two must (will necessarily) exist.

In order to answer the question whether a norm and its negation-norm are, in the sense defined, mutually exclusive, we ought to give criteria for the possible co-existence of norms. This we shall do in the next section. It will then be seen that the answer to our question is affirmative—though with an important qualification (cf. below Section 7).

The question whether a norm and its negation-norm are, in the sense defined, jointly exhaustive, leads to the problem of necessary existence of norms. It, too, will be discussed later (Section 8). We shall find that the answer to the question concerning joint exhaustiveness is negative. By virtue of this, the notion of negation in prescriptive discourse has a certain resemblance to the intuitionist notion of negation.[1]

5. Possibility of co-existence of norms, we could say, is the ontological aspect or significance of the formal notion of *compatibility* of norms. Before we turn to the ontological aspect we shall have to define and comment on the formal notion.

The compatibility of two or more norms we shall also call the mutual consistency of two or more norms. A set of compatible norms will be called a *consistent set* of norms.

It will be assumed throughout that the norms whose compatibility we are defining and discussing are (*self-*)*consistent* norms. How the problem of compatibility is to be treated for norms which do not satisfy the condition of (self-)consistency, I shall not discuss in detail. The problem seems of minor importance. A *set* of norms, at least one member of which is not (self-)consistent, may on that account be called an inconsistent set.

The problem before us can now be put as follows: Which conditions should a set of (self-)consistent norms satisfy in order that the set be consistent, the norms compatible?

We shall conduct the discussion in three steps. First, we define consistency for a given set of norms, all of which are norms of the O-character. Then we assume that a given set of norms contains only norms of the P-character. Finally, we define consistency for a given set of norms, some of which are of the O- and others of the P-character.

We can speak of the three kinds of sets of norms as an O-set, a P-set, and an $O + P$-set (or 'mixed set') respectively.

To the sets of norms there answer sets of norm-formulations, *i.e.* (atomic) O- and/or P-expressions. It is convenient to conduct the investigation, speaking in the first place of the expressions and their formal properties—not forgetting that the relevance of our talk is ultimately for the norms themselves. When talking of the O- and P-expressions it will throughout be assumed that the *df*-expressions in them are in the positive normal form. It will be assumed, moreover, that the normal forms are made *uniform*

[1] Cf. my paper "On the Logic of Negation" in *Soc. Sci. Fenn. Comm. Phys.-Math.* XXII 4 (1959).

(Ch. IV, Sect. 8) with regard to all atomic p-expressions (variables p, q, etc.), which occur in the entire set of O- and/or P-expressions.

(i) We consider a set of O-norms and a corresponding set of O-expressions.

We make a list of all the atomic p-expressions which occur in the O-expressions. Let the number of atomic p-expressions be n. Thereupon we list the 2^n state-descriptions which answer to these n atomic p-expressions. Next we list the $2^n \times 2^n$ change-descriptions which answer to these 2^n state-descriptions. These change-descriptions constitute a complete list of the conditions of application of the O-expressions, *i.e.* norms in the set.

For each one of the conditions of application we make a list of those parts, if any, of the (uniformed) normal forms of the df-expressions in the respective O-expressions which answer to those conditions. These lists tell us what the individual norms require to be done under the respective conditions. Thereupon we form the *conjunction* of the members of each of these lists. These conjunctions tell us what the totality of norms requires to be done under the respective conditions. It is not certain that there are as many conjunctions as there are conditions of applications in the complete list. For it can happen that under some of the conditions none of the norms applies.

The conjunctions are df-expressions. We examine whether they are consistent. This can be done according to several methods. We can, for example, transform the conjunctions into their positive normal forms. If this is not-vanishing the conjunctions are consistent. The result of these transformations, however, can be immediately read off from the conjugated expressions themselves. These are parts of the uniformed positive normal forms of the df-expressions in the O-expressions of our set. They are thus disjunctions of conjunctions of elementary d- and f-expressions. The conjugated disjunctions are consistent if, and only if, they have at least one common disjunct, *i.e.* conjunction of elementary d- and f-expressions. Otherwise they are inconsistent.

Assume that *none* of the conjunctions is inconsistent. Then, and then only, the O-set of norms is consistent, its members compatible.

Assume that *some* (at least one) of the conjunctions are inconsistent. Then the O-set of norms is inconsistent, its members incompatible.

Assume, finally, that *all* conjunctions are inconsistent. Then we have a special form of inconsistency and incompatibility, which we shall call 'absolute'.

When the conjunction which answers to a given condition of application of the norms is consistent we shall also say that the set of norms is consistent, and its members compatible, *under those conditions*. When a given conjunction is inconsistent we say that the set of norms is inconsistent and its members incompatible, *under those conditions*.

Thus, on our definitions, a consistent set of O-norms is consistent under *all* conditions of application of the norms—but an inconsistent set may be consistent under *some* conditions of application.

Our definition of a consistent set of O-norms amounts to this: a set of commands is consistent (the commands compatible) if, and only if, it is logically possible, under any given condition of application, to obey *all* commands (collectively) which apply on that condition.

(ii) We next consider a set of self-consistent P-norms.

Such a set is *ipso facto* consistent. Permissions never contradict each other. This is one of the basic logical differences between commands and permissions. To take the simplest possible illustration: a command to do a certain thing is incompatible with a command to forbear this same thing on a given occasion (see Section 6). But a permission to do a certain thing is not incompatible with a permission to forbear this same thing on a given occasion. The 'ontological' significance of this difference between commands and permissions we shall discuss later.

(iii) We finally consider a mixed set of self-consistent O- and P-norms, commands and permissions, and the corresponding set of expressions.

To find and formulate the conditions of consistency of the set we first divide it into two parts or sub-sets. One consists of all the O-norms in the set, the other of all the P-norms. We call the two sub-sets the O-part and the P-part of the mixed set. The P-part is *ipso facto* consistent. It is a condition of the consistency of the whole set that the O-part should be consistent. But this is not the sole condition of consistency.

We make a list of all the atomic p-expressions which occur in the O- and P-expressions of our mixed set. We then construct the corresponding lists of state- and change-descriptions. The list of change-descriptions includes all conditions of application of the norms in our mixed set.

Consider now the sub-set which consists of the O-part of the whole set and one of the members of the P-part.

For each of the conditions of application we list the parts, if any, of the normal forms of the *df*-expressions which occur in the O-expressions and the one P-expression of our sub-set (of expressions). We form the conjunctions of the members of each list and test the conjunctions for consistency.

If *all* conjunctions are consistent we say that the sub-set of norms is consistent and the members of the sub-set compatible. We then also say that the one P-norm is *compatible with* the (set of) O-norms.

If *some* (at least one) conjunction is inconsistent the sub-set of norms is inconsistent, and, in particular, the one permissive norm incompatible with the (set of) commands.

If *none* of the conjunctions is consistent the sub-set is absolutely inconsistent. If none of the conjunctions which answer to the several conditions of application of the P-norm is consistent, then the permissive norm is absolutely incompatible with the commands.

We repeat this procedure for *all* the members individually, *i.e.* one by one, of the P-part of our mixed set of norms. The definition of consistency of the mixed set is as follows:

A mixed set of norms is consistent, its members compatible if, and only if, each one of the members of its P-part is, individually, compatible with its O-part.

If some member of the P-part of the set is incompatible with the O-part, then the mixed set is inconsistent.

Our definition of consistency and compatibility also amounts to this: a set of commands and permissions is consistent (the norms compatible) if, and only if, it is logically possible, under any given condition of application, to obey *all* the commands collectively and avail oneself of *each one* of the permissions individually which apply on that condition.

6. We shall next mention and comment on some consequences of our definitions of compatibility and incompatibility of norms.

A first consequence is that a norm and its negation-norm (Section 4) are, on our definition, incompatible. This is seen as follows:

A norm and its negation have opposite characters. It can thus not happen that both are permissions. (Permissive norms never contradict one another.) Their contents are internal negations of one another. This entails that the two norms have the same conditions of application. The conjunction of those parts of the normal forms of the expressions for the contents of the two norms which answer to given conditions of application is inconsistent. (This follows from the definition of internal negation.) Hence the two norms are incompatible. Since, moreover, they are incompatible under *all* their conditions of application, they are *absolutely* incompatible.

It follows at once from this that two norms of O-character, whose contents are the internal negations of one another, are (absolutely) incompatible. For example: the commands expressed by $Od(\sim pTp)$ and $Of(\sim pTp)$ are absolutely incompatible.

The above results concerning the incompatibility of norms hold also for the general case when the contents are internally incompatible, and not only for the special case when the contents are the internal negations of one another. Thus two norms of opposite character, whose contents are internally incompatible, are (absolutely) incompatible. And two norms of O-character, whose contents are internally incompatible, are (absolutely) incompatible.

For example: The commands expressed by $O(d(pTp)$ & $d(qTq))$ and $O(d(pTp)$ & $f(qTq))$ are incompatible, and so are the command expressed by $O(d(pTp)$ & $d(qTq))$ and the permission expressed by $P(d(pTp)$ & $f(qTq))$.

The results can easily be generalized to *sets* of norms. A set of commands is inconsistent if the contents of two of its members are internally incompatible. A permission is incompatible with a set of commands if the content of the permission is internally incompatible with the content of one of the commands. (These incompatibilities of norms are not necessarily absolute.)

It is important to observe that mere incompatibility of the contents of two commands or of a command and a permission does not, on our definition, entail an incompatibility of the norms. The incompatibility of the contents must be *internal*.

The case when there is external but not internal incompatibility between the norm-contents has sometimes interesting logical peculiarities. We shall here consider one such peculiarity. It will first be illustrated by means of an example.

Consider the two commands $Od(\sim pTp)$ and $Od(pT\sim p)$. We could think of the first as an order to open a window and of the second as an order to close this same window. Do the commands contradict each other? Are they incompatible? Perhaps in some special sense of 'contradict' and 'incompatible', but certainly not in the sense which we have here given to the terms. The reason why, on our definition, the norms are not incompatible, although their contents contradict each other, is that they have no common condition of application. The second command applies to a world in which the state of affairs described by p obtains and does not independently of action vanish; the first to a world in which this state does not obtain and does not independently of action come into existence.

Compare the above commands with $Od(\sim pTp)$ and $Of(\sim pTp)$, for example with an order to open a window and an order to leave this same window closed. They contradict each other, on our definition, because, whatever an agent does on an occasion when both commands apply, he will necessarily disobey one of them. On an occasion when a certain window is closed and does not open of itself an agent who masters the art of window-opening will necessarily either open this window or leave it closed. But he will *not* necessarily either open this window or close it. Therefore he will necessarily disobey one of the pair of orders $Od(\sim pTp)$ and $Of(\sim pTp)$, but not necessarily disobey one of the pair of orders $Od(\sim pTp)$ and $Od(pT\sim p)$. The last order he can neither obey nor disobey on the occasion in question.

Let it be assumed that the two orders $Od(\sim pTp)$ and $Od(pT\sim p)$ are given for one single occasion only. Then they mean, in terms of our window-illustration, that the agent to whom the orders are given should close the window if it is open, and open it if it is closed (on that occasion). In practice, an authority would give *both* orders only if he does not himself know what the state of the world is or will be on the occasion in question. There is nothing uncommon or odd about such cases.

Let it be assumed that the two orders are general with regard to the occasion (see Ch. V, Sect. 11). Then they mean, in terms of our illustration, that the agent to whom the orders are given should close the window whenever he finds it open, and open it whenever he finds it closed. Now assume that the first order applies to the situation at hand, and that the agent obeys and closes the window. Thereby he creates a situation to which the second order becomes applicable. He ought now to open the window. If he obeys, he creates a situation to which the first order applies. And so forth *ad infinitum*. The case is noteworthy—also from a logical point of view.

I shall say that the two general orders jointly constitute a pair of *Sisyphos-orders*. Generally speaking: a set of orders which are general with regard to the occasion will be said to constitute a set of Sisyphos-orders if, and only if, obedience to all the orders which apply under given conditions of application necessarily creates new conditions of application (of some or all of the orders).

One could introduce a notion of *deontic equilibrium*. The world, we shall say, can be brought to deontic equilibrium with a (consistent) set of orders if it is possible to obey all the orders which apply to any given state of the world without creating *ad infinitum* a new state of the world to which some of the orders apply. The two orders to open a certain window whenever possible, and to close it whenever possible form a consistent set —but the world cannot be brought to deontic equilibrium with it.

To issue Sisyphos-orders such as 'Open the window whenever it is closed, and close it whenever it is open' may be cruel. But it is not nonsensical in the same sense in which to issue inconsistent orders such as 'Open the window, but leave it closed' is nonsensical.

7. In order to see the ontological significance of the conditions of consistency (and compatibility), we shall consider in some detail the case of two commands, the content of one of which is the internal negation of the content of the other. *Why* is it, let us ask, that a command to open a window and a prohibition to do this, *i.e.* a command to leave it closed, contradict each other, are incompatible?

It is here pertinent to note that the two commands (the command and the prohibition) can be reasonably said to contradict each other only if they refer to the same window, are addressed to the same agent, and are for the same occasion. If, on an occasion when a certain window is closed, I ask a person to open it, and on another occasion, when this same window is again closed, I ask the same or another person to leave the same window closed, there is no contradiction between my orders. But if I command a person to open a window and command the same person to leave the same window closed on the same occasion, then, it would seem, I can rightly be accused of contradicting myself logically. The two commands annihilate one another, they cannot exist together 'in logical space', as one might put it.

But on the other hand: if x orders z to open a window and y prohibits z to open the same window on the same occasion, is there then contradiction? It is true that it is logically impossible for z to obey both orders. But is it logically impossible for the two orders to coexist? Is there not room for them both in logical space? It seems off-hand reasonable to think that they *can* coexist. On the view which I have here taken of the nature of commands and prescriptions generally, this seems plausible too. On this view, the coexistence of the two commands which we just mentioned (normally) means that x wants z to open the window and y wants z to leave it closed on the same occasion. This is no logical contradiction; but it can truly be called a 'conflict'. It is an instance of what I shall call a *conflict of wills*.

Now then: Why is it logically possible for x to command z to open the window and for y to command z to leave it closed, but not logically possible for x to command z to open the window and at the same time to prohibit him to do this? Or is this last, after all, possible too? Can commands, or norms in general, ever contradict one another?

I wish I could make my readers see the serious nature of this problem. (It is much more serious than any of the technicalities of deontic logic.) It is serious because, if no two norms can logically contradict one another, then there can be no logic of norms either. There is no logic, we might say, in a field in which everything is possible. So therefore, if norms are to have a logic, we must be able to point to something which is impossible in the realm of norms. But that we can do this is by no means obvious.

It is important to realize that it will *not* do to answer the question why it should be called logically impossible to command and prohibit the same thing by saying that this is impossible because it is logically impossible for one and the same man both to do and forbear one and the same thing at the same time. For if I order a man to do something and you prohibit him to do the

148

same it is also logically impossible that the man should obey both of us, but nevertheless perfectly possible that there should be this command and this prohibition.

Commands, as we have said earlier, manifest efforts to make people do or forbear things. It is clear that one cannot, on the same occasion, *make* the same man do and forbear the same thing, since it is logically impossible for a man to do and forbear the same thing at the same time. It is also clear that I can *try* to make him do the thing and you *try*, on the same occasion, to make him forbear the thing—although it is logically impossible that we should both succeed. So *why* could it not be that *one* man, on the same occasion, should *try* to make another agent both do and forbear the same thing? Well, how does a norm-authority try to make people do or forbear things? By threats of punishment before the act and by punitive measures when disobedience has taken place, and in other ways (cf. Ch. VII, Sect. 14). If someone were to punish a child in one way, if it does a certain thing, and also to punish it, though perhaps in a somewhat different way, if the child abstains from doing this same thing—can he then be said both to *try* to make the child do this thing and to *try* to make him abstain from doing it? In the absence of criteria, we can say nothing at all. The concept of trying has still to be moulded to fit this case. But we should certainly feel inclined to say that such behaviour as that which we just described looks queer and purposeless. And if the agent described to us his own action by saying that he tries to make the punished child do and also tries to make it forbear the same act we should say that we do not understand him or that he behaves irrationally or perhaps even that he is mad.

We can illustrate the problem in pictures. A man *a* is walking along with another man *s*. *a* has a cane or whip in one hand and holds a rope with the other hand. The rope is tied round the waist of *s*. (It may be more attractive to the imagination to think of *s* as a dog rather than as a man.) They pass by various objects. Sometimes when they come to an object *a* drives *s* towards the object with the whip. Sometimes he pulls him back with the rope. Sometimes he lets *s* go towards the object, if *s* wants to. Sometimes he lets *s* turn away from the object. These four cases answer to the four basic norm-situations of positive and negative command and positive and negative permission respectively.

149

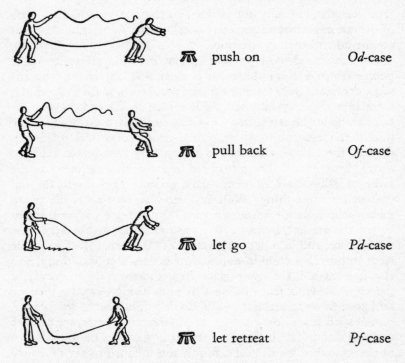

Now comes another man *b*. He also has a whip in one hand and a rope in the other. He ties the rope round *s*'s waist. *a* and *b* both walk along with *s*. Sometimes when *a* threatens *s* with the cane and urges him towards an object, *b* pulls him back. Then *a* and *b* try to make *s* do opposite things. *s* cannot please both his masters; it is logically impossible for him to do so. But this does not make it impossible for *a* to go on hitting *s* with the whip or for *b* to pull in the rope. There is nothing illogical or even irrational in this.

Remove *b* from the picture. *a* is alone with *s*. When they pass by a certain object, *a* drives *s* on to it with the whip and holds him back with the rope. *Can s* do this? I just described it in intelligible terms. We, as it were, see it happen in the imagination. The question is very much like this: Can a man both push and pull in opposite directions one and the same object at the same time? He can pull it with one hand and push it with the other, and the object will move in the direction of whichever hand is the stronger. He could do this to test which hand of his is the stronger. But if he said that he does this because he wants to make the object move in the one direction and also wants to make it move in the other direction, we should think that he was joking with us or was mad. A psychologist would perhaps speak of him as a 'split personality'. He acts as two men would act, who contested about the object.

The upshot of this argument is as follows:

That norms can contradict each other logically is not anything which logic, 'by itself', can show. It can be shown, if at all, only from considerations pertaining to the nature of norms; and it is far from obvious whether it can be shown even then. The only possibility which I can see of showing that norms which are prescriptions can contradict one another is to relate the notion of a prescription to some idea about the unity and coherence of a will.

Of the will which does not make incompatibilities its objects, it is natural to use such attributes as a *rational* or *reasonable* or *coherent* or *consistent* will.

The ontological significance of the formal notion of compatibility of norms is possibility of coexistence, we said at the beginning of Section 5. We now realize that, at least so far as prescriptions are concerned, the identification of compatibility with possibility of co-existence is subject to an important qualification. *The prescriptions must have the same authority.* (This was the qualification to which we alluded at the end of Section 4.)

I shall here introduce the notion of a *corpus* of norms. By this I understand a set of prescriptions which all have the same authority.

Thus, for prescriptions, the ontological significance of compatibility is the possibility of coexistence within a corpus. The consistency of a set of prescriptions means the possibility that the set constitutes a corpus. Incompatibility of prescriptions means the impossibility of their coexistence within a corpus. The inconsistency of a set of prescriptions, finally, means the impossibility, *i.e.* necessary non-existence, of a certain corpus.

Contradiction between prescriptions can be said to reflect an inconsistency (irrationality) in the will of a norm-authority. One and the same will cannot 'rationally' aim at incompatible objects. But one will may perfectly well 'rationally' want an object which

151

is incompatible with the object of another 'rational' will. Because of the first impossibility, prescriptions which do not satisfy our formal criteria of compatibility cannot coexist with a corpus of norms. Because of the second possibility, prescriptions which do not satisfy these criteria can yet exist within different corpora, and *in this sense* coexist.

In terms of the will-theory of norms, the inconsistency of a set of commands means that one and the same norm-authority wants one or several norm-subjects to do or forbear several things which, at least in some circumstances, it is logically impossible conjunctively to do or forbear.

In terms of the will-theory, the inconsistency of a set of commands and permissions means this: one and the same norm-authority wants one or several norm-subjects to do or forbear several things and also lets them do or forbear several things. Something which the authority *lets* the subject(s) do or forbear is, however, at least in some circumstances, logically impossible to do or forbear together with *everything* which he *wants* them to do or forbear. This, too, we count as irrational willing.

That permissions never contradict each other means that it is not irrational to *let* people do or forbear several things which it is not logically possible to do or forbear conjunctively on one and the same occasion. To let them do this is to let them freely choose their mode of action.

8. Self-inconsistent norms, we have said, cannot exist. They thus have what might also be called necessary non-existence. The question may be raised: are there norms which must exist or which have necessary existence?

The question can conveniently be divided into three:

(*a*) Are there norms which necessarily exist *simpliciter*?
(*b*) Are there norms which necessarily exist, *if* certain other norms (as a matter of fact) exist?
(*c*) Are there norms which necessarily exist, *if* certain other norms (as a matter of fact) do *not* exist?

The second of the three questions is the most important. It is virtually the same as the question of *entailment* between norms. We shall discuss it in the next section.

The first question may present interesting aspects, *e.g.*, in connexion with a theonomous view of morality. If God is a being endowed with necessary existence and if he has given a moral law to man, must we then not also think that the moral commands exist 'of necessity'? This *kind* of question we do not discuss in the present work at all. I have no idea how to answer or even how to tackle the question. But I do not think it can be dismissed as pure nonsense.

The only comment on question (*a*) which I shall make here concerns the notion of what I propose to call a *tautologous* norm. A norm of *O*- or of *P*-character will be called tautologous if, and only if, its content satisfies the following requirement: the positive normal form of the *df*-expression for the content contains as disjuncts *all* the act-descriptions which answer to some or several of the conditions of applications of the norm.

An example of a tautologous norm is the command expressed by $O(d(\sim pTp) \vee f(\sim pTp))$. The symbolic expression for its content is in normal form. The normal form enumerates all the modes of action which are possible under the conditions expressed by $\sim pT \sim p$. Another example is the command expressed by $O(d(\sim pTp) \vee d(\sim pT \sim p) \vee f(\sim pTp) \vee f(\sim pT \sim p))$. The normal form of its content enumerates all modes of action which are logically possible under the conditions expressed by $\sim pTp$ and by $\sim pT \sim p$. A third example of a tautologous norm is the permission expressed by $P(d(pTp)$ & $d(qTq) \vee d(pTp)$ & $f(qTq) \vee f(pTp)$ & $d(qTq) \vee f(pTp)$ & $f(qTq))$. The modes of action which its content covers are all the modes which are possible under the conditions expressed by $(pT \sim p)$ & $(qT \sim q)$.

What does the command expressed by $O(d(\sim pTp) \vee f(\sim pTp))$ require of the subject to whom it is addressed? Let p stand for 'The window is open'. The demand then is to open or leave closed a window which is closed (and does not open 'of itself'). Whatever the agent does in the situation in question, he necessarily either opens the window or leaves it closed. (Assuming that this is an act which he *can do*.) The command, therefore, does not, properly speaking, 'demand' anything at all. This is why we call it tautological.

What does the above tautologous permission permit? It applies to a situation when both of two given states of affairs obtain, but vanish unless prevented from vanishing. The permission is to prevent both from vanishing, or to prevent the one but not the other, or to let both vanish. Since this is what the agent will do anyway, the permission, properly speaking, does not 'permit' anything at all.

Tautologous prescriptions are thus commands which do not demand anything, or permissions which do not permit anything in particular. It is easily seen that the negation-norms of tautologous prescriptions are self-inconsistent prescriptions. Since these latter necessarily do *not* exist, shall we say that the former do necessarily exist?

We could say this, and no harm would follow. But we need not say this. The logically most appropriate reaction to the case seems to me to be to deny tautologous prescriptions the status of ('real') prescriptions. We exclude them from the range of the concept. The justification for this may be sought in our ontology of prescriptions. There *is* no such thing as *making* or ('actively') *letting* people do things which they will necessarily do in any case. Therefore it makes no sense to say that people are commanded or permitted to do such things either.

The only comment on question (*c*) which we shall make here concerns the relation of a norm to its negation-norm.

We have so far left open the question whether a norm and its negation-norm form an exhaustive alternative (cf. the discussion in Section 4). If they do, then we could conclude from the factual non-existence of a norm to the existence of its negation-norm. The existence and non-existence of either norm may be, in itself, contingent. What would be necessary is that either the one or the other exists.

Let the norm be, *e.g.*, the command expressed by $O(d(pTp)$ & $d(qTq)$ v $f(pTp)$ & $f(qTq))$. Its negation-norm is then the permission expressed by $P(d(pTp)$ & $f(qTq)$ v $f(pTp)$ & $d(qTq))$. Must it necessarily be the case that an agent is either *commanded* to continue both of two states or to let them both vanish or *permitted* to continue one of them and to let the other vanish?

It is easily recognized that the problem whether a norm and its negation-norm form an exhaustive disjunction is a generalization of the problem which we discussed in Ch. V, Sects. 13–16, of the mutual relations of the norm-characters of command and permission.

If we accept the view that a norm and its negation-norm form an exhaustive disjunction, then we are forced to accept the inter-definability of the two norm-characters also. Permission would then be mere absence of a command (prohibition) 'to the contrary', but also command would be absence of permission 'to the contrary.' The exact meaning of the phrase 'to the contrary' is explained in terms of the relation between a norm and its negation-norm.

Since we have decided *not* to accept the view of permission as absence of prohibition (cf. Ch. V, Sect. 16), we are therefore also forced to reject the idea that a norm and its negation-norm form an exhaustive disjunction. A norm and its negation-norm cannot both exist, *i.e.* coexist within a corpus. But they *can* both be absent from a corpus.

9. We shall now define the notion of *entailment* between norms.

Consider a consistent set of self-consistent norms *and* a self-consistent norm. We want to determine the conditions under which this single norm shall be said to be entailed by the set of norms.

We consider the negation-norm of the single norm. We add it to the set. We test the enlarged set of norms for consistency under each one of the conditions when the negation-norm applies. There are three possibilities as regards the results of the test. Either they are all positive, or some are negative, or they are all negative. In the third case we say that the negation-norm is *absolutely incompatible* with the original set of norms (cf. above Section 5). This is the possibility which is of relevance to entailment. For we define:

A consistent set of self-consistent norms entails a given self-consistent norm if, and only if, the negation-norm of the given norm is absolutely incompatible with the set.

Consider the command expressed by $Od(\sim pTp)$. We want to know whether an order to produce the state of affairs described by p is entailed by a set of prescriptions which have already been given. We consider the negation-norm expressed by $Pf(\sim pTp)$. We test whether a permission to leave this state unproduced is absolutely incompatible with the prescriptions of the set. That there is absolute incompatibility means that under no circumstances (conditions of application) could one avail oneself of a permission to leave the state in question unproduced without disobeying some of the commands (prohibitions) in the set of

155

prescriptions. In other words: Only by producing the state in question can one obey the commands (prohibitions) which have already been given. In this sense, the original set of prescriptions will be said to entail a command to produce this state.

Consider the prohibition expressed by $Of(\sim pTp)$. Is a prohibition to produce the state of affairs described by p entailed by a set of given prescriptions? Test the permission expressed by $Pd(\sim pTp)$ for compatibility with the set. Assume that it is absolutely incompatible with the set. This means that under no circumstances could one (avail oneself of a permission to) produce the state in question without disobeying some of the commands (prohibitions) in the set of prescriptions. Only by observing the prohibition to produce this state can one, under all circumstances, obey the commands (prohibitions) which have already been given. In this sense, the original set of prescriptions entails the new prohibition.

Consider the permission expressed by $Pd(\sim pTp)$. Is a permission to produce the state of affairs described by p entailed by a set of prescriptions? We test the prohibition expressed by $Of(\sim pTp)$ for compatibility with the set. Assume that there is absolute incompatibility. This means that in no circumstances could one observe the prohibition to produce the state described by p without either disobeying some command or not being able to avail oneself of some permission among those which have already been given. Only by actually producing the state described by p can one, under all circumstances, obey all the commands, and avail oneself of any one of the permissions which have already been given. In this sense, the original set of prescriptions entails a permission to produce this state.

To the case of the negative permission expressed by $Pf(\sim pTp)$ applies, *mutatis mutandis*, what was said of the positive permission expressed by $Pd(\sim pTp)$.

When a set of norms entails a further norm we shall also say that the norms of the set jointly ('conjunctively') entail this further norm.

10. Prescriptions which are entailed by a given set of norms I shall call *derived* commands, prohibitions, and permissions.

One could speak of derived prescriptions as the *commitments* of a norm-authority or lawgiver. If it turns out that a lawgiver *cannot* under any conditions, consistently with the prescriptions which he has already given, order a certain act to be done, then he *has*, in fact, permitted its forbearance. If he *cannot* consistently prohibit an act, then he *has*, in fact, permitted it. If he *cannot* permit it he *has* forbidden it. If he *cannot* permit its forbearance he *has* commanded its doing.

The ontological significance of the word 'cannot' should be plain from our discussion (in Section 7) of compatibility. That an authority 'cannot' give a certain prescription consistently with other prescriptions which he has already given means that an attempt to give this prescription would signalize an inconsistency in his will. He would then want or allow things to be done which for reasons of logic cannot be done.

When we call the derived prescriptions 'commitments' this should be understood in a *factual*, and not in a *normative*, sense. We did not say that if a lawgiver cannot consistently prohibit an act, then he *ought to* permit it, etc. But we said that if he cannot forbid it, he *has* permitted it, etc.

That an authority has prohibited something entails that he can and is prepared to see to it that this thing is not done. He threatens prospective trespassers with punishment, and takes steps to punish those who in fact disobey. In what sense, if any, can the authority be said to do this also with regard to the entailed prohibitions? Is it not logically possible that the authority shows great anxiety to make his will effective as far as his manifest prohibitions and orders are concerned, but is completely indifferent towards the conduct of the norm-subjects as far as the derived prescriptions are concerned?

The answer to the last question is that such an attitude on the part of the norm-authority is *not* logically possible. For let us recall what, on our definition, it means to say that a certain prohibition is entailed by a given set of prescriptions. It means that it is not logically possible in any circumstances to do the prohibited thing without disobeying some orders or breaking some prohibitions which have already been given (are in the set). If therefore the authority manifests anxiety to make the norm-subjects obey these latter commands and prohibitions, *e.g.*, by punishing the disobedient, he *ipso facto* also manifests anxiety to make the subjects observe the entailed prohibition.

The derived commands, prohibitions, and permissions of a

corpus of prescriptions, we could say, are as much 'willed' by the norm-authority as the original commands, prohibitions, and permissions in this corpus. The derived norms *are*, necessarily, in the corpus with the original ones. They are there, although they have not been expressly promulgated. Their promulgation is concealed in the promulgation of other prescriptions.

11. We shall now use the proposed definition of entailment for the purpose of proving some important entailment-relations between norms.

First, we show that a O-norm of a given content entails a P-norm of the same content. For short: Ought entails May, or Obligation entails Permission.

We conduct the proof in terms of an example. Its general significance should be immediately clear.

Consider the command expressed by $Od(pTp)$ and the 'corresponding' permission expressed by $Pd(pTp)$. The negation of the permissive norm is the command (prohibition) expressed by $Of(pTp)$. We have to show that the first and the third norms are absolutely incompatible. This we have already done in Section 6. Thus, the first norm entails the second.

Consider why it is not the case that May entails Ought, *e.g.*, that the permission expressed by $Pd(pTp)$ entails the command expressed by $Od(pTp)$. The negation of the command is the permission $Pf(pTp)$. It is true that one cannot, on one and the same occasion, avail oneself both of a permission to do and of a permission to forbear one and the same thing. But this impossibility does not, on our definition, mean that the permissions were incompatible. Hence the proposed entailment does not follow either.

12. Consider an order to do one (or both) of two things, each one of which *can* be done under the same conditions of application. An order to a person to stop smoking or to leave the room would be an example. I shall call this a *disjunctive order* (disjunctive obligation). A disjunctive order does not mean that the subject *ought to* do one thing or *ought to* do another thing. It means that the subject ought to *do* one thing or *do* another thing. The subject is, normally, free to choose between the two modes of conduct.

Compare this with an order to do one of two things which

cannot be done under the same conditions of application. An order to a person to open a door or keep it open would be an example. This should be called neither a 'disjunctive order' nor a 'disjunction of orders'. The order amounts, in fact, to *two* orders. The one is an order to do a certain thing should certain conditions be satisfied, *e.g.*, a certain door be closed. The other is an order to do a certain other thing should certain other conditions be satisfied, *e.g.*, a certain door be open but would close unless prevented. The two conditions are incompatible. The two orders can therefore never be both executed on the same occasion. The obedient subject will execute one *or* the other, if there is an opportunity of executing either. The subject is here never free to choose between two modes of conduct. Instead of the disjunctive form of the order 'Open the door *or* keep it open', one could use the conjunctive form 'Open the door, if it is closed, *and* keep it open, if it is (already) open'. The conjunctive form makes it more plain that, in fact, two orders are being given.

The form of words 'Open the door and keep it open' would normally be used to enunciate an order *first* to open a door which is (now) closed, and *then* keep it open, *i.e.* not let it close (again). This is an order of different logical structure from either of the two orders which we have just compared, *viz.* the disjunctive order and the 'conjunction' of two orders. It commands two things to be done in a certain order of time. It cannot be resolved into two orders which are given for the same occasion. In this it differs from the order enunciated with the words 'Open the door or keep it open'. But it may become resolved into two orders, one for an earlier occasion and another for a later occasion. In the theory of norm-kernels, which we are now studying, it is assumed that the norms under consideration are given for the same occasion. The theory of norm-kernels is therefore not, in its present form, adequate to deal with orders of the type of 'Open the door and keep it open'.

Consider now an order expressed in symbols by $O(d(\sim pTp)$ v $d(pTp))$. An instantiation would be the above example of an order to open a door or keep it open. It may easily be shown that, on our definition of entailment, this order entails the order expressed by $Od(\sim pTp)$. We form the negation of this last order. It is the permission, expressed by $Pf(\sim pTp)$, to leave the state of affairs described by p unproduced. Its sole condition of application is given by the change-description $\sim pT \sim p$. This is one of the two conditions of application of the disjunctive order. The disjunctive order requires that, under this condition, the state described by p be produced. The permission leaves the subject free to leave the state unproduced. Obviously, it is logically impossible to obey the order and avail oneself of the permission. Hence the order expressed by $Od(\sim pTp)$ is entailed.

By exactly similar argument it is shown that the order expressed by $O(d(\sim pTp) \vee d(pTp))$ entails the order expressed by $Od(pTp)$.

We can also show that, on our definition of entailment, the two orders expressed by $Od(\sim pTp)$ and $Od(pTp)$ jointly entail the order expressed by $O(d(\sim pTp) \vee d(pTp))$. The negation of the last is the permission expressed by $P(f(\sim pTp) \vee f(pTp))$. It has two conditions of application. The one is also the condition of application of the first of the two orders. The other is also the condition of application of the second of the two orders. It is logically impossible both to obey an order to produce a certain state and to avail oneself of a permission to leave it unproduced. It is also logically impossible both to obey an order to continue a certain state and to avail oneself of a permission to let it vanish. Hence the permission expressed by $P(f(\sim pTp) \vee f(pTp))$ is absolutely incompatible with the set of two orders. Hence, finally, the two orders jointly entail the order expressed by $O(d(\sim pTp) \vee d(pTp))$.

The generalization of the example should be clear to the reader. Let an order have n conditions of application. It is then equivalent to a set of n orders, each of which has only one condition of application. The contents of these n orders are those 'parts' of the contents of the first order which answer to its several conditions of application. (That the order and the set of orders are 'equivalent' means that the order entails each one of the orders of the set individually *and* that it is entailed by all the orders of the set jointly.)

I shall call this the *Rule of O-distribution*.

13. A permission to do at least one of two things which can both be done under the same conditions, I shall call a *disjunctive permission*. Often, when there is a disjunctive permission to do one of two things there is also a permission to do the one *and* a permission to do the other. But this is not necessarily the case. A

disjunctive permission is not equivalent to a set of several permissions.

A permission to do one of several things, no two of which can be done under the same conditions, is, however, equivalent to a set of permissions. A permission, for example, to open a window *or* to close it is tantamount to a permission to open the window if closed, *and* a permission to close it if open.

It is easily seen that the order expressed by $Of(\sim pTp)$ is absolutely incompatible with the permission expressed by $P(d(\sim pTp) \vee d(pT\sim p))$. Hence the permission expressed by $Pd(\sim pTp)$ is entailed by the first permission. By similar argument it is shown that the permission expressed by $Pd(pT\sim p)$ is entailed by it.

It is also the case that the order expressed by $O(f(\sim pTp) \vee f(pT\sim p))$ is absolutely incompatible with the set of two permissions expressed by $Pd(\sim pTp)$ and by $Pd(pT\sim p)$. Hence the permission expressed by $P(d(\sim pTp) \vee d(pT\sim p))$ is entailed by the set.

I shall call the generalization of these findings the *Rule of P-distribution*.

14. Thanks to the rules of distribution, every prescription with several conditions of application may become 'resolved' into a set of prescriptions, each one of which has only one condition of application. The members of the set of prescriptions we call the *constituents* of the original prescription. Depending upon the character of the original prescription, we distinguish between O- and P-constituents.

We can make a systematic list of all the possible O- and P-constituents which can be expressed in terms of a given number n of (atomic) states of affairs. We start from the systematic list of all possible state-, change-, and act-descriptions which can be thus expressed (see Ch. IV, Sect. 5). We consider the set of act-descriptions which answer to a given change-description. There are 2^n such act-descriptions. We then consider the set of *disjunctions* of act-descriptions which can be formed of these 2^n act-descriptions. Counting the act-descriptions themselves as one-membered disjunctions, there are in all $2^{(2^n)}-1$ such disjunctions. Each of them is the content of one possible O-constituent and one possible P-constituent. Thus, we get in all $2(2^{(2^n)}-1)$ constituents which answer to a given change-description. Since there are in all 2^{2n} change-descriptions, the total number of constituents which answer to n states of affairs is $2^{2n} \times 2(2^{(2^n)}-1)$ or $2^{2^n + 2n + 1} - 2^{2n + 1}$.

For $n = 1$ the formula yields the value 24. For $n = 2$ it yields 480.

One single state of affairs thus determines 24 possible norm-constituents. Their formation is a simple matter. We begin with the two act-descriptions $d(pTp)$ and $f(pTp)$, which answer to the change-description pTp. Of them only one disjunction can be formed, *viz.* $d(pTp) \vee f(pTp)$. We thus get three O-constituents $Od(pTp)$ and $Of(pTp)$ and $O(d(pTp) \vee f(pTp))$, and three P-constituents $Pd(pTp)$ and $Pf(pTp)$ and $P(d(pTp) \vee f(pTp))$, answering to the change-description pTp. In a similar manner, we form the six constituents answering to $pT \sim p$, the six answering to $\sim pTp$, and the six answering to $\sim pT \sim p$.

Of these 24 constituents, however, the 8 which have a disjunctive content express what we have called (Section 8) *tautologous* norms. We may not wish to count them as genuine prescriptions at all. If we omit them the number of constituents is reduced to 16.

Generally speaking, if the tautologous constituents are excluded the total number of constituents which answer to n states of affairs is reduced by $2^{2n + 1}$ and becomes $2^{2^n + 2n + 1} - 2^{2n + 2}$. For $n = 1$ the formula yields the value 16, and for $n = 2$ it yields 448.

Two single states of affairs determine 2^{2n} change-descriptions. If the states are described by p and q the first change-description in the list is (pTp) & (qTq). To it answer four act-descriptions, *viz.* $d(pTp)$ & $d(qTq)$ and $d(pTp)$ & $f(qTq)$ and $f(pTp)$ & $d(qTq)$ and $f(pTp)$ & $f(qTq)$. Of these, six two-termed disjunctions can be formed, four three-termed disjunctions, and one four-termed disjunction. Counting the four act-descriptions themselves as one-termed disjunctions, we thus get in all 15 disjunctions. They are the contents of 15 O- and 15 P-constituents. Not counting the two tautologous constituents, the contents of which is the four-termed disjunction $d(pTp)$ & $d(qTq) \vee d(pTp)$ & $f(qTq) \vee f(pTp)$ & $d(qTq) \vee f(pTp)$ & $f(qTq)$, we have in all 28 constituents. Since there are 16 change-descriptions in the list, the total number of not-trivial constituents will be 16 times 28, which is 448.

15. If the content of a norm is an internal consequence of the content of another norm, then the first norm is entailed by the second. This is true independently of the character of the norm.

For example: the mode of action described by $d(pTp)$ & $d(qTq)$ v $d(pTp)$ & $f(qTq)$ is an internal consequence of the mode of action described by $d(pTp)$ & $d(qTq)$. The internal negation of the first is described by $f(pTp)$ & $d(qTq)$ v $f(pTp)$ & $f(qTq)$. This last is internally incompatible with the mode of action described by $d(pTp)$ & $d(qTq)$. From this incompatibility (and our definition of entailment) it follows both that the command expressed by $O(d(pTp)$ & $d(qTq))$ entails the command expressed by $O(d(pTp)$ & $d(qTq)$ v $d(pTp)$ & $f(qTq))$ and that the permission expressed by $P(d(pTp)$ & $d(qTq))$ entails the permission expressed by $P(d(pTp)$ & $d(qTq)$ v $d(pTp)$ & $f(qTq))$.

If the content of a command or permission is an internal consequence of the conjunction of the contents of two or more commands, then the first command (permission) is entailed by the set of commands.

Consider, for example, the two commands expressed by $O(d(pTp)$ & $d(qTq)$ v $d(pTp)$ & $f(qTq))$ and by $O(d(pTp)$ & $f(qTq)$ v $f(pTp)$ & $d(qTq))$. The conjunction of their content is the act described by $d(pTp)$ & $f(qTq)$. One can obey both commands only by doing this act. Its internal negation is the act described by $d(pTp)$ & $d(qTq)$ v $f(pTp)$ & $d(qTq)$ v $f(pTp)$ & $f(qTq)$. One could avail oneself of a permission to do this last act only by disobeying at least one, or possibly both, of the commands in question. Hence the command expressed by $O(d(pTp)$ & $f(qTq))$ is entailed by the first two commands jointly.

If the content of a permission is an internal consequence of the conjunction of the contents of one or several commands and of one permission, then the first permission is entailed by the set of one or several commands and one permission.

Consider, for example, the command expressed by $O(d(pTp)$ & $d(qTq)$ v $d(pTp)$ & $f(qTq))$ and the permission expressed by $P(d(pTp)$ & $f(qTq)$ v $f(pTp)$ & $d(qTq))$. The internal negation of the conjunction of their contents is the act described by $d(pTp)$ & $d(qTq)$ v $f(pTp)$ & $d(qTq)$ v $f(pTp)$ & $f(qTq)$. One can obey the first command and a command to do this last act only by doing the act described by $d(pTp)$ & $d(qTq)$. But this would make it impossible to avail oneself of the above permission. Hence the three-termed disjunctive action cannot be commanded. Its internal negation must be a permitted action. This means that the permission expressed by $P(d(pTp) \& f(qTq))$ is entailed by the first command and the first permission jointly.

It is possible to merge the three theorems concerning entailment which have been mentioned in this section into two. Let us adopt the convention that the phrase 'the conjunction of the content of a command (permission) with the contents of *none* or one or several command(s)' shall mean 'the content of a command (permission) or the conjunction of the content of this command (permission) with the content(s) of one or several command(s)'. Then we have the following two entailment-theorems:

(i) If the content of a command (or permission) is an internal consequence of the conjunction of the content of a command with the contents of none or one or several other commands, then the first command (permission) is entailed by the second command or by the set of it and the other commands.

(ii) If the content of a permission is an internal consequence of the conjunction of the content of a permission with the contents of none or one or several commands, then the first permission is entailed by the second permission or by the set of it and the commands.

The rule that Ought entails May is easily seen to be a special case of the first of these two theorems.

It is essential to the entailment-theorems which we have been discussing in this section that the consequence-relations between norm-contents should be of the kind which we have called *internal*. For external consequences the theorems are not valid.

Thus, for example, $d(pTp) \vee d(pT\sim p)$ is an external consequence of $d(pTp)$. But from, say, $Od(pTp)$ does not follow $O(d(pTp) \vee d(pT\sim p))$. That it must be thus is easily understood. For, by virtue of the Rule of O-distribution, $Od(pT\sim p)$ follows from $O(d(pTp) \vee d(pT\sim p))$. If therefore $O(d(pTp) \vee d(pT\sim p))$ followed from $Od(pTp)$, then one could conclude by transitivity that $Od(pT\sim p)$ follows from $Od(pTp)$. This means that one could deduce an order to destroy a state from an order to continue it.

It is intuitively obvious that no norm can entail another norm

164

to the effect that something ought to or may or must not be done under conditions when the first norm does not apply. A norm can only have consequences for the circumstances in which it applies itself. This is reflected in the formal theory by the fact that only internal relationships of consequence between norm-contents have repercussions in the form of relationships of entailment between norms.

16. We have distinguished between a *descriptive* and a *prescriptive* interpretation of the (atomic) *O*- and *P*-expressions. The meta-logical notions of (self-)consistency, compatibility, and entailment, which we have defined in this chapter, are in the first place relevant to the prescriptive interpretation. They concern the logical properties of the norms themselves. The ontological significance of those properties, however, has to be explained in terms of the (possible) existence of norms. Hence this significance will be reflected in the descriptive interpretation too. For, on the descriptive interpretation, the *O*- and *P*-expressions express norm-propositions. And norm-propositions are to the effect that such and such norms exist.

O- and *P*-expressions, descriptively interpreted, and their molecular complexes we have called *OP*-expressions.

Every *OP*-expression expresses a truth-function of the propositions expressed by the atomic *O*- and/or *P*-expressions which are the constituents (descriptively interpreted) of the atomic *O*- and/or *P*-expressions, of which the given *OP*-expression is a molecular complex. We shall call these constituents of its atomic components the constituents of the *OP*-expression itself.

Which truth-function of its constituents a given *OP*-expression is can be investigated and decided in a truth-table. If this truth-function is the tautology we shall call the given expression an *OP-tautology* or *deontic tautology*.

It may be of particular interest to know whether the proposition expressed by one *OP*-expression entails the proposition expressed by another *OP*-expression. In order to find out this, we form a third *OP*-expression, which is the material implication of the first and the second. We test it in a truth-table. If, and only if, it is a deontic tautology the (proposition expressed by the) first *OP*-expression entails the (proposition expressed by the) second *OP*-expression.

The truth-tables of deontic logic differ from ordinary truth-tables (of propositional logic) in that certain combinations of truth-values in the constituents of the tables are excluded as being impossible. Which the excluded combinations are, is determined by the definitions of consistency, compatibility, and entailment for norms (and theorems derived from these definitions).

This is the rule for the construction of truth-tables in Deontic Logic:

Given an OP-expression. We replace the atomic O- and/or P-expressions in it by the *conjunctions* of their constituents. The constituents are made uniform with regard to the atomic p-expressions (variables $p, q, \ldots$), which occur in the entire OP-expression.

The distribution of truth-values over *all possible* constituents, which are determined by the atomic p-expressions in the whole OP-expression, is subject to the following restrictions:

(i) If the content of an O- or P-constituent is inconsistent the constituent must be assigned the value 'false' (cf. above, Section 3).

(ii) If the contents of two or more O-constituents or of one or several O- and one P-constituent are internally incompatible all constituents cannot be assigned the value 'true' (cf. above, Section 6).

(iii) If an O- and a P-constituent have the same content, then if the first constituent is assigned the value 'true' the second constituent must also be assigned the value 'true' (cf. above, Section 11).

(iv) If the content of an O-constituent is an internal consequence of the content of another O-constituent or of the conjunction of the contents of several O-constituents, then if the latter are all assigned the value 'true' the former must also be assigned the value 'true' (cf. above, Section 15).

(v) If the content of a P-constituent is an internal consequence of the content of another P-constituent or of the conjunction of the contents of one P-constituent and one or several O-constituents, then if the latter are all assigned the value 'true' the former must also be assigned the value 'true' (cf. above, Section 15).

When the truth-table of the given OP-expression is being constructed care must be taken that only such distributions of

166

truth-values occur in the table as are allowed by the rules for the distribution of truth-values over *all possible* constituents which can be formed in terms of the atomic *p*-expressions in the entire *OP*-expression. (These constituents *may* all occur in the truth-table, but some *may* also be missing.)

These are examples of deontic tautologies:

$$Od(pTp) \rightarrow Pd(pTp)$$
$$Od(pTp) \rightarrow \sim Of(pTp)$$
$$Od(pTp) \rightarrow \sim Pf(pTp)$$
$$O(d(pTp) \text{ v } d(pT \sim p)) \rightarrow Od(pTp)$$
$$Od(pTp) \text{ \& } Od(pT \sim p) \rightarrow O(d(pTp) \text{ v } d(pT \sim p))$$
$$P(d(pTp) \text{ v } d(pT \sim p)) \rightarrow Pd(pTp)$$
$$Pd(pTp) \text{ \& } Pd(pT \sim p) \rightarrow P(d(pTp) \text{ v } d(pT \sim p))$$
$$O(d(pTp) \text{ v } d(pT \sim p)) \text{ \& } O(d(pTp) \text{ v } d(\sim pTp)) \rightarrow Od(pTp)$$
$$O(d(pTp) \text{ v } d(pT \sim p)) \text{ \& } P(d(pTp) \text{ v } d(\sim pTp)) \rightarrow Pd(pTp)$$

The reader will immediately recognize how these formulae may be said to 'reflect' the very rules for the construction of truth-tables in Deontic Logic. Their proof in a truth-table is therefore completely trivial. The non-trivial aspect of the proof of those tautologies is an application to the particular formulae in question of the definitions of consistency, compatibility, and entailment for norms.

IX

DEONTIC LOGIC: HYPOTHETICAL NORMS

1. HYPOTHETICAL prescriptions order or permit or prohibit a certain mode of action to some subject(s) on some occasion(s), assuming that the occasion(s) satisfy certain conditions—in addition to providing an opportunity for performing the action.

Formally, hypothetical prescriptions differ from categorical ones in the statement of their conditions of application. The conditions of application of categorical prescriptions can be 'read off' from a statement of their contents. The conditions are that the occasion(s) for which the prescription is given should provide an opportunity for performing the commanded, permitted, or prohibited action. The conditions of application of hypothetical prescriptions require special statement. The requirement is usually fulfilled by appending an 'if-then'-clause to the norm-formulation. For example: 'If it starts raining, shut the window', 'If you have finished your homework before dinner, you may see your friends in the evening', 'If the dog barks, don't run'.

Our first problem concerns the nature of the *conditionality* which is characteristic of hypothetical prescriptions (and other hypothetical norms). We could also say that it concerns the 'formalization' of the 'if-then'-clause which normally occurs in their formulation.

2. Compare the following two types of schematic sentence: 'One ought to (may, must not), should such and such contingen-

cies arise, do . . .' and 'Should such and such contingencies arise, then one ought to (may, must not) do . . .'. Ordinary usage does not maintain a sharp distinction between two meanings here. But the two different orders of words may be said to hint at a distinction, which the logician has to note.

The second schema contains a deontic sentence as a part. The deontic sentence appears in the consequent of a conditional sentence, whose antecedent contains the sentence 'Such and such circumstances arise'. Shall we say that the schema is that of a descriptive sentence which conditions a prescriptive sentence? I do not think we should say this. Deontic sentences, it will be remembered, have a typical ambiguity. They can be understood prescriptively or descriptively. In the kind of context now under consideration they should, I think, be interpreted descriptively (or else we shall become involved in logical difficulties). The schema will then be that of a descriptive sentence which conditions another descriptive sentence. The whole thing says 'If such and such is (will be) the case, then such and such is (will be) the case too'. The antecedent speaks of things which happen. The consequent speaks of norms (prescriptions) which there are (will be). I shall say that the schema is of a sentence which expresses a *hypothetical norm-proposition*. The proposition is true or false, depending upon whether there are (will be) such and such norms, should such and such things happen. It is clear that hypothetical norm-propositions are quite different from hypothetical norms (prescriptions).

The first schema may be said to be itself a deontic sentence. As such it admits of a descriptive and a prescriptive interpretation. Descriptively interpreted it expresses a norm-proposition. This proposition is to the effect that a certain norm (prescription) exists. The norm-proposition is categorical and not hypothetical. It says that there is such and such a norm—not that, should such and such be the case, there is a norm. Prescriptively interpreted, however, the schema is of a norm-formulation. The norms (prescriptions) which sentences of that form are used for enunciating are *hypothetical norms*.

The scope of the deontic operator in the formulation of a hypothetical norm includes or stretches over the conditional clause in the formulation. What is subject to condition in the norm is the *content*, *i.e.* a certain action. The *character* is not conditioned.

We could also say that a hypothetical norm does not contain a categorical norm as a part.

3. We have distinguished between hypothetical and technical norms (cf. Ch. I, Sect. 7). Technical norms are concerned with that which ought to or may or must not be done for the sake of attaining some end. They, too, are normally formulated by means of a conditional clause. 'If you want to escape from becoming attacked by the barking dog, don't run.' Here not-running is thought of as a means to escaping attack by the dog.

The *reason* why a hypothetical prescription is given is often or perhaps normally that the prescribed action is thought of as a means to some end. In the 'background' of a hypothetical prescription there is thus often a technical norm. The reason, for example, why the order 'If the dog barks, don't run' is given to somebody may be anxiety that the subject of the order should not be bitten by the dog.

Wanting something as an end can be regarded as a contingency which may arise (in the life of a person). A hypothetical prescription can be given for such cases too. 'Should you want to climb that peak, consult him first.' This could express a genuine hypothetical order. There *may*, but *need not*, be any means–end connexion between consulting that person and success in the projected enterprise of climbing the hill. That is: the order can 'exist' independently of the existence of any such causal ties. This observation should make it clear that a technical norm is not the same as a hypothetical norm for the special case, when the conditioning circumstances happen to be the pursuit of something as an end.

It seems to me that a difference between hypothetical and technical norms is that the answer to the question, what is subject to a *condition*, is different for the two types of norm. In the case of a hypothetical norm it is the *content* of the norm which is subject to a condition. In the case of a technical norm it is the *existence of the norm* which is subject to condition. The 'if–then'-sentence says: Should you want that as an end (but not otherwise), then you ought to (may, must not) do thus and thus. The 'if–then'-sentence is of the second rather than of the first of the two schematic types which we mentioned and discussed in Section 2. It is a descriptive sentence. The proposition expressed by it is a hypothetical norm-proposition.

170

If this is a correct view of the matter the technical *norm* itself is categorical and not hypothetical. The *existence* of the norm, however, is hypothetical. The 'if–then'-sentence is not a norm-formulation, but a statement of the conditions under which something will become imperative (permissible) for an agent.

4. For our theory of hypothetical norms we need an extension of our previous Logic of Action. We need a logical theory of *conditioned action*, *i.e.* action performed on occasions which satisfy certain conditions (in addition to affording opportunities for performing the actions themselves).

We introduce a new symbol /.

By an *elementary* /-expression we understand an expression which is formed of an elementary *d*- or *f*-expression to the left and an elementary *T*-expression to the right of the stroke /. For example: $d(pTp) \mid qTq$ is an elementary /-expression.

By an *atomic* /-expression we understand an expression which is formed of a (atomic or molecular) *df*-expression to the left and a (atomic or molecular) *T*-expression to the right of /. For example: $(d(pT \sim p) \vee f(\sim qTq)) \mid rTs$ is an atomic /-expression.

By /-*expressions*, finally, we understand atomic /-expressions and molecular complexes of atomic /-expressions. For example: $d(pTp) \mid qTq \,\&\, \sim(f((p\,\&\,r)\,T\,(\sim p\,\&\,\sim r)) \mid \sim sT \sim s)$ is a /-expression.

A /-expression describes a generic action which is performed by an unspecified agent on an unspecified occasion, when a certain generic change takes place (independently of the action). The generic change, be it observed, can also be a non-change. For example: The elementary /-expression $d(pTp) \mid qTq$ describes that which an (unspecified) agent does, who on some (unspecified) occasion, when the state described by *q* obtains and remains independently of action, prevents the state described by *p* from vanishing.

/-expressions belong to (formalized) descriptive discourse. They are schematic representations of sentences which express propositions. Their combination by means of truth-connectives to form molecular complexes is therefore entirely uncontroversial.

5. *df*-expressions may be regarded as degenerate or limiting cases of /-expressions.

Thus, for example, $d(pTp)$ and $d(pTp) \mid (qTq \text{ v } qT \sim q \text{ v } \sim qTq$ v $\sim qT \sim q)$ obviously describe the same action. The first expression says that the state of affairs described by p is continued (prevented from vanishing). The second says that the state described by p is continued on some occasion, when the state described by q either is and remains or is but vanishes or is not but comes into being or is not and remains absent. Since what is being said about the state described by q is trivially true, the end part of the second description can be omitted as vacuous. The df-expression and the $/$-expression say, in fact, the same.

Generally speaking: any df-expression may be regarded as a degenerate form of a $/$-expression, in which the df-expression in question stands to the left of $/$ and an arbitrary T-*tautology* stands to its right.

But may not $d(pTp)$ be regarded as a degenerate form of $d(pTp) \mid pT \sim p$ also? Generally speaking: May not any df-expression be regarded as a degenerate form of a $/$-expression, in which the df-expression in question stands to the left of $/$ and a description of the conditions for performing the action described by the df-expression to the right of $/$?

As will be seen presently, the answer to these questions is affirmative. There are thus two senses or ways in which df-expressions may be said to represent limiting cases of $/$-expressions. The second of these two conceptions of df-expressions as limiting cases is, however, provable on the basis of the first with the aid of other principles of our logical theory of $/$-expressions.

6. As will be remembered, there are four types of elementary T-expressions and eight types of elementary df-expressions. Since thus the expression to the left of $/$ in an elementary $/$-expression may be any one of eight types and the expression to the right any one of four types, it follows at once that there are 32 types of elementary $/$-expressions. We could list them, beginning with $d(pTp) \mid qTq$ and ending with $f(\sim pT \sim p) \mid \sim qT \sim q$.

Since elementary T-expressions and also elementary df-expressions of the same variable but of different types are mutually exclusive, it is obvious that any two elementary $/$-expressions of different types, but containing the same variable to the left of $/$ and the same variable to the right of $/$, are mutually exclusive also.

172

The 32 elementary types of /-expression do not *ipso facto* form an exhaustive disjunction. They do it only on condition that the eight elementary types of *df*-expression in them form an exhaustive disjunction. This condition is fulfilled for an arbitrary agent and state of affairs, provided it is within the ability of the agent in question to continue and produce and destroy and suppress the state in question, when there is an opportunity (cf. above, Ch. IV, Sect. 2). We shall here assume that this condition is actually satisfied for any agent and state that may enter our consideration.

7. Consider an atomic /-expression. Assume that the *df*-expression to the left is self-inconsistent, *i.e.* expresses a *df*-contradiction. This means that it describes a logically impossible mode of action. It is clear that, on this assumption, the /-expression too is inconsistent. An action which it is logically impossible to perform in any case, cannot be performed under certain conditions either. Assume next that the T-expression to the right is self-inconsistent, *i.e.* expresses a T-contradiction. This means that it describes a logically impossible transformation of the world. It is clear that on this assumption, the /-expression, too, is inconsistent. Under logically impossible conditions no action is possible either.

An atomic /-expression is thus inconsistent if the *df*-expression to the left or the T-expression to the right of the sign / (or both) is inconsistent. This, however, is not the sole condition of inconsistency.

The occasion on which the action described by an atomic /-expression is done has (*i*) to satisfy the conditions stated by the T-expression to the right of /, and (*ii*) to afford an opportunity for doing the action described by the *df*-expression to the left of /. It can happen that the conditions stated by the T-expression and the conditions for doing the action described by the *df*-expression are consistent in themselves but *mutually incompatible*.

Consider, for example, the expression $d(pTp) / pTp$. The *df*-expression to the left is consistent, so far as the laws of the Logic of Action are concerned. The T-expression to the right is consistent, so far as the laws of the Logic of Change are concerned. But the /-expression itself is obviously inconsistent. It says that somebody prevents the state described by p from vanishing in a situation when this state obtains and does *not* vanish, unless destroyed. But under such circumstances it is not (logically) possible to 'prevent' the state in question from vanishing. This can be done only in a situation when the state in question obtains and *does* vanish, unless prevented.

Formally, the inconsistency of $d(pTp) \mid pTp$ is reflected in the incompatibility, in the Logic of Change, of the expressions pTp and $pT \sim p$. The first states the condition which the occasion for doing the action in question has to satisfy *in addition to* affording an opportunity of doing the action. The second states the condition which the occasion has to satisfy *in order to* afford an opportunity of doing the action. The two conditions are incompatible. (pTp) & $(pT \sim p)$ expresses a T-contradiction.

These observations relating to the self-inconsistency of the expression $d(pTp) \mid pTp$ can easily be generalized. An atomic $\mid$-expression is inconsistent, if the T-expression to the right of $\mid$ is, in the Logic of Change, incompatible with the T-expression, which states the conditions for doing the action described by the df-expression to the left of $\mid$. An atomic $\mid$-expression is inconsistent, we could also say, if the conjunction of the two T-expressions in question expresses a T-contradiction.

From the meaning of $\mid$-expressions, as we have explained it, the validity of the following principle is obvious:

If we replace the T-expression to the right of $\mid$ in a given $\mid$-expression by the conjunction of itself and the T-expression which states the conditions for doing the action described by the df-expression to the left of $\mid$, then the new $\mid$-expression is logically equivalent with the original $\mid$-expression.

For example: $(d(\sim pTp)$ & $f(\sim qTq)) \mid rTr$ is logically equivalent with $(d(\sim pTp)$ & $f(\sim qTq)) \mid ((\sim pT \sim p)$ & $(\sim qT \sim q)$ & $(rTr))$.

We can, accordingly, speak of a 'shorter' and 'longer' form of any given atomic $\mid$-expression. In the longer form the T-expression to the right states both the conditions which the occasion has to satisfy in order to afford an opportunity of action and the conditions which the occasion has to satisfy in addition to affording an opportunity of action. The variables which appear in the df-expression to the left all appear in the T-expression to the right. But the T-expression may contain additional variables.

When an atomic $\mid$-expression is in the longer form it is, in fact, consistent if, and only if, the T-expression to the right of the symbol $\mid$ is consistent.

8. Consider two atomic /-expressions. The two df-expressions to the left may or may not contain the same variables. The same holds good for the two T-expressions to the right.

Let the variable p occur in one of the df-expressions, but not in the other. Then p can be made to appear in this latter by conjoining to it the eight-termed disjunction $d(pTp) \lor \ldots \lor f(\sim pT \sim p)$. By this procedure one can procure that the two df-expressions contain exactly the same variables.

Let the variable p occur in one of the T-expressions, but not in the other. Then p can be made to appear in this latter by conjoining to it the four-termed disjunction $(pTp) \lor \ldots \lor (\sim pT \sim p)$. By this procedure one can achieve that the two T-expressions contain exactly the same variables.

Atomic /-expressions which contain the same variables in the df-expressions to the left of / and the same variables in the T-expressions to the right of / will be called *uniform* (with regard to the variables).

Uniform atomic /-expressions which are in the 'longer' form will satisfy the additional condition that the variables which occur in the df-expressions to the left of / form a sub-set of the variables which occur in the T-expressions to the right of /.

9. Every /-expression expresses a truth-function of elementary /-expressions. That this must be the case is intuitively obvious from considerations about distributability.

We consider an atomic /-expression. We assume that the df-expression to the left and the T-expression to the right are both in the positive normal form.

Let, for example, the expression be $d(pTp) \mid (qTq \lor qT \sim q)$. A state of affairs is prevented from vanishing on an occasion when another state obtains and either remains or vanishes independently of action. Obviously this means the same as $(d(pTp) \mid qTq) \lor (d(pTp) \mid qT \sim q)$.

Let the expression be $d(pTp) \mid (qTq \ \& \ rTr)$. This means the same as $(d(pTp) \mid qTq) \ \& \ (d(pTp) \mid rTr)$.

Let the expression be $(d(pTp) \lor d(pT \sim p)) \mid qTq$. This means the same as $(d(pTp) \mid qTq) \lor (d(pT \sim p) \mid qTq)$.

Let, finally, the expression be $(d(pTp) \ \& \ d(qTq)) \mid rTr$. This means the same as $(d(pTp) \mid rTr) \ \& \ (d(qTq) \mid rTr)$.

It is important to remember that the whole /-expression refers

175

to one and the same agent and occasion. Assume, for example, that $(d(pTp) / qTq) \vee (d(pTp) / qT \sim q)$ meant that either some agent on some occasion, when the state described by q is and remains, prevents the state described by p from vanishing, *or* some agent on some occasion, when the state described by q is but vanishes, prevents the state described by p from vanishing. Then the expression would *not* be identical in meaning with $d(pTp) / (qTq \vee qT \sim q)$.

If atomic /-expressions are truth-functions of elementary /-expressions, then all /-expressions must be truth-functions of elementary /-expressions.

10. Consider an arbitrary /-expression. It is a molecular complex of atomic /-expressions. We make its atomic constituents uniform (with regard to the variables) according to the procedure described in Section 8. We replace the *df*-expressions to the left and the T-expressions to the right of / in the atomic /-expressions by their positive normal forms. Thereupon we carry out the four types of distribution mentioned in Section 9. The original /-expression has then become transformed into a molecular complex of elementary /-expressions. The elementary /-expressions we call the /-*constituents* of the original /-expression.

Which truth-function of its /-constituents a given /-expression is can be investigated and decided in a truth-table. The distribution of truth-values over the constituents is subject to the following two restrictions:

(i) Uniform elementary /-expressions are mutually exclusive and jointly (all 32 of them) exhaustive.
(ii) Inconsistent elementary /-expressions must be assigned the value 'false'. An elementary /-expression is inconsistent if, and only if, the T-expression to the right contradicts the condition of doing the action described by the elementary d- or f-expression to the left.

If a /-expression is the tautology of its /-constituents we call it a /-*tautology*. If it is the contradiction of its constituents we call it a /-*contradiction*.

11. Let there be an arbitrary /-expression. We replace it, according to the transformations described in Section 10, by a

complex of its /-constituents. This complex we transform into its perfect disjunctive normal form. This is a disjunction of conjunctions of elementary /-expressions and/or their negations. We replace every negation of an elementary /-expression by a 31-termed disjunction of elementary /-expressions, which are uniform with the first and form with it an exhaustive disjunction. We transform the expression obtained after these replacements into *its* perfect disjunctive normal form. This will be a disjunction of conjunctions of (unnegated) elementary /-expressions. We call it the *positive* normal form of the original /-expression.

12. In Section 5 we showed that *df*-expressions may be regarded as degenerate or limiting cases of /-expressions. Unconditioned action, we could also say, is a limiting case of conditioned action. It is the limiting case when the condition of action is tautological.

Similarly, categorical norms may be regarded as degenerate or limiting cases of hypothetical norms.

Consider the expression $d(pTp)$. According to what was said in Section 5, it may become 'translated' into the /-expression $d(pTp) \mid (qTq \vee qT \sim q \vee \sim qTq \vee \sim qT \sim q)$. If the letter O or P is prefixed to the first expression we obtain the symbol for the norm-kernel of a categorical command and permission respectively. If the letter O or P is prefixed to the second expression we obtain the symbol for the norm-kernel of a hypothetical command and permission respectively. 'Axiomatically', we shall regard the two symbols for norm-kernels as 'intertranslatable'. A command or permission to do something unconditionally may be regarded as a command or permission to do something under conditions which are tautologously satisfied.

Since there is no restriction on the choice of a variable for the tautologous T-expression to the right of /, the expression $d(pTp)$ may also become 'translated' by $d(pTp) \mid (pTp \vee pT \sim p \vee \sim pTp \vee \sim pT \sim p)$. By virtue of the distribution-principles mentioned in Section 9, the last expression is equivalent to $d(pTp) \mid pTp \vee d(pTp) \mid pT \sim p \vee d(pTp) \mid \sim pTp \vee d(pTp) \mid \sim pT \sim p$. According to the criteria of consistency given in Section 7, the first, the third, and the fourth disjunct in this four-termed disjunction of elementary /-expressions is inconsistent. The whole expression is thus tautologically equivalent to $d(pTp) \mid pT \sim p$. Generally speaking: any *df*-expression may become 'translated' into a /-expression, in which the given *df*-expression stands to the left of / and a statement of the condition of doing the action described by it stands to the right of / (cf. Section 5).

Corresponding to the two ways in which *df*-expressions may be regarded as limiting cases of /-expressions, there are two ways in which categorical norms may be regarded as limiting cases of hypothetical norms. $Od(pTp)$ may be regarded as an 'abbreviation' of an expression of the form $O(d(pTp) / (qTq \vee qT \sim q \vee \sim qTq \vee \sim qT \sim q))$, or of the form $O(d(pTp) / pT \sim p)$. And the corresponding is true of $P(pTp)$.

We can now generalize the notion of an *OP*-expression, which we introduced in Ch. V, Sect. 4.

By an *atomic O*-expression (*P*-expression) we understand an expression formed of the letter O (P) followed by a *df*- or by a /-expression. The atomic *O*- and *P*-expressions are thus symbols of norm-kernels of categorical or of hypothetical norms.

By an *OP*-expression we understand any atomic *O*- or atomic *P*-expression or molecular complex of atomic *O*- and/or *P*-expressions.

An *OP*-expression, in the general sense of the term, can thus be a molecular compound containing symbols both of categorical and of hypothetical norm-kernels. The symbolic statement of many of the theorems which we are going to prove will be such 'mixed' *OP*-expressions. When 'mixed' expressions are handled for the purposes of proofs it is often convenient to replace expressions of categorical norm-kernels in them by such expressions of hypothetical norm-kernels, of which the first may be regarded as degenerate or limiting cases.

13. The principles of the logic of categorical norms (norm-kernels) which we discussed in the last chapter are, with minor modifications, also the principles of the logic of hypothetical norms. The logic of hypothetical norms (norm-kernels) has no new, independent principles of its own.

The 'minor modifications', to which we referred, concern the notions of the content, the conditions of application, and of the negation-norm of a given norm. They have to be redefined so as to become applicable also to hypothetical norms.

Consider an atomic *OP*-expression, in which the /-expression following after the letter O or P is *atomic*. By the *content* of the hypothetical norm in question we understand the action described by the *df*-expression to the left of / in the /-expression.

By the *condition of application* of the norm we understand the conjunction of the change, which is the condition of doing the action described by the *df*-expression to the left of /, and the change described by the *T*-expression to the right of /.

By the *negation-norm* of the given norm, finally, we understand a norm of opposite character, whose content is the internal negation of the content of the original norm, and the conditions of application of which are the same as those of the original norm.

For example: the content of the hypothetical command expressed by $O(d(pTp) \mid qTq)$ is the action described by $d(pTp)$. Its condition of application is the change described by $pT \sim p$ & qTq. Its negation-norm, finally, is the norm whose kernel is expressed by $P(f(pTp) \mid qTq)$.

These definitions will have to be generalized for the case when the /-expression following after the letter O or P in the OP-expression is not atomic. In this case we have to think of the /-expression as being in the positive normal form. It is then a disjunction of conjunctions of elementary /-expressions. Consider such a conjunction in the normal form. We form the conjunction of the elementary *d*- and/or *f*-expressions to the left of the symbols / in it. Thereupon we form the conjunction of the *T*-expressions stating the conditions of doing the acts described by these *d* and/or *f*-expressions *and* the *T*-expressions to the right of the symbols /. These two operations are performed on each one of the conjunctions in the normal form. The operations give us two conjunctions for each conjunction in the normal form. The one is a conjunction of elementary *d*- and/or *f*-expressions; the other is a conjunction of elementary *T*-expressions. The disjunction of all the conjunctions of the first kind states the *content* of the hypothetical norm in question; the disjunction of all the conjunctions of the second kind states its *conditions of application*. The *negation-norm* of the given hypothetical norm, finally, is a norm of opposite character, whose content is the internal negation of the content of the original norm, and the conditions of application of which are the same as those of the original norm.

For example: The content of the hypothetical norm with the norm-kernel $O(d(pTp) \mid qTq \lor d(pT \sim p) \mid qT \sim q)$ is the action described by $d(pTp) \lor d(pT \sim p)$. Its condition of application is the change described by $(pT \sim p \,\&\, qTq) \vee (pTp \,\&\, qT \sim q)$. The symbol for the norm-kernel of its negation-norm, finally, is $P(f(pTp) \mid qTq \vee f(pT \sim p) \mid qT \sim q)$.

Having redefined the notions of content, conditions of application, and negation-norm, the definitions of the notions of compatibility and entailment can, without further modification, be transferred to the theory of hypothetical norms. The notion of consistency we define as follows: The norm-kernel of a hypothetical norm is consistent if, and only if, the $\mid$-expression after the letter O or P in the symbol of this norm-kernel is consistent.

14. We easily prove that the following formula is a deontic tautology: $Od(pTp) \rightarrow O(d(pTp) \mid qTq)$. The proof is as follows: We replace, in accordance with the principles of 'translation' given in Section 12, the antecedent of the implication-formula by $O(d(pTp) \mid qTq \vee qT \sim q \vee \sim qTq \vee \sim qT \sim q)$. The $\mid$-expression after the letter O can be replaced by $d(pTp) \mid qTq \vee d(pTp) \mid qT \sim q \vee d(pTp) \mid \sim qTq \vee d(pTp) \mid \sim qT \sim q$. If we apply the Rule of O-Distribution (Ch. VIII, Sect. 12) to the above implication-formula we get the formula $(O(d(pTp) \mid qTq) \,\&\, O(d(pTp) \mid qT \sim q) \,\&\, O(d(pTp) \mid \sim qTq) \,\&\, O(d(pTp) \mid \sim qT \sim q)) \rightarrow O(d(pTp) \mid qTq)$. This is easily recognized as a tautology of the Logic of Propositions.

In the above proof we assumed the validity of the Rule of O-Distribution for hypothetical norms. We could, however, have proved the same formula without this assumption, directly on the basis of our definition of entailment. We would then have to show that the negation-norm of $O(d(pTp) \mid qTq)$, which is $P(f(pTp) \mid qTq)$, is absolutely incompatible with $Od(pTp)$. The two norms have only one condition of application in common, $viz.\ pT \sim p \,\&\, qTq$. The conjunction of their contents under this condition is $d(pTp) \,\&\, f(pTp)$. This conjunction is inconsistent. $P(f(pTp) \mid qTq)$ has no condition of application which is not also a condition of application of $Od(pTp)$. Hence $P(f(pTp) \mid qTq)$ is not only incompatible but *absolutely* incompatible with $Od(pTp)$. It follows that $O(d(pTp) \mid qTq)$ is entailed by $Od(pTp)$.

Similarly, we establish the tautological character of the formula $Pd(pTp) \rightarrow P(d(pTp) \mid qTq)$, either directly on the basis of our definition of entailment, or with the aid of the Rule of P-distribution and principles of the Logic of Propositions.

Generalizingly, we can state the two theorems which we have proved in this section as follows:

If something is unconditionally obligatory, then it is also obligatory under any particular circumstances, and if something is unconditionally permitted, then it is also permitted under any particular circumstances.

15. In this and the next few sections I shall take up for discussion some principles of deontic logic, which I have acknowledged as true in previous publications and which other writers in the field seem, on the whole, to have accepted. It will be seen that the principles in question will either have to be rejected altogether or reformulated so as to avoid some error which was implicit in their original formulation. I shall refer to my previous system of deontic logic with the name 'the old system'.

In the old system the O-operator was conjunctively distributive. In the symbolism of that system the formula $O(A \& B) \leftrightarrow OA \& OB$ expressed a deontic tautology. The idea was that one ought to do two things jointly if, and only if, one ought to do each one of the things individually. For example: One ought to open the window and shut the door if, and only if, one ought to open the window and ought to shut the door.

Is this a logical truth? Doubts are raised by the following considerations: A command to open a window *and* shut a door applies to a situation when a certain window is closed and a certain door is open. A command to open a window applies to a situation when a certain window is closed—irrespective of whether a certain door is open or not. The two commands have different conditions of application. How could then the one entail the other?

The nearest formal analogue in the new system to the above formula of the old system would be $O(d(\sim pTp) \& d(\sim qTq)) \leftrightarrow Od(\sim pTp) \& Od(\sim qTq)$. It may easily be shown that this formula does *not* express a deontic tautology. To this end we need only show that $O(d(\sim pTp) \& d(\sim qTq))$ does not entail $Od(\sim pTp)$. This is done as follows:

The negation-norm of $Od(\sim pTp)$ is $Pf(\sim pTp)$. It has four conditions of application in terms of the two states described by p and by q respectively. These conditions are the changes described by $\sim pT \sim p \& qTq$ and $\sim pT \sim p \& qT \sim q$ and $\sim pT \sim p \& \sim qTq$ and $\sim pT \sim p \& \sim qT \sim q$. The norm expressed by

$O(d(\sim pTp)$ & $d(\sim qTq))$ has only one condition of application, *viz.* the change described by $\sim pT \sim p$ & $\sim qT \sim q$. Under this one condition of application the two norms are incompatible, as shown by the fact that $f(\sim pTp)$ & $d(\sim pTp)$ & $d(\sim qTq)$ is inconsistent. But the mere fact that the first of the two norms applies under conditions in which the second does not apply is enough to warrant that their incompatibility is not absolute. Hence, on our definition of entailment, $O(d(\sim pTp)$ & $d(\sim qTq))$ does not entail $Od(\sim pTp)$.

An order to produce both of two states does not entail an order to produce the first of them unconditionally. But it obviously entails an order to produce the first of them on condition that the occasion in question affords an opportunity for producing the second as well. $O(d(\sim pTp)$ & $d(\sim qTq))$, in other words, entails $O(d(\sim pTp) \mid \sim qT \sim q)$. This is easily proved as follows:

The negation-norm of $O(d(\sim pTp) \mid \sim qT \sim q)$ is $P(f(\sim pTp)\mid \sim qT \sim q)$. The sole condition of application of the norms $O(d(\sim pTp)$ & $d(\sim qTq))$ and $P(f(\sim pTp) \mid \sim qT \sim q)$ is the change described by $\sim pT \sim p$ & $\sim qT \sim q$. Under this condition the two norms are incompatible. Their incompatibility, moreover, is absolute. Hence the categorical norm expressed by $O(d(\sim pTp)$ & $d(\sim qTq))$ entails the hypothetical norm expressed by $O(d(\sim pTp) \mid \sim qT \sim q)$. By similar argument we show that it entails the hypothetical norm $O(d(\sim qTq) \mid \sim pT \sim p)$. Very easily too it is shown that the two hypothetical norms jointly entail the categorical norm. The following formula is a deontic tautology: $O(d(\sim pTp)$ & $d(\sim qTq))\leftrightarrow O(d(\sim pTp) \mid \sim qT \sim q)$ & $O(d(\sim qTq)\mid \sim pT \sim p)$.

A conjunctive categorical obligation may thus become resolved into a conjunction of hypothetical obligations. The tendency to think that it may become resolved into a conjunction of categorical obligations probably arises from the fact that we think of the norms as having the same conditions of application, and ignore that there may be conditions under which some of them apply and others not.

16. In the old system the P-operator was disjunctively distributive. In the symbolism of this system the formula $P(A \lor B)\leftrightarrow PA \lor PB$ expressed a deontic tautology. The idea was that one may do at least one of two things if, and only if, one may do the one

or may do the other. This principle was the very cornerstone on which the old system of deontic logic rested.

The principle, however, has to be rejected. From the fact that one is unconditionally permitted to do one or the other of two things, it does not follow that one is unconditionally permitted to do the one *or* unconditionally permitted to do the other. (The converse entailment, however, is valid.)

As was shown in Section 14, if something is unconditionally permitted it is permitted also under any particular conditions. Now it may happen that, whatever the conditions are, one is permitted to do one or the other of two things, but that under *some* conditions doing one thing is forbidden and under some *other* conditions doing the other thing is forbidden. One may, for example, be permitted always to leave either the door or the window of a certain room open, but not permitted to leave the door open at night and not permitted to leave the window open in the morning. These considerations should convince us that the principle of the disjunctive distributivity of the P-operator is not a logical truth.

One can sustain this insight by formal considerations. Let there be an unconditional permission, expressed by $P(d(pTp)$ & $f(qTq)$ v $f(pTp)$ & $d(qTq))$. Some agent is on some occasion unconditionally allowed either to continue one state and let another vanish or to let the first vanish and continue the second. Let there further be a hypothetical order to that same agent for that same occasion, expressed by $O((d(pTp)$ & $d(qTq)$ v $f(pTp)$ & $d(qTq)$ v $f(pTp)$ & $f(qTq)) / rTr)$. This is a prohibition to continue the first state and let the second vanish, should a third state (r) obtain on the occasion in question and remain, unless destroyed through action. Let there, finally, be a hypothetical order to that same agent for that same occasion, expressed by $O((d(pTp)$ & $d(qTq)$ v $d(pTp)$ & $f(qTq)$ v $f(pTp)$ & $f(qTq)) / rT \sim r)$. This is a prohibition to let the first state vanish and continue the second, should a third state (r) obtain on the occasion in question, but vanish unless continued through action. The three norms, *viz.* the categorical permission and the two hypothetical prohibitions, are compatible. The reader can easily convince himself of this by constructing a table in which are listed the conditions of application and the parts of the contents of the various norms which apply under the respective conditions.

It may easily be shown that, if there is a categorical disjunctive permission, then it is impossible that both the disjunct modes of action should be *categorically* prohibited. It is also impossible that both should be hypothetically prohibited under the *same* conditions. But it *is* possible that one of the modes of action is prohibited under *some* conditions and the other under some *other* conditions. From the fact that it is impossible that both modes of action are *categorically* prohibited it does not follow that at least one of them must be *categorically* permitted.

17. Sometimes when an agent does something he thereby becomes *committed* to doing something else. *If* he does the first he ought to do the second. Promising might be given as an example. By giving a promise an agent commits himself to doing the act which fulfils the promise.

In the old system of deontic logic the symbol $O(A \rightarrow B)$ was proposed as a formalization of the notion of commitment. It was suggested that the symbol might be read as follows: 'It is obligatory to do B if one does A' or, alternatively, 'It is forbidden to do A without also doing B'.

Some theorems on commitment were proved in the system. One of them was the formula $PA \,\&\, O(A \rightarrow B) \rightarrow PB$. Another was the formula $O(A \rightarrow B) \,\&\, O \sim B \rightarrow O \sim A$. The first was read: 'Doing something permitted can commit one only to doing something else which is also permitted.' And the second: 'An act, the doing of which commits one to a forbidden act, is itself forbidden.'

The suggested formalization of commitment is highly problematic and the reading of formulae is very free indeed. It is obvious that a much more refined symbolism is needed for coping adequately with the notion of commitment and for expressing the ideas aimed at in the above theorems.

How, then, should the notion of commitment be formalized? I do not think the question has a unique answer. For by 'commitment' one can mean several things of rather different logical character.

One sense of 'commitment' has to do with the very notion of a hypothetical norm. Consider, for example, the command expressed by $O(d(\sim pTp) \mid qTq)$. It orders the production of the state of affairs described by p, if the state described by q obtains and

184

remains unless destroyed through action. Assume now that this second state can be produced through action. If, then, an agent produces the change described by $\sim qTq$ and the state thus produced does not vanish 'of itself' unless prevented, he thereby *commits* the agent, who is the subject of the hypothetical command, to produce the change described by $\sim pTp$. If the agent who produces the first change is the same as the subject of the hypothetical command we can speak of *auto-commitment*. If the agents are different we can speak of *alio-commitment*. Both cases are of obvious importance in many legal and moral contexts. Agreement, contract, and promise may be regarded as instances of auto-commitment.

A satisfactory account of *this* notion of commitment is not possible within our theory of norm-kernels. For commitment in this sense involves action on at least two distinct, though related, occasions for acting. *First* one state *is* transformed, and *then* another state, which exists simultaneously with the result of the transformation, ought in its turn to be transformed. This can be formalized only within a symbolism which has signs for occasions. Thus it cannot be formalized within the theory of norm-kernels.

There is, however, another notion of commitment, which concerns action on one occasion only. Its study falls within the theory of norm-kernels.

The definition of commitment in the old system was based on the notion of an 'implication-act'. Commitment was defined as the obligatoriness of an act of this kind. The act was symbolized by a material implication formula, which obeyed the laws of the Logic of Propositions and no special rules of its own. This symbolism is inadequate. The question therefore is urgent, how the notion of an 'implication-act' shall be formalized in the notation of our Logic of Action.

The formula $p \rightarrow q$ is a schematic description of a compound state of affairs. Does the 'implication-act' consist in the production, through action, of a state of this kind? In that case its symbolic expression would be $d(p \ \& \ \sim qTp \rightarrow q)$. The 'implication-act' would consist in the transformation, through action, of a $p \ \& \ \sim q$-world into either a $p \ \& \ q$-world or a $\sim p \ \& \ q$-world or a $\sim p \ \& \ \sim q$-world. Commitment would be the obligatoriness of such action.

It may be of some interest to study acts of the schematic

185

description $d(p$ & $\sim qTp \rightarrow q)$. It seems to me excluded, however, that their study would be of relevance to the notion of commitment. The reading of $Od(p$ & $\sim qTp \rightarrow q)$ as 'one ought to do q, if one does p' does not appear at all natural.

The idea of producing (or having to produce) one state, *if* one produces another, obviously applies to an initial situation in which neither of these two states obtains. The notion which we are trying to 'formalize' concerns action in a world described by $\sim p$ & $\sim q$. The mode of action in question consists in this, that this world is *not* transformed into a p-world *unless* it is also transformed into a q-world. Or conversely, *if* it is transformed into a p-world it is also transformed into a q-world. It is not unnatural to call this mode of action an 'implication-act'. Obligatoriness of this mode of action means that it is forbidden to produce the first of two states and forbear to produce the second.

The symbolic expression of the prohibition to produce the state of affairs described by p and forbear to produce the state described by q is $O(d(\sim pTp)$ & $d(\sim qTq)$ v $f(\sim pTp)$ & $d(\sim qTq)$ v $f(\sim pTp)$ & $f(\sim qTq))$. This is the nearest formal equivalent in the new deontic logic to the symbol $O(A \rightarrow B)$ of the old system.

Is it a logical necessity that, if one is categorically permitted to produce the state of affairs described by p and categorically prohibited to produce p and forbear to produce q, then one is also categorically permitted to produce q? The answer obviously is negative. A categorical permission to produce q is a permission to produce it also on an occasion which does not afford an opportunity for producing p. And it is clear that a permission to produce q on such an occasion cannot be deduced from norms which do not apply to this occasion at all. These considerations show—as may also be intuitively felt—that there is a logical flaw involved in the entailment theorem of the old system, which was given the wording 'Doing something permitted can commit one only to doing something else which is also permitted'.

This, however, is a valid formula of deontic logic: $Pd(\sim pTp)$ & $O(d(\sim pTp)$ & $d(\sim qTq)$ v $f(\sim pTp)$ & $d(\sim qTq)$ v $f(\sim pTp)$ & $f(\sim qTq)) \rightarrow P(d(\sim qTq)/\sim pT \sim p)$. In words: If one is unconditionally permitted to produce a certain state of affairs but unconditionally forbidden to produce this state and forbear to produce a certain other state, then one is also permitted to produce this second state under circumstances which constitute an opportunity

186

for producing the first state. The proof, which is easy, is left as an exercise to the reader.

This, too, is a valid formula of deontic logic: $O(d(\sim pTp)$ & $d(\sim qTq)$ v $f(\sim pTp)$ & $d(\sim qTq)$ v $f(\sim pTp)$ & $f(\sim qTq))$ & $Of(\sim qTq) \rightarrow O(f(\sim pTp) \mid \sim qT\sim q)$. In words: If one is unconditionally forbidden to produce (the state of affairs described by) p and forbear to produce q, whose production is itself unconditionally forbidden, then one is also forbidden to produce p under circumstances which constitute an opportunity for producing q.

The last two formulae are what correspond in the new system to the formulae PA & $O(A \rightarrow B) \rightarrow PB$ and $O(A \rightarrow B)$ & $O \sim B \rightarrow O \sim A$ of the old system.

18. In the old system this was a valid formula: $O \sim A \rightarrow O(A \rightarrow B)$. It was read: 'Doing the forbidden commits one to doing anything.' This was an analogue in deontic logic to one of the well-known Paradoxes of Implication. Another analogue was $OB \rightarrow O(A \rightarrow B)$. It was read: 'Doing anything commits one to doing one's duty.' We could call these two formulae Paradoxes of Commitment.

The impact of the paradoxes is that they make debatable the attempt to formalize the notion of commitment by means of $O(A \rightarrow B)$. As we know, there are, independently of the 'paradoxes', conclusive reasons for regarding this formalization as inadequate.

It is an observation of some interest that corresponding 'paradoxes' arise for the suggested formalization of commitment through $O(d(\sim pTp)$ & $d(\sim qTq)$ v $f(\sim pTp)$ & $d(\sim qTq)$ v $f(\sim pTp)$ & $f(\sim qTq))$. For it may easily be shown that this expression is entailed both by $Of(\sim pTp)$ and by $Od(\sim qTq)$.

These findings are not 'paradoxical' if we render them in words as follows: If it is categorically forbidden to do a certain thing, then it is also forbidden to do this thing in conjunction with any other thing; and if it is categorically obligatory to do a certain thing, then it is also obligatory to do this thing irrespective of whether one does or forbears to do a certain other thing. The air of paradox comes in when we speak of the conjunctive prohibition and obligation as a 'commitment'.

The proper conclusion to be drawn from these 'paradoxes' is, in my opinion, that the suggested formalization of the notion of commitment is not (entirely) satisfactory. The way out of these 'paradoxes' is not, however, to abandon the notion of commitment which we are trying to formalize, in favour of *that* notion of commitment which concerns action on different occasions. My suggestion is that we should replace the suggested formalization by the following amplified form of it: $O(d(\sim pTp) \ \& \ d(\sim qTq) \ v \ f(\sim pTp) \ \& \ d(\sim qTq) \ v \ f(\sim pTp) \ \& \ f(\sim qTq)) \ \& \ P(d(\sim pTp) \ / \sim qT\sim q) \ \& \ P(f(\sim qTq) \ / \sim pT\sim p)$.

It may be shown that this expression entails $P(f(\sim pTp) \ / \sim qT\sim q)$ and also $P(d(\sim qTq) \ / \sim pT\sim p)$.

The amended definition of commitment amounts to the following: The fact that it is prohibited to do a certain thing and forbear a certain other thing on some occasion gives rise to a *commitment* to do the second thing, *if* one does the first, then, and then only, when the agent is normatively free, *i.e.* permitted, to do or forbear the first thing and also normatively free, *i.e.* permitted, to do or forbear the second thing on the occasion in question.

In the notion of commitment there is thus involved not only the notion of obligation but also the notion of permission. This is not surprising. To commit oneself normatively is to 'bind oneself' normatively, to give up a freedom. Therefore one cannot commit oneself *to* an action which one is already normatively bound to do. Nor can one commit oneself *by* action from which one is normatively bound to abstain.

The two theorems of deontic logic which we discussed in the last section retain their validity as theorems. But they cease to be theorems on commitment. If, in the two formulae under discussion, we replace the originally suggested formalization of commitment by the amended formalization the formulae reduce to tautologies of the Logic of Propositions.

X

NORMS OF HIGHER ORDER

1. CAN norms themselves be the contents of norms? Can, for example, a prohibition be itself commanded or permitted or prohibited?

If, for some reason, it be thought that norms cannot be the contents of norms the question may be raised whether norm-propositions can be so. Could it, for example, not be permitted *that* a certain thing is prohibited?

It appears more plausible to think that norm-propositions could be the contents of norms than that norms themselves could be so.

That a norm-proposition is true means that a certain norm *exists*. That a norm-proposition is the content of a norm would consequently mean that a certain state of affairs, *viz.* the existence of a certain norm, ought to or may or must not be (Ch. V, Sect. 2). A norm with this content would be a norm of the type which we have called *ideal rules* (Ch. I, Sect. 9).

It is doubtful whether there can be ideal rules about the existence of (other) norms. We shall not here inquire into *this* possibility.

Instead let us ask: How does the state of affairs, which is the existence of a norm, come to be? If the norm is a positive prescription, *i.e.* a prescription with an empirical agent as its authority, the answer is that it comes into being as a result of human action. Someone has given or issued the norm. Issuing norms is human action too. For action of this type we have previously coined the term *normative action*.

189

Even if it were not the case that the *existence* of norms could be meaningfully subject to norm, it seems obvious that the human *acts* through which norms come into existence may themselves be obligatory or permitted or forbidden. And it may be suggested that *this* is what is really meant by the idea that norm-propositions sometimes are the contents of norms, and also by the even more obscure idea that norms themselves may function as such contents.

By norms of higher order I shall here exclusively understand norms whose contents are normative acts. Since normative action is the giving of prescriptions, norms of higher order are, in a characteristic sense, 'about' prescriptions. They *may* be prescriptions themselves. But they *need not* be so.

It may be thought that legislation in a state, or the giving of prescriptions generally, could be subject to some norms which are *not* themselves prescriptions but norms of a 'moral' or kindred nature. The idea that the laws of the state have (or should have) a 'foundation' in a Law of Nature postulates the existence of higher-order norms which are not themselves prescriptions but 'govern' (the giving of) prescriptions.

Norms of higher order which are prescriptions are of great importance to the legal order of a state and to other 'hierarchies of commanding power', such as, *e.g.*, an army.

Here we shall only be dealing with such norms of higher order which are (positive) prescriptions.

The interesting peculiarities of a logic of higher-order prescriptions have to do with relationships between norm-authorities and between norm-authorities and norm-subjects. These peculiarities cannot be treated within a theory of norm-kernels. For this theory takes into account only the character, content, and conditions of application of norms—omitting from consideration authority and subject.

The formal apparatus for dealing with norm-kernels which we developed in Chapters VIII and IX is therefore inadequate for dealing (interestingly) with norms of higher order. We shall not in this work, however, extend the scope of the strictly formal theory beyond the theory of the kernels. Our comments on the logic of higher-order norms will be 'informal'. I hope they will invite formal treatment by making it plain that here is another virgin land of logical inquiry awaiting exploration.

2. Besides the acts of giving prescriptions there is another type of act, which I shall also call normative, *viz.* acts of *cancelling* (voiding, withdrawing) prescriptions.

The act of issuing a norm transforms a world of which the negation of a certain norm-proposition is true into a world of which this norm-proposition itself is true.

The act of cancelling a norm again introduces a change into a world in which a certain norm exists, *i.e.* of which a certain norm-proposition holds true. But which state of affairs does the cancellation produce? Two answers seem possible.

According to the first answer, the state produced by the cancellation is simply one of which a formerly true (generic) norm-proposition is no longer true.

According to the second answer, cancellation—like issuing—brings a new norm into existence. This new norm is the *negation-norm* of the cancelled norm.

On the second view of cancellation, to cancel a command to do a certain thing thus entails issuing a permission to forbear this same thing and vice versa; and to cancel a prohibition to do, *i.e.* command to forbear, a certain thing entails issuing a permission to do this same thing, and vice versa.

The question which is the 'right' concept of cancellation: the idea that cancellation simply dissolves or annihilates an existing normative relationship or the idea that cancellation creates a new norm, is as such pointless. These are just *two* concepts of cancellation. But whether within normative orders of certain types, such as, *e.g.*, the laws of the state, cancellation actually is of the one kind or the other, and what further consequences a choice between the alternative possibilities has, can, I think, be problems of considerable interest. We shall not, however, discuss these problems here.

3. Norms whose contents are acts other than normative acts, I shall call norms of *the first order*.

A norm of higher order is a norm of the second order, if the normative act which is its content is the act of issuing or cancelling certain norms (prescriptions) of the first order. A norm is of the third order if the normative act which is its content is the act of issuing or cancelling certain norms (prescriptions) of the second order. In an analogous manner we define norms of the fourth, fifth, . . . *n*th order.

The subjects of norms of higher order, *i.e.* the agents whom those norms address, are themselves authorities of norms of lower order. We may call the authority of a norm of the first order an authority of the first order, the authority of a norm of the second order an authority of the second order, etc.

The authority who issues one norm may also issue another norm, and the norms may be of different order. When we say of an authority that he is of order *n* we are therefore speaking of him *as* authority of one or several norms of this order *n*, and not *as* authority of norms of some higher or lower order.

If the normative act which is performed by an agent a_1 when he issues a norm is itself the content of a norm which has been given by an agent a_2 to this agent a_1, then a_1 in issuing this norm will be said to be acting as *sub-authority* relative to or under a_2.

If the normative act of issuing a certain norm is *not* itself the content of any higher order norm, then the agent who performs this act (issues this norm) will be said to act as *sovereign* or *supreme authority* of the norm in question.

4. It is probably right to say that among norms of the first order commands and prohibitions hold the most prominent position. Among norms of higher order the relative prominence of the various types of norm appears to be different. It is probably right to say that higher-order permissions are of peculiar interest and importance.

A higher-order permission is to the effect that a certain authority *may* issue norms of a certain content. It is, we could say, a norm concerning the competence of a certain authority of norms. I shall call permissive norms of higher order *competence norms*.

In the act of issuing a competence norm, *i.e.* a permissive norm of higher order, the superior authority of higher order may be said to *delegate power* to a *sub-authority* of lower order. 'Power' here means 'competence, by virtue of norm, to act as an authority of norms'. I shall also speak of it as *normative* competence or power.

An important aspect of the study of norms of higher order is therefore the study of the logical mechanism of the phenomenon known in legal and political philosophy as *the delegation of power*.

It is essential to what I here call 'the delegation of power' that the norm delegating power should be permissive. If an authority *commands* or *prohibits* an agent to issue norms of such and such a content we shall not say that he is delegating power to the sub-authority. For an aspect of what we call the sub-authority's power is that he should be free to issue or not to issue the norms which it is within his competence to issue.

Are the permissions whereby power is delegated tolerations or rights? This question will for the time being be left open. (We shall presently decide that they are rights.)

It is, however, a noteworthy fact that the delegation of power to a sub-authority is often combined with an *order* to this authority to issue norms about certain *types* of act. The city magistrates, for example, may have the right to issue specific traffic-regulations about, say, speed limits and parking and the use of the horn when driving in the street, but at the same time be ordered to issue *some* regulations about these things, *i.e.* be ordered not to leave these things unregulated. Then it is *not* within the competence of the magistrate to decide whether there are going to *be* traffic-regulations or not, but only to decide *which* these regulations will be.

It is easy to see what could be the *raison d'être* for this combination of a higher-order permission with a higher-order command. The supreme authority wants to have certain things subject to regulation, perhaps for the sake of that which is also called the common good. But he leaves the details of the legislation to a lesser authority, which has a better insight into what are the specific requirements of this end, the common good, in the particular case.

The *limits* of delegated power are often set by certain prohibitions. The authority *may* issue norms of a certain kind, but *must not* issue norms of certain other kinds. It may be argued that norms, the issuing of which is not expressly permitted to the authority, are in fact forbidden to him to issue. This, however, cannot be deduced from the nature of permission as such. The prohibition, if there is such a prohibition, is a norm in its own right.

In Section 14 of Chapter V we briefly discussed the principle *nullum crimen sine lege*. We said that it could not be regarded as a *logical principle* to the effect that whatever is not prohibited is thereby *ipso facto* permitted. But it may be regarded as being itself a *permissive norm* to this effect. Such a norm, which confers a normative status upon all human acts which are not already subject to norm, may be said to *close* the system of norms to which it belongs.

As far as norms of the first order are concerned, it seems natural to take the view that everything which is not forbidden is permitted, but not very natural to take the converse view that everything which is not permitted is forbidden. It may, in fact, easily be shown that this latter view involves a contradiction, unless either the doing or forbearing of every conceivable human act has already been individually permitted. For otherwise both the doing and the forbearing of acts which are not expressly permitted would be forbidden. This, as we know, is an impossibility (cf. Ch. V, Sect. 14).

As far as norms of higher order, *i.e.* norms regulating normative activity, are concerned, it appears much more natural to think that 'whatever is not permitted is forbidden' than to think that 'whatever is not forbidden is permitted'. If we understand the 'whatever' as referring only to the *doing* and not to the *forbearing* of normative acts there is no contradiction in this idea (cf. Ch. V, Sect. 14). There is, however, another logical difficulty to be noted:

A prohibition to the effect that *no* norm-authority must issue norms which he has not an explicit permission to issue would prohibit all normative activity whatsoever, including the act through which it itself came into existence, unless some permissive norms had first been issued. If a contradiction is to be avoided the sovereign authority, who delegates power to a sub-authority, must be exempt from the prohibition in question. Only the sub-authorities can be its subjects. *Their* normative acts may consistently be regarded as forming a normatively closed field of acts in the sense that these authorities are allowed to exercise only such normative power as has been delegated to them, and no other. Whether this is an altogether reasonable view of the competence of subordinate norm-authorities, I shall not discuss here. But it is a logically possible view.

5. Within a theory of higher-order norms we can illuminate one of the most controversial and debated notions of a theory of norms, *viz.* the notion of *validity*.

What is meant by the 'validity' of a norm? There are at least *two* different, relevant meanings of the words 'valid' and 'validity' in connexion with norms. Several controversies in the theory of norms will be seen to be futile when we realize that apparently opposed opinions really pertain to different notions of validity.

One sense in which a norm can be said to be valid is that it *exists*. A person comes across something which he interprets as a norm-formulation, say, on a notice-board or in a statute-book. He concludes that such and such a norm has been issued and thus also has existed, at least for some time in the past. But he may be curious to know whether it still exists, or whether it has been cancelled or has passed out of existence by what in jurisprudence is called *desuetudo*. The question 'Does this norm still exist?' is often couched in the words 'Is this rule still valid?', and the answer 'It still exists' in the words 'It is still valid'. Since validity here means existence, it would perhaps be better not to use the word 'validity' at all. For this word is also used with a quite different meaning.

Under this other meaning the validity of a norm means that the norm exists and that, in addition, there exists another norm which permitted the authority of the first norm to issue it. If we decide to call the act of issuing a norm *legal* (or lawful) when there is a norm permitting this act, then we may also say that *the validity*, in the sense now contemplated, *of a norm means the legality of the act of issuing this norm*.

The words 'valid' and 'validity', when applied to a norm, thus sometimes refer to the *existence*, as such, of the norm and sometimes to the *legality* of the act as a result of which this norm came to be. In English, a norm or law which is valid in the sense that it exists is also said to be *in force* (cf. Ch. VII, Sect. 8). To say of a norm that it 'exists' is not ordinary usage, but philosophic jargon invented for special purposes. The question 'Is this law valid?' can often be rendered more unambiguously by 'Is this law in force?' In German, however, one would nearly always use the same word 'gültig' (*i.e.* 'valid') for the two cases. And in the Swedish language 'gällande rätt', which literally means 'valid law', is the technical term for *law which is in force*, and thus, in our philosophic terminology, for existing law or law in existence. These peculiarities of various languages may offer a partial explanation of the fact that philosophers of law, at least in Germany and Scandinavia, have found it hard to see that there are two utterly different concepts covered by the same word 'valid', and have often thought that an account of *one* meaning of the word could cover both concepts. Some philosophers, such as Hans Kelsen in his early period, have tended to identify validity with the legality of norm-giving acts and to ignore or under-emphasize the factual aspect of law as the efficacy of a commanding will. Others, such as Axel Hägerström, have put *all* the emphasis on efficacy, on 'law as fact', ignoring the normative notion of validity as legality.

For the sake of avoiding ambiguities I shall here always under-stand 'validity' in the normative sense of 'legality', and never in the factual sense of existence or being 'in force'.

Some authors have thought of validity as a parallel attribute to truth. Statements of fact (propositions) are true or false; norms, it is said, are not true or false, but valid or invalid. What truth-value is in the world of propositions, validity is in the world of norms.

The analogy between validity and truth is a bad one, and should therefore not be used. Validity is neither a 'substitute' for nor a 'parallel' to truth in the realm of norms.

The notion of validity which we are discussing is a *relative* notion. A norm is valid, if at all, *relative to* another norm permitting its issuing or coming into existence.

This relativity of the notion of validity, however, must not be misinterpreted. It does *not* mean that the issued norm is valid *if* the norm permitting its issuing is *valid*. The first norm does not 'get' its validity from the validity of the second. The validity of a norm, in the sense now under discussion, is not validity relative to the *validity* of another norm. It is validity relative to the *existence* of another norm, hierarchically related to the first in a certain way.

In this respect validity is *unlike* truth. By saying that a proposi-tion is true 'relative to' another proposition one could hardly mean anything else, but that *if* the second proposition is *true*, then the first proposition is true also. The first proposition 'gets' its truth from the truth, if it be true, of the second proposition.

If we do not see clearly the difference between validity and truth, but believe that they are analogous concepts, we are easily led to the following mistaken idea: If validity of a norm is validity relative to the validity of another norm of higher order, the validity of this higher-order norm will in its turn mean validity relative to a third norm of still higher order, and so forth. If this chain is infinite the concept of validity would seem to lose all meaning, or be hanging in the air. If again the chain is *not* infinite, then the validity of the norm in which the chain terminates cannot mean 'validity relative to some other valid norm', since there are no other norms to refer to. It must mean validity 'absolutely' or 'in itself'. The relative notion of validity is thus thought to require or presuppose an absolute notion in much the same sense in which a notion of relative truth can rightly be said to presuppose a notion of absolute truth.

But this argument is fallacious. The notion of relative validity which we have been explaining does not, by logical argument, force upon us a notion of absolute validity. The relative notion is self-sufficient, so to speak. But as we shall see later, the notion can be supplemented in a way which may be said to create an analogue to an absolute notion.

To the notion of validity, which we have here explained, corresponds a notion of *invalidity*. We shall say that a norm is invalid if the issuing of that norm by a certain authority is forbidden to this authority by virtue of some higher-order norm. If we decide to call the act of issuing a norm *illegal* when there is a norm prohibiting this act, then we may also say that *the invalidity* (in the sense now under discussion) *of a norm means the illegality of the act of issuing such a norm.*

It should again be observed that the *standard of invalidity* of a norm is the *existence* and not the *validity* of a certain other norm, hierarchically related to the first in a certain way.

It is clear that a norm need be neither valid nor invalid in the senses here defined. A sovereign norm, for example, cannot be valid or invalid.

It may happen that a norm which is valid relative to one norm of higher order is invalid relative to another. A norm can thus be both valid and invalid.

There is nothing illogical (contradictory) about this. One and the same norm *n* is both valid and invalid when there is one higher-order norm which permits and another higher-order norm which prohibits the authority of the norm *n* to issue the norm *n*. If, however, one and the same norm happened to be both valid and invalid, then the permissive norm validating it and the prohibiting norm invalidating it must emanate from different authorities. For one and the same authority cannot both permit and prohibit the same act to the same agent on the same occasion.

It is a straightforward application of this rule that one and the same superior authority cannot both permit and prohibit the same sub-authority to issue a certain norm. But one superior authority may permit and another superior authority prohibit the same inferior authority to issue a certain norm. And if then the inferior authority issues this norm the norm which thus comes into existence is both a valid norm and an invalid norm.

6. Assume that x orders or permits y to order or permit z to issue some norms. Assume further that y actually orders or permits z to issue these norms, and that z does this.

On these assumptions we shall say that y, in giving the norm to z, acts as *immediate* subordinate to x, and that z, in giving norms to some further agent or agents, acts as immediate subordinate to y and as *remote* subordinate to x.

Conversely, we may also say that y acts as z's immediate superior, and that x acts as y's immediate but as z's remote superior. And what we say of the agents in these respects we may also say of their acts, and, since these acts are normative acts, also of the norms in which they result.

Of these three acts, of x and y and z, and of the norms in which they result we shall say that they form a chain of subordinated acts and norms or simply a *chain of subordination*. We shall do this notwithstanding the fact that the first act in the chain is not subordinate to any other act in the chain.

We shall call the acts of x and y and z and the corresponding norms *links* in the chain, in that order. The act of x constitutes the first, the act of y the second, the act of z the third link. The first act and norm, we shall say, is linked to the third act and norm thanks to the *intermediary* of the second act and norm.

A chain of subordination may, of course, contain more than two links. Links may be omitted from either end of the chain, and what remains—if the remainder is at least two links—is still a chain of subordination. But one cannot omit links from other places in the chain but the ends, without 'breaking' the chain.

It is essential to the notion of a chain of subordination, as I have explained it here, that each link in the chain—with the exception of the first link—is a *valid* norm (and normative act) relative to the next superior link in the chain. A norm is valid when the act of issuing this norm is permitted. It is a theorem of deontic logic that, if an act is commanded, then it is also permitted. Therefore, an order to issue norms entails that the norms issued under that order are also valid, *i.e.* their issuing is permitted because commanded. We can also say that each inferior link in the chain is, by transitivity, valid relative to every superior link in the chain, and that each inferior link *derives its validity immediately* from the next superior link, *remotely* from those superior to this, and *ultimately* from the first link in the chain.

By saying that one norm (and normative act) can be ('*normatively*') *traced back* to another norm (and normative act), we shall understand that there exists a chain of subordination of which the first norm is an inferior and the second a superior (relative to the first) member.

A norm which cannot be traced back to any other norm cannot, by definition, be valid relatively to any other norm. It will be either *invalid* relatively to some norm of next higher degree or it will be neither valid nor invalid, *i.e. sovereign.*

If the number of individual norms which have been issued is finite the process of tracing back norms will always in a finite number of steps take us to a norm which can no longer be traced back to yet another norm. This assumption of finitude we can, I think, safely make. Thus, we are entitled to say that any finite chain of subordination terminates in or originates from a norm which is either sovereign *or* invalid.

All the norms which are links in at least one chain which originates from the sovereign norms issued by *one and the same authority* will be said to belong to one and the same normative *hierarchy* or *order* or *system*. The sovereign norms themselves we shall include, by definition, in the system. A system of norms is thus a class of one or several sovereign norms which are issued by one and the same authority, and norms which may, through chains of subordination, be traced back to these sovereign norms.

We can make use of the notion of a system of norms for defining a new concept of validity of a norm. This new concept will be called *validity in a system* or *absolute validity*. That a norm is absolutely valid will mean simply that it can be traced back to a sovereign norm. This, as we have already seen, is not trivially the case with every norm. For the process of tracing back may terminate in an invalid norm.

Since the notion of 'tracing back' a norm is defined by means

199

of the notion of relative validity, it follows that the notion of 'absolute validity', as defined by us, presupposes or is secondary to the notion of relative validity. The opposite is the case with the notions of absolute and relative truth. That a proposition is true relatively to another proposition means that the first is true absolutely if the second is true absolutely. The notion of relative truth is secondary to the notion of absolute truth, since it is defined in terms of absolute truth.

The question may be raised: Do the laws of the state constitute a normative system (hierarchy, order) *in the sense here defined*? If they do, who is the sovereign authority in a state? These are no doubt extremely interesting questions of political and legal philosophy. The questions can be raised empirically for the law of a given country. They can also be discussed as purely conceptual questions. The answers to the conceptual questions will depend on how we mould our concept of the state. The answers to the empirical questions again will depend on how well those empirical phenomena of an enormously complex structure, which we know as so-called sovereign states, conform to the concept as moulded by the political philosopher. I shall not, however, discuss these problems in the present work.

7. Suppose that a chain of subordination terminates in an invalid norm. This means that there exists some norm which prohibits the authority of the invalid norm to issue it. The act of the sub-authority was therefore an act of *insubordination* relative to this higher-order norm. In issuing the invalid norm he transgressed the limits of his normative competence as set by the superior authority. He seized or usurped a power which had not only not been delegated to him but which had been expressly denied to him. Invalid normative acts might therefore also be called acts of *usurpation*.

It should be noted that, on the definition which we have given, the invalid norm and the norm relative to which it is invalid are both in force (exist). The authorities who issue them succeed in establishing normative relationships between themselves and the subjects of their norms. The authority of the invalid inferior norm is the subject of the superior norm. That the superior norm is in force and that the authority of the invalid norm is its subject entails that the authority of the superior norm tries to make the authority of the inferior norm forbear such illegal acts. He may, for example, order him to be prosecuted for disobedience and punished. He will also, probably, take steps to dissolve the relationships under norm which the usurper had succeeded in establishing. There might be a whole chain of such 'illegal' relationships. If the superior authority is successful the illegal norm and its possible repercussions in the form of norms subordinate to it will vanish, cease to exist.

The outcome of the struggle of authorities may, however, also be the reverse. The usurper of power is successful. The normative relationships which he has established remain, acquire relative permanence. The authority who was superior to the usurper resigns in his efforts to make the usurper obey. This means that the superior norm, relative to which the usurper's act was invalid, passes out of existence—perhaps dies as a consequence of an act of cancellation. If this happens the usurper's norm ceases to be invalid. It is now neither valid nor invalid relatively to any other norm. *It has become a sovereign norm*. The chain or chains of subordination to which it has given origin will then, together with possible further normative acts of the same ex-usurper, constitute a normative system in its own right. And the norms which may be traced back to this once invalid norm will not only be valid relatively, but valid absolutely, in the sense that they are valid within a system.

One may distinguish two kinds of acts of usurpation.

Assume that x has prohibited to y the issuing of commands to z. y nevertheless issues a command to z to do something. This act on y's part is an act of usurpation.

Assume further that, in addition to the prohibition from x to y and the command from y to z, there is also a prohibition from x to z to do the very same act which y has ordered z to do. A positive and a negative command, with different authorities but identical content, subject, and occasion we have previously called *conflicting commands*. In the case under discussion we thus have an invalid order from y to z which conflicts with a (sovereign or) valid order from x to z. Then we shall say that y's invalid normative act was not only usurpatory but also *revolutionary*. y, in issuing the invalid order, did not only himself violate a prohibition by transgressing the limits of his normative competence as assigned

201

to him by x. y also urged another agent, z, who takes orders from x, to disobey orders from that quarter. This *is* the 'logic of revolution': seizing illegal normative power and urging the citizens to disobey existing regulations. 'Revolution' is very much the *mot juste* to describe the case. For, if the usurper is successful in the sense that his illegal commands become effective, *i.e.* generally obeyed by those to whom they are addressed, then, since his commands conflict with existing valid commands, these latter will have to become ineffective, cease to be generally obeyed by the citizens. Two conflicting commands, as we know, can coexist and 'contend' with each other, at least for some time. But it is logically impossible that they should both become effective in the sense of being generally obeyed by their subjects. A revolutionary usurpation of norm-giving power, which is successful, will therefore necessarily overthrow an existing effective legal order, or a part of it, and institute a new effective order in its place.

8. No normative act can be both sovereign and subordinate. But one and the same authority of norms may perform both sovereign and subordinate normative acts. When Mr. X, who is a judge, sentences a thief in court he performs a subordinate normative act. But when he orders his children to go to bed he acts as sovereign (unless there is a norm to the effect that parents are entitled to give orders to their children).

The example also shows that the normative acts of one and the same authority of norms may belong to different systems of norms. This is a fairly trivial observation. Of more interest is it to observe that one and the same normative act may belong to two or more different systems of norms. It is conceivable that two agents x and y, whose normative acts cannot be traced back to the same sovereign act—*e.g.*, because they both act as sovereigns themselves—authorize (permit) a third agent z to issue norms to w. If z makes use of the power delegated to him, *i.e.* if he actually issues a norm to w, then the normative act of z can be traced back both to the normative act of x, whereby x gave him this power, and to the normative act of y, whereby y gave him this same competence. Since the two normative acts of x and y respectively belong to different systems, and therefore also the norms in which they result, the act of z will be a common member of two systems of normative acts. And the norm which z issued to w will belong to at least two systems of norms.

If two systems of norms and normative acts have common members the two systems will be said to *intersect*. If they do not intersect they are *independent*.

9. A command which belongs to one system S may conflict with a command which belongs to another system S^1. That the commands conflict means that they demand incompatible modes of conduct of the same subject on some occasion. A special case of conflict is when the one command requires the subject to do and the other requires him to forbear the same thing on the same occasion. In this case the two conflicting prescriptions are related to one another as command and prohibition with identical content.

When two systems contain conflicting commands we shall say that there is a conflict between the systems. For example: x and y are two sovereign commanders. x orders z to do a certain thing. y prohibits z to do this same thing. Then there is conflict between the system emanating from x and the system emanating from y.

Conflict between systems of norms is a special case of that which we have previously (Ch. VIII, Sect. 7) called *conflict of wills*. We have just studied another case of conflict of wills in the realm of norm, *viz*. the case when a revolutionary usurpation of power takes place. The normative concept of a revolution necessarily entails a conflict of commanding wills.

Can conflicting commands coexist *within* one system of norms? Revolution, it should be observed, is not an example of conflict between norms belonging to the same system. Revolution entails conflict between norms, but it also presupposes the occurrence of an invalid act of usurpation of power. And the norm which is the result of the invalid normative act, by definition, does not belong to the system, but marks a recession from the system.

In order to find out whether conflicting norms can coexist within a system we must first make it clear what such a conflict would mean.

10. That a conflict of commanding wills occurs within a system of norms means the following: Some agent w receives from an authority y an order to do something on a certain occasion and

203

from another authority z an order to do something else on that same occasion. Both orders can be traced back to sovereign norms issued by an authority x. But the contents of the two orders are incompatible modes of conduct.

Let us assume, for the sake of argument, that x has permitted y to command w to do a certain thing, and that x has also permitted z to prohibit w to do this same thing. The question may now be raised whether there is anything 'illogical' about the case which makes its factual occurrence impossible. Can such cases happen?

That w received the conflicting orders from y and z is certainly possible. This is just as possible as *any* conflict of will is possible. If there is anything 'illogical' about the case it can only be because the conflicting orders were both *valid* relatively to norms of *the same* supreme authority. By permitting y to order w to do a certain thing and z to order w to forbear this same thing, x as it were 'endorses' a possible conflict of commanding wills within the system. The conflict need not arise. The competent sub-authorities need not make use of their power. But the conflict *may* validly arise. This must be the 'illogicality', *if* there is one.

Thus the problem before us is this: Can x issue the two permissions, to y and z respectively, without somehow 'contradicting himself'? I find this question very puzzling. One cannot settle the difficulty by saying that since x, on our assumption, has permitted those acts to y and z, this shows that this can happen and therefore is logically possible. This is no answer, since the question is whether x can do anything which can be truly described as giving two permissions of the kind now under discussion. He can, of course, *say* to y 'I permit you to command w to produce the state p' and to z 'I permit you to command w to forbear the production of p'. But this is not to say that x can *permit* y to command w to do a certain thing and z to command w to forbear this same thing.

In order to answer our question, we must therefore first become clear about what x is supposed to do when he gives the two permissions. It is the problem of the nature of permissions recurring.

If we take the view that a permission is a 'toleration', then x's two permissions are two declarations of intention or two promises, to the effect, roughly speaking, that x will leave y in peace, should he choose to give a certain command to w, and that x will leave z in peace, should *he* choose to give a certain other command to w (cf. Ch. V, Sect. 16). And since these two acts by y and z are simultaneously possible, albeit conflicting, it is difficult to see that there could be any logical inconsistency concealed in x's two permissive normative acts.

If, on the other hand, the two permissions (or at least one of the two) amounted to *rights* the situation would be different. A right, we have suggested (Ch. V, Sect. 15), entails a prohibition to others to do that which one has resolved or promised not to do oneself, *viz.* hinder the holder of the right from availing himself of his permission. Now assume that x grants a right to y to command w to do a certain thing. This entails that x prohibits z to interfere with y's action, should y command w to do this thing, *i.e.* should he take certain steps to make w do it. If z has this prohibition from x he cannot at the same time hold a permission from x to prohibit w to do the thing in question, *i.e.* a permission to make or try to make w forbear it. For an attempt on the part of z to make w forbear this thing falls under the prohibition, issued to him by x, to interfere with y's attempts, should he make such attempts, to make w do it. Hence a permission to z to prohibit w to do a certain thing would conflict with the prohibition to z to interfere with y's attempts to make w do this thing, and consequently with y's right to command w to do it. It follows, finally, that x cannot consistently (without inconsistency) permit y to command w to do a certain thing and permit z to prohibit w to do this same thing, if one of the permissions (or both) are rights.

The upshot of the discussion is thus as follows:

It is logically *possible* for a sovereign agent to endorse a conflict of will within a system of norms, *if* endorsing the conflict means to permit, in the weak sense of tolerate, the issuing of conflicting commands by two sub-authorities. But it is *not* logically possible for a sovereign to endorse a conflict of commanding wills within a system of norms, if endorsing the conflict means to permit, in the stronger sense of granting a right, the issuing of conflicting commands. By granting such rights the authority is contradicting his own will.

The answer to the question whether a conflict of commanding wills is logically possible within a system of norms thus depends upon how we understand the permission whereby superior authorities in the system delegate power to inferior authorities. If these permissions amount merely to declarations or promises that the superior authority is going to tolerate certain normative actions on the part of the inferior authorities, then there *may* occur a conflict of commanding wills in the system. But if the power-delegating permissions amount to rights to issue certain norms, *i.e.* if the superior authority undertakes to protect the normative actions of the subordinate authorities by prohibiting other agents to interfere with such actions, then conflicts of will are logically impossible within the system.

A system of norms which is, in the sense explained, logically immune to conflict possesses the same coherence and unity which is characteristic of that which we have called a *corpus* of norms. A corpus is a class of norms which have the same authority (see Ch. VIII, Sect. 7). Within a corpus a conflict between prescriptions is excluded as being contrary to the nature of a rational will. In a system of norms there are (normally) several authorities. But in a system which is logically immune to conflict, and thus has the coherence of a corpus, the sub-authorities cannot contradict the will of the sovereign, but only 'transmit' it. In a sense, therefore, there is only *one* commanding and permitting will within such a system, *viz*. the sovereign will.

We could sharpen our definition of validity in such a way that to say that a norm is valid shall mean that the authority who issues it has a permission amounting to a right to issue the norm. Normative competence or power would then mean permissions in the stronger sense of rights to perform certain normative acts. Such redefinitions of the notions of competence and validity would give to the notion of a normative system the coherence of a corpus. I think that this reshaping of our definitions should take place. The higher-order permissions of which we have here been talking should be regarded as rights.

I would not, however, myself say that these findings support the view that (all) permissions 'essentially' are rights. Permissions as 'mere' tolerations have a normative status of their own. But it is most illuminating, I think, in regard to the logical nature of this much-debated and controversial idea of permissive norms, to see clearly that only permissions which are rights may serve the purpose of giving to a normative system the concord of commanding wills which is characteristic of rational willing, and which it is at least highly reasonable to think that a class of norms such as, say, the laws of a state should possess. This also makes the idea—entertained by so many philosophers—that *legal* permissions are rights, more understandable.

INDEX

Ability, 45, 48–55, 57–58, 108–116, 121–128, 173
Act, v–vii, 35–55, 86, 88, 116
-category, v, 36–37, 39, 50, 55, 111, 122, 171
-description, 62, 153, 161, 162
elementary a., 42, 56–58
generic a., *see* act-category
-individual, v, 36–37, 50, 55, 111, 122
Action, 48
condition of a., 43–45, 64–66, 73–74, 172, 174, 177–180
conditioned a., 171, 177
consequence of a., 39–41, 116
Logic of A., vii, 36, 56–69, 129, 130, 134, 171–178, 185
normative a., *see* Normative
result of a., 39–41, 42, 44, 49, 50, 75, 88, 116, 118, 119, 126
Activity, 35, 41–42, 49–50, 51, 52, 71–72, 116, 117
Agent, 36, 37–39, 44–45, 75, 77, 109, 118, 119, 123, 125, 184, 185, 189
collective a., 38, 45, 76, 77, 79, 80
empirical a., 38, 75
impersonal a., 38, 76, 77
individual a., 38, 76, 77
personal a., 38, 76, 77

Agent (*contd.*)
super-empirical (-natural) a., 38, 75
Alio-commitment, 185
Anankastic (connexion, relation, proposition, sentence, statement), 10, 11, 95, 101, 103
Aristotle, 87
Austin, 82, 83
Authority, *see* Norm-authority
Auto-commitment, 185
Autonomous norm, *see* Norm

Blackmail, 128
Blackstone, 82, 83
Broad, v
Brusiin, 102

Can do (*see also* Ability), 48–55, 58, 108–116, 121–125, 135, 152, 153
Cancellation (of norms), 191, 195, 201
Capacity, 50
Categorical norm, *see* Norm
Change, vii, 28–29, 35–37, 39–41, 42–45, 134, 171
-description, 33, 142, 143, 144, 160, 161, 162
Logic of Ch., vii, 36–47, 129, 134, 173, 174
Claim, 89–90

209